Teaching Oral Communication
in Grades K–8

Teaching Oral Communication in Grades K–8

Ann L. Chaney
Formerly of The College of William and Mary

Tamara L. Burk
The College of William and Mary

Allyn and Bacon

Boston   London   Toronto   Sydney   Tokyo   Singapore

Library of Congress Cataloging-in-Publication Data

Chaney, Ann L.
    Teaching oral communication in grades K–8 / Ann L. Chaney,
Tamara L. Burk.
        p.   cm.
    Includes bibliographical references and index.
    ISBN 0-205-18938-5
    1. Oral communication—Study and teaching.   2. Oral communication—
Problems, exercises, etc.   I. Burk, Tamara L.   II. Title.
LB1572.C43   1998
372.62´2--dc21

                                                           98-48560
                                                             CIP

Printed in the United States of America
10 9 8 7 6 5 4 3 2 1   01 00 99 98 97

To Jason and Kirt

Contents

Foreword

This book represents a very real groundbreaking activity in the world of language arts instruction in that it focuses exclusively on the art and science of oral communication. Although there are many texts available that give lip service to this area, none look at the process in a systematic way that honors its integrity as a full partner in language arts curriculum and instruction.

The authors of this text are highly qualified to offer the world of education such a text. Each has been instrumental here at The College of William and Mary in developing the Oral Communication Program for undergraduates and in pioneering new approaches for assessing it over the past several years. Moreover, they have worked with our Center for Gifted Education in developing curriculum for high-ability learners and with teachers to implement the oral communication component. Both Ann and Tamara have an excellent grasp of how oral communication can contribute effectively to the world of K through 12 language arts instruction in schools.

At a time when language arts practitioners are hard pressed to show that students are learning challenging material, this book has the opportunity to help make manifest the spirit of curriculum reform because it offers a practical yet theoretically sound way to promote both constructivist and symbolic interactionist perspectives on teaching. Their definition of oral communication is especially central to this emphasis: "the building and sharing of meaning using verbal and nonverbal symbols in a variety of communication contexts." The authors' continued emphasis throughout the book on the integration of the language arts skills of listening, speaking, reading, and writing with thinking places their ideas soundly in the realm of current emphasis on embedding the teaching of thinking in a content-relevant way. And the authors not only provide models for how to practice oral communication techniques, they also share important authentic approaches for assessing it in a variety of contexts.

Both practitioners and professors alike should find *Teaching Oral Communication* a very useful tool in enhancing language arts instruction for all learners in their classrooms.

JOYCE VAN TASSEL-BASKA
The College of William and Mary

Preface

Teaching Oral Communication in Grades K–8 was inspired by our involvement in a project to develop a language arts curriculum for K through 8 high-ability learners. Directed by Dr. Joyce Van Tassel-Baska (Center for Gifted Education, The College of William and Mary) and funded by the U.S. Department of Education and the Javits Act Program (BOCES, Saratoga Springs, New York), participants collaborated to design content standards and curriculum guidelines for K through 8 high-ability learners with accompanying curriculum units integrating reading, writing, thinking, and oral language.

In the process of consulting with language arts teachers about contemporary issues in oral communication pedagogy, we learned that there are very few resources readily available to teachers that address oral communication competency in the K through 8 classroom. We were also struck by the lack of interdisciplinary scholarship on oral communication. Most of the literature we reviewed was either highly theoretical and directed toward an audience of speech communication professionals; or, at the other extreme, directed toward language arts practitioners, but subject to some significant theoretical misconceptions (noted below) about the nature of oral language and its interrelationship to other strands of the language arts. Several of the most useful and theoretically sound books were written more for an audience of undergraduate or secondary speech communication educators rather than for the K through 8 classroom teacher, education graduate student, or curriculum supervisor.

Three primary misconceptions occur frequently in oral language instruction. First, while there is much evidence to suggest that oral communication is a vital aspect of literacy and critical thinking development, a prominent misconception that oral communication is merely the ability to talk has nonetheless persisted. The result has been a significant under-emphasis on oral communication within the language arts. A second factor inhibiting the effectiveness of oral language instruction is the misconception that oral communication skills central to life management, work, and learning competence are acquired naturally as a child develops and thus need less emphasis following the achievement of basic literacy skills. A third, and corollary, misconception is that writing skills are highly transferable into oral communication skills, an assumption recently undermined by strong scholarly criticism.

In writing this book, it was our intention to address these three persistent misconceptions about oral communication and literacy and, thus, to help bridge the interdisciplinary gap between contemporary oral communication theory and its actual application in the K through 8 classroom. We have tried to explain fundamental concepts in contemporary oral communication instruction while suggesting practical strategies for implementing a competency-based approach to oral communication, both within the individual classroom and as part of a larger curriculum development effort. Toward this end, the first four chapters of the book constitute a theoretical foundation for practical strategies suggested in later chapters.

Chapter 1 presents a view of oral communication-as-process and suggests that it is appropriate to place a stronger emphasis on oral language competency within the integrated language arts classroom. Chapter 2 addresses the creation of a communication-friendly climate in the classroom and discusses the impact of climate on communication competency, self-concept, and communication apprehension. Gender and cultural sensitivity are discussed here as well. Chapter 3 presents a theoretical scope and sequence for a variety of oral communication contexts, including formal informative and persuasive public speaking, debate, conversation, small-group discussion, dramatic performance, and media literacy. Chapter 4 is devoted exclusively to active listening. It reviews the four primary functions of listening and how they interrelate to four primary speaking functions.

The second part of this book is more practical in its discussion of teaching and assessment strategies. Chapter 5 tackles the practical assessment issues facing teachers who would like to include a greater emphasis on oral communication in their classroom, including a discussion of authentic performance assessment, assessment methods, and tips on informal classroom evaluation. Chapter 6 suggests practical ways in which teachers can make the most of basal and traditional language arts texts in teaching oral communication as process. Chapters 7 through 9 contain exercises for three levels (K–2, 3–5, and 6–8) for use with integrated language arts programs and for those programs that integrate the language arts around a social studies content focus.

Chapter 10 reviews the value of oral communication co-curricular and extracurricular activities, and includes an explanation of competitive activities such as those fostered by the newly created National Junior Forensics League (speech and debate). Finally, the appendix explores two cost-effective ways to build and maintain an oral communication lab and resource center with audiovisual and teaching resources.

Many language arts and speech communication professionals graciously contributed their time and expertise to this project. *Teaching Oral Communication in Grades K–8* merges many different experiences and perspectives about contemporary oral communication instruction, and we hope it will be useful for anyone seeking to foster a classroom community of enthusiastic and communicative learners.

Acknowledgments

We very much appreciate the efforts of the many individuals who contributed their expertise and support to the completion of this book: Joyce Van Tassel-Baska, Dana T. Johnson, and Linda Neal Boyce of the Center for Gifted Education, The College of William and Mary; our colleagues in the Department of Theatre and Speech, The College of William and Mary, especially Patrick H. Micken; Martha D. Cooper, Northern Illinois University; Eric E. Peterson and Kristin M. Langellier, University of Maine; Stephen E. Lucas, University of Wisconsin–Madison; Mike Cronin and George L. Grice, Radford University, Radford, Virginia; Sherwyn Morreale, University of Colorado, Colorado Springs; John Morello, Mary Washington College, Fredericksburg, Virginia; Jean Slattery, Dick Stear, and Ann Brown, Rochester City School District, Rochester, New York; Pat Arneson, University of Northern Colorado, Greeley, Colorado; the faculty, students, and parents of Toano Middle School, Toano, Virginia, and D. J. Montague Elementary School, Williamsburg, Virginia; Carolyn Pereira, Diana Hess, Ruth Woodruff, and Diane Farwick, Constitutional Rights Foundation Chicago; the National Forensics League; the National Speech Communication Association; Jim Graupner, Minnesota Debate Teacher's Association; Morris Snively, Belleville High School, Belleville, Virginia; Rick Olsen, Regent University, Virginia Beach, Virginia; Lauretta Olson; Diane Sudbury; Jillian L. Nickless; Jason B. Jones; and Kirt E. Moody, photographer par excellence and drafter of the appendix on oral communication labs and resource centers.

We also wish to thank Allyn and Bacon, especially Virginia Lanigan, our editor; Nihad Farooq, editorial assistant; and our reviewers Susan Trostle of the University of Rhode Island, Gail Donahue of St. Mary of the Mills School, and Pamela Monk of Boynton Middle School, whose careful reading and thoughtful comments substantially improved the manuscript.

About the Authors

Ann L. Chaney practices law in Chicago, Illinois, and consults and writes about oral communication and education. She is a former Communication Studies Instructor and intercollegiate debate coach at The College of William and Mary in Virginia, and she has trained teachers and created specialized curricula for middle school, high school, and college classrooms. Recently, she authored "Oral Communication: Thinking in Action," in *Developing Verbal Talent*, edited by VanTassel-Baska, Johnson, & Boyce (1996, Allyn and Bacon). Ann holds an M.A. in Communication Studies from Northern Illinois University and a J.D. from Loyola University of Chicago School of Law.

Tamara L. Burk is the Director of the Oral Communication Program and teaches Communication Studies courses at The College of William and Mary in Virginia, where she regularly serves as a consultant for faculty and administrators interested in developing, delivering, and assessing oral communication instruction across the curriculum. Tamara holds an M.A. in Speech Communication from the University of Maine and an Ed.S. from The College of William and Mary, and she is Vice President of the Virginia Association of Communication Arts and Sciences. Her current research interests and publications focus on the pedagogical process as it relates to oral communication skill development.

Teaching Oral Communication in Grades K–8

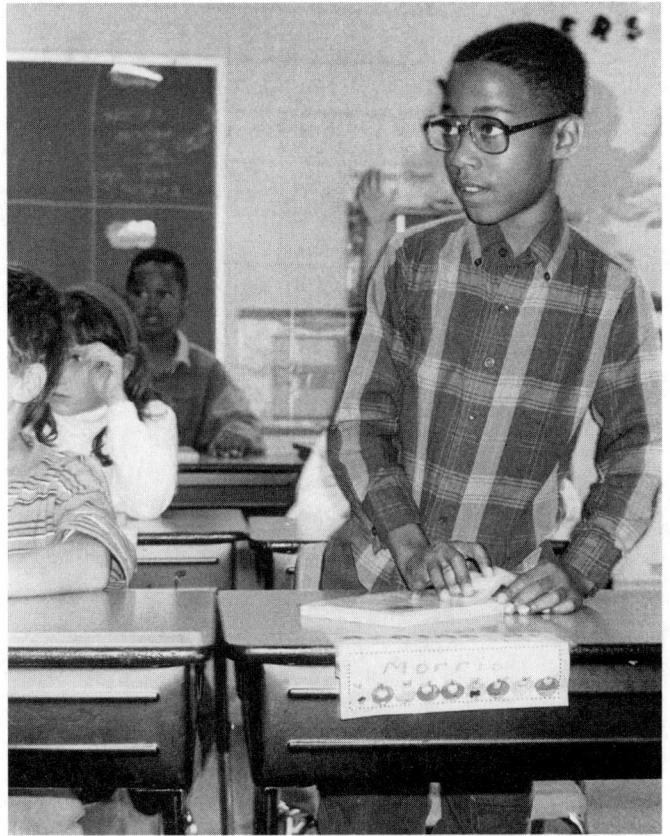

1

Positioning Oral Communication Within the Language Arts

OVERVIEW

Teaching the integrated language arts involves a constant search for balance among competing philosophies, desired outcomes, and practical realities. On one level, educational reform movements such as whole language, back to the basics (phonics and spelling), national standards, and multiculturalism vie for attention and loyalty. On another level, state education departments and school districts must make difficult choices about how to parcel out scarce funds for books, resources, and teacher training. In the classroom, teachers struggle to find time for experiential learning and performance-based assessments while devoting attention to students who may have widely ranging levels of literacy and related special needs.

In the midst of it all, language arts and communication educators have called for yet another recalculating of the balance—placing greater weight on oral language as a component of the language arts curriculum. In pursuit of that challenge, this chapter identifies and explores the merits of a competency-based approach to teaching oral communication as process.

PRACTICALLY SPEAKING

What is oral communication?

Why is it important to teach oral communication as a strand of the language arts?

What is competency-based instruction?

Why adopt a competency-based approach to oral communication within the language arts?

How might a competency-based approach fit within an integrated curriculum?

WHAT IS ORAL COMMUNICATION?

Oral language has long been recognized as an important step in the development of literacy (Modaff & Hopper 1984). The physical act of talking through a problem enables children to name, organize, and process information while learning to read and write (Barnes 1992). A holistic view of oral language is sometimes obscured, however, by the very words *oral* and *language: oral* because it does not adequately reference the nonverbal communicative behaviors associated with speaking and listening; and *language* because we are not accustomed to thinking of listening as a linguistic activity.

For these reasons and others we will discuss shortly, it may be helpful to reframe *oral language* as *oral communication* and to define it as the process of building and sharing meaning through the use of verbal (spoken) and nonverbal (unspoken) symbols in a variety of contexts. The components of this definition merit some discussion.

Process

Like reading and writing, oral language is a communicative process that uses language to make meaning (Allen & Brown 1976). There are seven key elements:

1. *Sender:* The person who initiates a message.
2. *Message:* Usually, the combination of verbal and nonverbal symbols intended to impart information for some communicative purpose. Some messages, however, are sent unintentionally.
3. *Channel:* The mechanism through which the message is conveyed—sight (observance of verbal and nonverbal symbols) and sound (aural reception of verbal and nonverbal symbols). Both sight and sound can be further mediated by electronic devices (telephone, television, radio, the Internet).
4. *Receiver:* The person who hears and responds to the message. A receiver need not be the *intended* receiver of a message.
5. *Interference:* Physical, psychological, or environmental barriers to interpretation of a message in the way the sender intended it to be interpreted. For instance, the loud, distracting noise of an ambulance siren may make it difficult to hear a speaker. Similarly, fear, anger, or fatigue may also interfere with communication by distorting a listener's frame of reference or willingness to listen.
6. *Situation:* The temporal or physical circumstances of a communication event, such as the occasion of the communication (formal ceremony or informal family talk), duration of the communication (a five-minute phone conversation or a three-hour committee meeting), place of the communication (outdoors in a park, indoors in a cafeteria), and demographics of the communication participants (gender, age, race or ethnic background, group membership, occupation, religion, and so on).

7. *Feedback:* Verbal and nonverbal symbols used by the receiver in reaction to a message. Feedback includes such activities as asking questions, making exclamations, shaking or nodding the head, creating facial expressions, varying eye contact, and using gestures.

The seven-step model of the oral communication process is often referred to as the SMCR (Sender–Message–Channel–Receiver) model of communication. A sender encodes—or puts together—a message of verbal and nonverbal symbols that she sends to the receiver. The receiver decodes—or interprets—that message by comparing it with his prior knowledge and experience. The receiver's interpretation of the message may be influenced by physical or internal interference, which he must overcome in order to comprehend the sender's intended meaning. Efforts to overcome interference may include sending feedback to the sender in the form of verbal or nonverbal symbols. The sender, in turn, acts as a receiver and interprets the feedback to adjust her message, and the cycle begins again.

Building Meaning

In defining oral communication, the word *building* is important because speakers and listeners build meaning when they interpret messages using their previous knowledge, background, and experiences. J. David Cooper (1993) explains in his book, *Literacy: Helping Children Construct Meaning,* that children comprehend what they read by relating new information to their prior knowledge. As a child reads a story, she compares information, symbols, and images from the text with those she already knows or finds familiar. Her prior knowledge serves as a foundation for interpretation, suggesting similarities or differences that help the learner construct new meaning.

In the oral communication process, learners construct meaning by comparing clues from the oral (and/or nonverbal) message to their store of prior knowledge. Unlike the process of reading and writing, however, oral communication usually involves opportunities for immediate feedback between communicators. This feedback further builds—reinforces or changes—the understanding between the communicators.

Sharing Meaning

The word *sharing* is important because both speaker (sender) and listener (receiver) must actively participate in the communication process in order to facilitate clarity and achieve their communication purposes. Sharing also implies that speakers and listeners simultaneously exchange verbal and nonverbal messages.

The word *sharing* is important in a definition of oral communication for another reason. Without the word sharing, a definition of oral communication might not adequately convey its transactional nature. We say oral communication is transactional because it is a form of relationship between persons, involving not only their roles as communicators, but their identities as persons. As Pamela J. Cooper (1995) notes in her book, *Communication for the Classroom Teacher*:

*A young student takes
questions from his peers*

[I]f our communication is to be truly effective, I must think of you as
a person, not just another student. Similarly, you must think of me as
a person, not just another teacher. This requires that we be person
oriented rather than role oriented. What the transactional view suggests
is that I must not only concentrate on my performance as a teacher and
be aware of you as a student, but I must also be aware of you as a
person—treat you as an individual and not as an object (p. 3).

If it were not for sharing, oral language might otherwise be viewed—as it
sometimes has been in the language arts—merely as the presenting of information
by a speaker to a listener; as talk instead of a process of communicating (Barnes
1992). With a lopsided emphasis on presenting, the listener's *role* is considerably
devalued. If the act of listening is unimportant, or less important than speaking,
the listener's *identity* may also be perceived as unimportant. Further, an emphasis
on speaking as the most important communication behavior raises a significant
question: What might we be teaching students about power in human relationships? How might we be shaping perceptions of persons who are shy, soft-spoken,
or who come from cultural backgrounds where an assertive manner of speaking is
considered rude? We will raise this topic again in later chapters when we discuss
gender, culture, and communication.

Symbols

An oral communicator masters a challenging array of complex verbal and nonverbal symbols. Words and phrases are not the only oral symbols that communicators employ. Vocal characteristics (such as pronunciation, articulation, pitch, tone,

rate, and volume) convey additional information about purpose and emotion. Silence—whether through deliberate pauses or a momentary inability to speak— also provides clues to meaning that are interpreted by the receiver. Nonverbal behaviors, including posture, gestures, facial expressions, and eye contact, can also have symbolic meanings. Nonverbal behaviors can increase a speaker's credibility, enhance a listener's understanding, or, conversely, lead to misperceptions and confusion.

Context

Oral communication behavior is highly context-dependent. Although context can be broadly construed to mean the major "genres" of communication (such as mass communication, interpersonal communication, or public speaking), it is used here in a narrower sense. In everyday life, the way people build and share meaning varies greatly according to rules and social conventions, physical surroundings, personalities, backgrounds, purposes, and expectations of the parties involved. Factors influencing communication context may also include the formality and informality of the occasion, the number of communicators participating in the event, and the direct or indirect nature of the communication. Examples of specific oral communication contexts could thus include a formal public presentation, storytelling between a parent and a child, a customer service encounter, a telephone conference call between corporate professionals, or a patron asking a reference librarian for information.

Two other factors unique to oral communication and affecting context deserve special attention: the immediacy and the impermanence of the spoken word (Backlund 1983).

Immediacy of Speech
Unlike the writer, who generally has opportunity to plan, write, and revise a communication before submitting it to an audience, an oral communicator rarely has a "text" or opportunities for revision. Such opportunities almost always occur in only the most formal kinds of public speaking. Oral communicators thus depend on a variety of critical thinking and behavioral skills to participate in successful communication. Most of an oral communicator's decisions about which words or symbols, tone of voice, nonverbal expression, or persuasive strategy to use will be made, for better or worse, in a split second. This need to simultaneously and continuously assess, respond, and adapt to the communication behavior of another person is known as the *immediacy* of speech.

Impermanence of Speech
Spoken and nonverbal messages are also impermanent—not easily recoverable or reviewable. Only with the aid of a recording device can we rewind, edit, and splice to change a spoken message once it has transpired. In most cases, a listener endeavors to understand a spoken message without benefit of a recording device or

Oral communication involves speaking and listening, frequently in informal contexts

a companion text. That is why organizational and critical thinking skills are central to the oral communication process. Some skills involved in active listening, such as concentration, note taking, maintaining eye contact, and using gestures—are also unique to oral communication and require practice and individual mastery (Brown et al. 1979).

WHY IS ORAL COMMUNICATION INSTRUCTION IMPORTANT?

The demand for oral communication competence in the workplace and in daily life is growing. This is a good reason to increase the emphasis on oral communication in the classroom.

In an increasingly service-based economy, students benefit professionally from frequent opportunities to learn and practice oral communication skills. A national survey of personnel managers reported that corporate employers of new college graduates look for excellent oral communication skills more than writing and technical expertise. Interpersonal and oral communication skills were also named in the same survey as the top two determinative factors in successful job performance (Curtis, Winsor, & Stephens 1989).

In the early 1990s, the American Bar Association concluded that legal employers considered oral communication skills more important to the success of young attorneys than research and writing skills, a significant departure from the mid-1970s when computer and library research skills were highest in demand (Stein 1993). The shift in skill preference from research and writing was explained in the study by a need to hire people who could build and maintain good working relationships with clients and colleagues. A subsequent study of attorneys ranked listening, building credibility, and adapting to a variety of different audiences as among the top ten oral communication skills for the legal profession (Chaney 1994).

Helping students achieve success in the professional world is only one benefit of a strong emphasis on oral communication instruction. Oral communication skills are vital for successful life management—listening skills, in particular. People from different cultures and backgrounds are more likely to live, work, and go to school with each other than in the past. Families are more likely than ever to be separated in some manner and to include new or nontraditional relationships between members. A commitment to open communication can thus be challenging for some in our modern society, but the quality of life is enriched when individuals choose to engage in ethical, constructive, self-aware communication with their families, friends, co-workers, neighbors, and fellow community members.

One example of how listening skills have received greater attention as life-management skills can be seen in efforts to counter the rising tide of violence in our society with elementary and secondary peer-mediation programs. Students trained as peer mediators assist other students in talking about their differences and drafting agreements to solve problems. Successful peer mediators must master the oral communication skills of active listening—including summarizing, reflecting, and maintaining direct eye contact—in order to assist the participants in clarifying the issues and generating solutions. As early as kindergarten, children can discuss examples of how conflicts may be resolved or have been resolved in the past without violence (Kriedler 1994).

Listening and thinking skills have also become more important with the rise of information technology as a powerful medium for persuasion. If we are not already inundated with messages conveyed by radio, television, and multimedia computers in our homes and places of work, we are certain to encounter a variety of electronically conveyed warnings, sales pitches, or announcements as we travel around town. Even soft-drink and video-game machines are capable of uttering salutations and attention-getting phrases.

Wolff and associates (1983) identify four types of listening (discussed in Chapter 4): *discriminative* (gathering information), *evaluative* (analyzing and determining the merits of persuasive messages), *empathic* (providing support and guidance), and *appreciative* (listening for enjoyment). Evaluative listening is arguably the most needed but the least emphasized in schools. According to psychologists, we live in a message-dense environment in which the average television viewer sees nearly 38,000 commercials alone annually; but people have less and less time to process and evaluate what they hear (Scott 1992). The skills of an evaluative listener—identifying hidden motives, recognizing fallacies in reasoning, distinguishing emotional appeals from logic, separating fact from opinion, and recognizing common forms of propaganda—are important tools for successful life management in the modern world. As listeners, both children and adults are vulnerable without the skills needed to objectively assess and respond to the merits of "image" advertising, 24-hour home shopping networks, and the claims of Internet-savvy persuaders. An active listener is, above all, a critical thinker.

WHAT IS ORAL COMMUNICATION COMPETENCE?

Communication competence is defined differently among disciplines. Linguists refer to *communicative competence* as "the total communication system, verbal and nonverbal" and the "knowledge that speakers have of how to construct and use language, rather than their actual skill in doing so" (Foster 1992, pp. 8–9). In contrast, performance-based perspectives in the language arts and speech communication disciplines are likely to include specific speaking, listening, and thinking skills that will assist a communicator on a daily basis (Backlund 1985). Rubin (1982, 1985) described communication competence as having knowledge, skill, and motivation dimensions while also viewing it as "an impression formed about the appropriateness of another's communication behavior" (1985, p. 173).

There is healthy debate over the nature and parameters of oral communication competence, but one underlying principle is certain: at its most fundamental level, oral communication competence includes abilities essential for the building and sharing of meaning, not merely the abilities necessary to "talk to" a passive, perhaps even anonymous, listener or audience. *Building and sharing* implies (1) that oral communication competence includes skills in three areas—speaking, listening, and thinking—so that a person may fully participate in the transactional process, and (2) that oral communication competence includes behavioral, cognitive, and affective components.

A Working Definition of Oral Communication Competence

1. Abilities essential for the process of building and sharing meaning, including:
2. behavioral, cognitive, and affective components;
3. allowing the communicator to function transactionally as speaker, listener, and critical thinker;
4. as the communication context requires.

The advantage of a working definition of competence is that it provides a set of flexible standards by which to measure individually tailored, locally developed programs. There may never be national agreement on the full range and depth of skills that should be included in oral communication competence, and arguably individual school districts and state departments of education are in the best position to design standards for each community of students and teachers. Several comprehensive efforts have been made in this direction, however, by the national Speech Communication Association, resulting in the skill inventory for elementary students (Speech Communication Association 1994) shown in Exhibit 1.1. The Speech Communication Association has also compiled a set of general standards in the areas of speaking, listening, and media literacy, for use by local communities in developing oral communication curricula (Speech Communication Association 1996).

Exhibit 1.1   Speaking and Listening Competencies for Elementary School Students

I. *Communication Codes.* Producing and responding to spoken English and nonverbal forms of communication such as gestures and facial expressions. The child, when communicating:
- Speaks clearly and expressively through appropriate articulation, pronunciation, volume, rate, and intonation
- Uses and understands spoken language appropriate to the communication context
- Uses nonverbal cues that emphasize meaning

II. *Functional Skills.* Communicating for specific purposes, such as informing, controlling, following social conventions, imagining, sharing feelings in particular communication contexts. The child, when communicating:
- Seeks, offers, and responds to information
- Seeks to influence others' beliefs and actions and reacts to others' persuasion
- Recognizes and participates appropriately in social conventions
- Uses spoken language creatively to enjoy and participate in imaginative situations
- Uses spoken language to express own and respond to others' feelings
- Asks appropriate questions to clarify meaning

III. *Interaction and Message Strategy Skills.* Participating in situations ranging from informal conversations to more planned and formal interactions. The child, when communicating:
- Maintains conversations through communication behaviors such as entering into the conversation, taking turns, responding to other's remarks, and closing the conversation
- Presents ideas in an orderly way
- Clarifies and supports ideas with necessary details such as examples, illustrations, facts, opinions

IV. *Receptive and Evaluative Skills.* Understanding and evaluating the messages of others. The child, when communicating:
- Listens effectively to spoken messages (e.g., hears the speaker, understands meaning, follows sequence of ideas and draws inferences)
- Recognizes and interprets nonverbal cues given by others
- Describes others' points and recognizes how they differ
- Distinguishes between different purposes in communication
- Provides effective and appropriate feedback
- Critically evaluates a spoken message

Excerpted and adapted with permission of the Speech Communication Association (1994).

A COMPETENCY-BASED APPROACH AND THE INTEGRATED LANGUAGE ARTS: BUILDING AND SHARING MEANING

An integrated curriculum treats reading, writing, speaking, and listening both as content areas and as communication modes that enable learning about content in other disciplines (Van Tassel-Baska 1993). The processes of writing and oral communication, for instance, share the elements of purpose, audience, symbol referents, ethics, encoding and decoding—among others. These concepts, skills, and attributes are reinforced for one strand as they are studied and applied in another. The thematic unit, which examines a particular topic across disciplines, is one form of integrated curricula that has successfully created challenging opportunities for learning content in the language arts, science, math, social studies, and art by using skills from all four strands.

Although there is overlap in the four language arts strands with respect to some concepts and skills—particularly those associated with critical thinking—there are significant differences between oral communication and the other language arts strands. Earlier in this chapter, we touched on some of those differences, including the immediacy and impermanence of speech and the subsequent need to think on one's feet in many oral communication contexts. An integrated language arts curriculum can effectively address such distinctions by providing a wide variety of learning situations.

The number one challenge facing oral communication instruction in an integrated language arts curriculum is that students are at risk of receiving inadequate content instruction to build their knowledge about oral communication and positive oral communication attributes. To a lesser extent, they are at risk of experiencing too few opportunities to apply oral communication skills in authentic contexts—even though that is an explicit goal of an integrated curriculum. Failure to adequately address oral communication as a strand of the language arts occurs (1) when we allow any one formal speaking context—such as an oral report or a creative reading—to serve as the sole measure of a student's speaking proficiency; (2) when we teach only listening to follow directions or to summarize a story; and (3) perhaps most auspiciously, when we provide for frequent cooperative learning activities in small groups, but do not provide any instruction about how to play roles in a small group. An integrated curriculum is at its most effective when we lay a foundation of knowledge for all activities.

A competency-based oral communication strand resolves this dilemma by identifying core competencies—knowledge, skills, and attitudes—thus providing a comprehensive set of guidelines as a target for proficiency levels. Students are prepared for success when they exit to the next grade level and when they engage in real world oral communication activities. Van Tassel-Baska (1993) suggests guidelines for developing an integrated language arts unit (Exhibit 1.2) that includes speaking and listening. We have added a few extra issues to consider.

**Exhibit 1.2   Key Questions to Answer While Developing
a New Language Arts Unit**

Topic/Content
- Is the area of study important to the understanding of the language arts?
- Does the area lend itself to interdisciplinary study?
- Can the selected concept be honestly represented in this area?

Whole Language Approach
- Does the unit integrate the language arts as much as possible?
- Are there interrelated opportunities for reading, speaking, listening, and writing?
- Do students engage with the richest literature possible?

Speaking and Listening
- Do the units provide opportunities for students to engage in active speaking and listening activities?
- Do the units generally address critical thinking skills through listening and speaking?
- Do the units specifically promote the use of critical thinking skills through evaluative listening and persuasive speaking?
- Do the units promote involvement of students in responding to each others' presentations through questions, discussions, and critique?
- Do the units promote positive attitudes toward communication?
- Do the units challenge students to achieve self-awareness of their communication styles and behaviors?

Adapted and reprinted with permission of J. Van Tassel-Baska (1993, pp. 71–74).

Although developmental limitations are known to affect communication abilities and motivation, communication research does not yet provide much evidence as to when these limitations ease so that students can be challenged to achieve higher levels of communication proficiency. Until more is known about the impact of biological development on the acquisition of communication skills, teachers and administrators can design instruction that merges theory with their own observations about student abilities. The 1991 SCA framework shown in Exhibit 1.3 locates skills and abilities by grade level (Speech Communication Association 1991, pp. 12–13).

Douglas Barnes (1992) noted that the most effective teachers are often those who intently observe their students as they play, read, and otherwise interact with their classmates. His philosophy has been supported by research from the Canadian Peels Project on Oracy, which espoused the virtues of "kidwatching." That project found that "kidwatching" teachers tended to learn more about their students' communication habits and abilities than teachers who observed oral communication only during testing and designated oral language activities (Booth & Thornley-Hall 1991a,b). At least one study has shown that teachers who actively observe their students are good predictors of their students' capabilities (Anderson et al. 1985).

Exhibit 1.3   Developmental Conception of a Communication Curriculum

Grade	Guidelines
Kindergarten	Learning activities should focus on the acquisition of basic oral linguistic skills.
First Grade	Learning activities should provide opportunities for students to increase their oral language options and choices.
Second Grade	Learning activities should provide opportunities for students to identify the range of relationships among roles, norms, and oral language choices.
Third Grade	Learning activities should provide opportunities for students to understand the range of options and possibilities which oral language creates in small-group and multicultural settings.
Fourth Grade	Learning activities should provide opportunities for students to be exposed to how oral language reflects and conveys values, particularly in terms of the choices alternatives, and consequences of the values embedded in oral communication.
Fifth Grade	Learning activities should provide students with opportunities to understand the social conventions regulating oral communication.
Sixth Grade	Learning activities should provide students with a formal exposure to the requirements and effective use of listening.
Seventh Grade	Learning activities should provide opportunities for students to identify, understand, and experience the requirements for effective interpersonal, nonverbal, and small-group communication.
Eighth Grade	Learning activities should provide opportunities for students to understand the effects of cultural systems on effective oral communication.

Reprinted with permission of the Speech Communication Association (1991, pp. 12–13).

An integrated language arts curriculum that places a strong emphasis on oral communication skills has been developed by the Rochester (N.Y.) City School District (RCSD). Rather than assigning competencies by grade level, the school district uses student content standards and developmental stages. Content standards as defined by the district are "specific statements that further define District goals—what students are expected to know, be able to do, and personify in terms of attributes and attitudes" (Rochester City School District 1995). Rochester (1995) defines developmental stages as follows:

> A means of reporting a student's progress toward the content standards in key areas of learning. The stages consist of a series of short statements called descriptors.* The descriptors are arranged in levels of achievement and are framed in positive terms. The stages themselves have

---

*Adapted from *The National English Profile. Trialling and Formal Consultation Draft.* Australian Education Council Curriculum and Assessment Committee, 1992.

breadth and depth, offering much richer information than is yielded by traditional grades such as "satisfactory," "unsatisfactory," or by a standardized test (Section 2, p. 1).

One of the outstanding characteristics of the Rochester curriculum is its commitment to a wide variety of challenging oral communication contexts, even at early grade levels. Efforts to link language arts content standards to performance in social studies are also comprehensive.

With the permission of the Rochester City School District, we have included their content standards and developmental stages for the primary school juncture (K–2) and the intermediate school juncture (3–5) as one example of how a school district can achieve a comprehensive, in-depth treatment of oral communication within the integrated language arts (see Appendices 1.1–1.5).

SUMMARY

Oral communication is the process of building and sharing meaning through the use of verbal and nonverbal symbols, in a variety of contexts. It differs fundamentally from written communication in that oral communication is immediate—interaction between speaker and listener can occur within a matter of seconds—and it is impermanent, necessitating strong critical thinking, comprehension, and recall skills. Oral communication competence includes behavioral, cognitive, and affective components allowing the communicator to function transactionally as a speaker, listener, and thinker as the context requires.

Oral communication instruction is important because oral communication is a mode of human communication that is used frequently, and competency is vital for academic, workplace, and life-management success. In the past, oral communication instruction was neglected because of misconceptions that the oral communication competence develops naturally over time and that the cognitive skills involved in writing automatically transfer to analogous oral communication skills.

A competency-based approach to oral communication identifies core competencies, sets proficiency levels, and designs instruction to target these levels. The goal of competency-based instruction is to prepare students for success when they reach the next exit level (progress to the next grade in school) and to prepare students for success in the real world. Teachers can determine appropriate competencies by observing students and merging those observations with theory about what students might be able to achieve at each grade level. Researchers are discovering that children can learn a broader and deeper array of oral communication competencies than has been taught previously in the language arts.

A competency-based approach to the language arts integrates essential oral communication skills with reading and writing activities. Authentic assessment of oral communication can include cooperative learning activities as well as traditional formal speeches or reports. Other appropriate activities for assessment include dramatizations, debate, mass media projects, self- and peer assessments of oral communication activities, and role-playing in listening.

REFERENCES

Allen, R. R., & Brown, K. (1976). *Developing communication competence in children.* Skokie, IL: National Textbook.

Andersen, J. F., Andersen, P. A., Murphy, M. A., & Wendt-Wasco, N. (1985). Teacher reports of students' nonverbal communication in the classroom: A developmental study in grades K–12. *Communication Education, 34,* 292–304.

Backlund, P. (1983). Methods of assessing speaking and listening skills. In R. B. Rubin (Ed.), *Improving speaking and listening skills: New directions for college learning assistance, No. 12* (pp. 59–73). San Francisco: Jossey-Bass.

———. (1985). Essential speaking and listening skills for elementary school students. *Communication Education, 34,* 185–195.

Barnes, D. (1992). *From communication to curriculum* (2nd ed.). Portsmouth, NH: Heinemann, Boynton/Cook.

Booth, D., & Thornley-Hall, C. (1991a). *Classroom talk.* Portsmouth, NH: Heinemann Educational Books.

———. (1991b). *The talk curriculum.* Portsmouth, NH: Heinemann Educational Books.

Brown, K., Backlund, P., Gurry, J., & Jandt, F. (1979). *Assessment of basic speaking and listening skills: State of the art and recommendations for instrument development,* 2 vols. Boston: Massachusetts Department of Education, Bureau of Research and Assessment.

Chaney, A. (1994). Attorney perceptions of oral communication competence: Toward a working definition. Paper presented at the annual meeting of the Speech Communication Association, New Orleans, October.

Cooper, J. D. (1993). *Literacy: Helping children construct meaning* (2nd ed.). Boston: Houghton Mifflin.

Cooper, P. J. (1995). *Communication for the classroom teacher* (5th ed.). Scottsdale: Gorsuch Scarisbrick.

Curtis, D., Winsor, J., & Stephens, R. (1989). National preferences in business and communication education. *Communication Education, 38,* 6.

Foster, S. H. (1992). *The communicative competence of young children: A modular approach.* New York: Longman.

Kriedler, W. J. (1994). *Teaching conflict resolution through children's literature: Grades K–2.* New York: Scholastic Professional Books.

Modaff, J., & Hopper, C. (1984). Why speech is basic. *Communication Education, 33,* 37–42.

Rochester City School District. (1995). Goals, measures, content standards: Language arts/social studies. Rochester, NY: Rochester City School District.

Rubin, R. (1982). Assessing speaking and listening skills at the college level: The communication competency assessment instrument. *Communication Education, 31,* 19–32.

———. (1985). The validity of the communication competency assessment instrument. *Communication Monographs, 52,* 173–185.

Scott, J. (1992). How they get you to do that. *New York Times,* July 23, A1.

Speech Communication Association. (1991). *Guidelines for developing oral communication curricula in kindergarten through twelfth grade.* Annandale, VA: Speech Communication Association.

———. (1994). *Speaking and listening competencies for elementary school students.* Annandale, VA: Speech Communication Association.

———. (1996). *Speaking, listening, and media literacy standards for K through 12 education.* Annandale, VA: Speech Communication Association.

Stein, A. (1993). Job hunting? Exude confidence. *ABA Journal,* November, 40.

Van Tassel-Baska, J. (1993). *Creating a new language arts curriculum for high ability learners.* Language Arts Topics Papers. Williamsburg, VA: College of William and Mary, Center for Gifted Education.

Wolff, F., Marsnik, N., Tacey, W., & Nichols, R. (1983). *Perceptive listening.* New York: Holt, Rinehart, & Winston.

APPENDIX 1.1
Rochester City School District
Content Standards and Examples of Applied Learning
SPEAKING AND LISTENING, Primary School Juncture (Pre-K–2)

FUNCTION	CONTENT STANDARDS	APPLIED LEARNING
Making Sense	Students make sense of the spoken word and make themselves understood by: • requesting essential information in formal or informal situations • listening actively and following directions • recalling and restating essential information from formal or informal communications • analyzing, reviewing, and expressing opinions on issues, ideas or experiences • presenting information clearly and logically, following preset guidelines • explaining their responses with reference to personal experiences and values	Some examples of how students can demonstrate competence: • ask questions during a field study • ask relevant questions; seek clarification persistently with regard for needs of others • tell what has been learned after listening to a formal presentation by a classroom visitor • engage in a discussion about a current event • talk about a shared class experience (e.g., unit of study, science investigation, math exploration) • retell scenes from stories/films/dramatic presentations
Demonstrating Range	Students demonstrate versatility by: • speaking to a variety of audiences for different purposes and in different situations • listening actively and responding appropriately in a variety of situations	Some examples of how students can demonstrate competence: • record audio/video tapes in different situations
Using Strategies	Students demonstrate an awareness of craft by: • recognizing and practicing appropriate speaking and listening strategies • making a presentation	Some examples of how students can demonstrate competence: • play-act familiar stories and rhymes (i.e., *Three Little Pigs, This Old Man, Head and Shoulder*) • plan and deliver a talk (include who/what/when/where/why/how)
Using Conventions	Students demonstrate command of conventions by: • using classroom conventions appropriately while being aware that home and school expectations may differ • recognizing and practicing appropriate speaking and listening conventions • making a presentation using appropriate grammar, syntax, tone, and language	Some examples of how students can demonstrate competence: • self-correct in response to modeling • reflect and self-correct by rephrasing to clarify meaning • speak audibly and clearly • use social conventions of speech (volume of voice, nonverbal signs, greetings, courtesy terms) • read prepared material with appropriate use of expression, slang, and jargon

APPENDIX 1.1   *Continued*

FUNCTION	CONTENT STANDARDS	APPLIED LEARNING
Taking Responsibility	Students demonstrate increasing independence by: • evaluating their own performance for content, organization, and delivery • recognizing and expressing feelings and attitudes • assuming assigned roles within a group	Some examples of how students can demonstrate competence: • participate in small-group discussions in which students take turns being listeners and speakers • resolve arguments without resorting to physical and verbal violence • discuss ideas and exchange information in everyday school situations • talk about a favorite literary character and give reasons for choice • participate appropriately in a cooperative learning task • observe rules in a structured group setting (raise hand to speak, take turns, listening attentively, answer questions, offer opinions and ideas)

Reprinted with permission of the Rochester City School District (1995).

APPENDIX 1.2
Rochester City School District
Developmental Stages Descriptors
SPEAKING AND LISTENING, Primary School Juncture (Pre-K–2)

LANGUAGE ARTS PROFILE: As children work to meet content and performance standards, they move through developmental stages. While not rigid, the stages are described by behaviors that tend to cluster (i.e., emerge at about the same time). Children's portfolios should contain concrete evidence of their progression through the stages.

Record the descriptor(s) in each stage that a child is consistently demonstrating (i.e., date initially, then highlight or check when behavior is consistent).

DEVELOPING
PORTFOLIO
DOCUMENTATION

STAGE A

Speaking
- Speaks clearly enough to be understood by an unfamiliar listener (NY)*
- Asks questions either nonverbally, or using single words or phrases
- Participates in conversations with other children and/or adults in unstructured situations
- Shares in group discussions
- Tells a familiar story, relying upon pictures and teacher support
- Participates in rhymes, fingerplays, songs, and childhood chants
- Uses language to communicate personal needs and wants, relate personal experience, ask what and where questions (NY)

Listening
- Demonstrates understanding, verbally and nonverbally
- Listens to stories with sustained interest
- Follows simple one- and two-step directions with support
- Listens to a peer's idea and helps carry it out
- Demonstrates an awareness of language patterns, rhythms, and sounds
- Listens actively when having a conversation in an instructional situation
- Listens to meet specific personal needs, respond to what/where questions and participate in social interactions (NY)

Oral Presentation

Teacher Observations

Tape/video recordings

Self-reflection

Commercial

Review of peer's
oral presentation

STAGE B

Speaking
- Communicates meaning using simple sentences
- Responds appropriately in instructional and social settings
- Uses language to relate stories and events, create dialogue in play situations, tell jokes, ask how/when/why questions

---

*The New York State–mandated kindergarten screening requires identification of problems in Receptive Language ("Listens . . ."), Articulation ("Speaks clearly . . .") and Expressive Language ("Uses language . . ."). These three areas in Speaking and Listening Stage A are designed for this purpose.

APPENDIX 1.2 *Continued*

STAGE B *(Continued)*

Listening
- Follows two- and three-step directions without reminders
- Listens to informational texts with sustained interest
- Listens to participate in completing a plan and responds to how/why questions

STAGE C

Speaking
- Gives simple instructions to others
- Asks for clarification in conversation, using who/what/when/where/how questions
- Contributes new and pertinent information to discussions and conversations
- Uses language to entertain, predict, give simple instructions, and relate stories or events in logical sequences

Listening
- Demonstrates attentiveness as a listener through body language and/or facial expression
- Listens to be entertained and extract pertinent information

STAGE D

Speaking
- Uses prepositions, conjunctions, and connectives appropriately
- Embeds phrases and clauses within sentences
- Converses on topics other than self
- Uses accurate pronunciation, and appropriate intonation, expression, and tone of voice
- Demonstrates an awareness of listener's needs in conversations
- Elaborates without prompting questions
- Uses language to describe real and imagined events, define, and reason

Listening
- Interprets increasingly complex language
- Recognizes the need to ask questions to understand what is heard
- Listens to form an image, formulate definitions, understand reasoning and recognize differing viewpoints

STAGE E

Speaking
- Uses prepositions, conjunctions, and connectives appropriately
- Embeds phrases and clauses within sentences
- Converses on topics other than self
- Uses accurate pronunciation, and appropriate intonation, expression, and tone of voice

Oral Presentation

Teacher Observations

Tape/video recordings

Recordings

Self-reflection

Commercial

Review of peer's oral presentation

(continued)

APPENDIX 1.2   *Continued*

STAGE E

Speaking *(Continued)*

(See previous performances.)

- Demonstrates an awareness of listeners' needs in conversations.
- Elaborates without prompting questions
- Uses language to describe real and imagined events, define, and reason

Listening

- Interprets increasingly complex language
- Recognizes the need to ask questions to understand what is heard
- Listens to form an image, formulate definitions, understand and recognize differing viewpoints

Reprinted with permission of the Rochester City School District (1995).

APPENDIX 1.3
Rochester City School District
Content Standards and Examples of Applied Learning
SPEAKING AND LISTENING, Intermediate School Juncture (3–5)

FUNCTION	CONTENT STANDARDS	APPLIED LEARNING
Making Sense	Students make sense of the spoken word and make themselves understood by: • connecting the main idea of a speech with supporting detail • paraphrasing, summarizing and extracting essential information • adhering to topic when speaking • conveying directions • listening actively and asking relevant questions • interpreting ideas effectively • following directions • listening critically to presentations for main ideas, sequence of events, facts or opinions	Some examples of how students can demonstrate competence: • debate an issue or a topic • give an oral presentation • make an announcement about an event • interview a peer and introduce him/her • summarize issues following a panel discussion • critique an oral presentation • identify fact, opinion, bias, stereotype, and emotion in spoken text • prepare questions and conduct a field study or interview • tutor another student
Demonstrating Range	Students demonstrate versatility by: • speaking to a variety of audiences for different purposes and in different situations • using language creatively to express ideas, point of view, reasoning and experiences • using language that is appropriate for the audience and situation • listening actively and responding appropriately in a variety of situations	Some examples of how students can demonstrate competence: • record audio/video tapes in different situations (presentation, play, meeting) • create a written plan for an informative speech and a summary of how the presentation went • write a story with dialogue and then read conversations between different characters aloud • contribute significantly and respect contributions from others in a group inquiry project
Using Strategies	Students demonstrate an awareness of craft by: • identifying the strategies used by a speaker to inform or entertain or to influence an audience • matching language and delivery style to different audiences • assuming different roles in collaborative/cooperative learning groups	Some examples of how students can demonstrate competence: • plan and deliver a campaign speech • evaluate a classmate's speech using an established format • serve as a peer mediator • serve as a school tour guide to visitors

(continued)

APPENDIX 1.3   *Continued*

FUNCTION	CONTENT STANDARDS	APPLIED LEARNING
Using Strategies *(Continued)*	• using a process to organize, develop, and deliver an oral presentation incorporating information from multiple sources and appropriate visual aids	• develop an audio/video tape along with a written plan
Using Conventions	Students demonstrate command of conventions by: • using syntax, tone, and language that is respectful of and sensitive to audiences from different backgrounds • choosing vocabulary that enriches, sustains, and clarifies meaning for an audience • speaking clearly and audibly with appropriate eye contact, expression and gestures	Some examples of how students can demonstrate competence: • see examples of performances linked with *Using Strategies*
Taking Responsibility	Students demonstrate increasing independence by: • contributing to and responding constructively during formal and informal discussions • monitoring, evaluating, and self-correcting while speaking • reflecting on and evaluating their own performances for content, organization, and delivery • participating actively in a community of learners	Some examples of how students can demonstrate competence: • organize and present information to a group in a clear and logical manner • share personal events/anecdotes in a context of a topic • evaluate own speech using audience response • take part in a literary discussion group (e.g., reader's circle) • develop special techniques to help themselves become active listeners • reflect on how they see themselves as a speaker and listener

Reprinted with permission of the Rochester City School District (1995).

APPENDIX 1.4
Rochester City School District
Developmental Stages Descriptors
SPEAKING AND LISTENING, Intermediate Juncture (3–5)

LANGUAGE ARTS PROFILE: As children work to meet content and performance standards, they move through developmental stages. While not
rigid, the stages are described by behaviors that tend to cluster (i.e., emerge
at about the same time). Children's portfolios should contain concrete
evidence of their progression through the stages.

Record the descriptor(s) in each stage that a child is consistently demonstrating (i.e., date initially, then highlight or check when behavior is
consistent).

DEVELOPING
PORTFOLIO
DOCUMENTATION

STAGE F

Speaking
- Gives multi-step directions to others
- Asks relevant questions to seek information and/or clarification
  during structured learning situations
- Contributes in learning groups by commenting constructively and
  persuasively with teacher support
- Paraphrases and summarizes to clarify meaning with guidance
- Uses body language that is appropriate for purpose and audience
  to reinforce the message
- Delivers developmentally appropriate presentations to inform
  and/or influence a variety of audiences
- Uses language to express emotions, to sequentially relate events
  and to retell stories
- Uses an expanded vocabulary to relate more elaborate messages

Listening
- Listens to developmentally appropriate presentations to form an
  image, formulate definitions, identify reasoning, recognize differing viewpoints and make inferences

STAGE G

Speaking
- Helps to plan and participate in a group presentation to inform
  and influence a variety of audiences
- Contributes by commenting constructively and persuasively in
  learning groups
- Experiments with new vocabulary to convey shades of meaning
- Paraphrases and summarizes to clarify meaning with support
- Uses a wider variety of prepositions, conjunctions and connectives
  appropriately (e.g., however, therefore, although)

Listening
- Listening to developmentally appropriate presentations to form
  an image, formulate definitions, identify reasoning, recognize
  differing viewpoints and make inferences.

Retelling

Peer mediation

Choral reading/speaking

Dramatic listening/
speaking

Discussion groups

Play/skit

Interview

Peer/cross-age tutoring

Role-playing

News bulletins/
PA announcements

Audio/Visual tapes

Book talks

Conferences

Anecdotal records

Assumption of different
roles in cooperative
groups

Notes, outlines, scripts

(continued)

APPENDIX 1.4   *Continued*

STAGE H

Speaking

(See previous
performances.)

- Uses an expanded vocabulary in a variety of situations to convey subtlety of meaning
- Explains a position taken on a controversial topic
- Delivers an extemporaneous speech using appropriate vocabulary and syntax
- Converses appropriately with a variety of people in different situations/settings
- Paraphrases and summarizes to clarify meaning

Listening

- Listens to developmentally appropriate presentations to form an image, formulate definitions, identify reasoning, recognize differing viewpoints, and make inferences

APPENDIX 1.5
Rochester City School District
Foundation Skills Linked to Language Arts Standards
SOCIAL STUDIES, Primary and Intermediate School Junctures (Pre-K–5)

FOUNDATION STANDARDS LINKED TO LANGUAGE ARTS STANDARDS	MEASURES/DOCUMENTATION/EXAMPLES/ GENERIC ASSESSMENT
Students will: • Develop social and political participation skills • Acquire information by using community resources and using primary and secondary source materials • Locate, select, and organize information from written sources, such as books, periodicals, and encyclopedias • Retrieve and use information by using computers and audio-visual media • Read and interpret maps, globes, models, diagrams, tables, graphs, charts, and pictures • Understand basic social studies vocabulary • Organize and express ideas clearly in writing and speaking • Record and interpret information from observation, field studies, and interviews • Read, interpret, and make time lines • Develop research strategies using a variety of resources (atlases, autobiographies, maps, globes, encyclopedias, tradebooks, etc.)	• Preparing and giving an oral report • Writing a critical analysis of relationships of concepts • Writing a personal narrative relating concepts to personal life • Self-assessing in terms of group work and/or project development • Interpreting information through graphs, charts, timelines, diagrams, flow charts, etc. • Constructing maps and models to demonstrate knowledge of content and concepts (e.g., latitude and longitude, geography, terms, etc.) • Keeping journals to demonstrate an understanding of historical perspectives • Competing in games (e.g., Geography Bee) to demonstrate factual knowledge • Participating in cooperative learning activities to demonstrate citizenship skills • Using a variety of resources to report on a topic • Using different forms of media to discuss/ summarize/report/analyze current events • Using oral history to report on past events and issues • Using primary sources (documents, charts, cartoons) to analyze an issue • Reporting on field trips and interviews • Role-playing historical characters in skits, as speakers, or as diary writers • Simulating political and economic activities • Simulating historical experiences (e.g., westward migration) using resources from a variety of disciplines

(continued)

APPENDIX 1.5   *Continued*

FOUNDATION STANDARDS LINKED TO LANGUAGE ARTS STANDARDS	MEASURES/DOCUMENTATION/EXAMPLES/ GENERIC ASSESSMENT
	• Exploring interdisciplinary topics in research activities • Using art, literature, music, and drama to examine or demonstrate historical, political, cultural, and/or economic circumstances • Using court simulations or debates of topics

Reprinted with permission of the Rochester City School District (1995).

Exploratory talk in pairs

2

The Importance of a Communication-Friendly Classroom

OVERVIEW

This chapter focuses on the importance of establishing and maintaining a communication-friendly classroom, the benefits of which are a more stimulating and productive learning environment, a positive learner self-concept, and reduction in high levels of anxiety about speaking and listening. A communication-friendly classroom helps students understand what it means to be competent communicators in the real world. Students learn that acting with respect for self and others is an important part of effective oral communication, leading to stronger interpersonal relationships and life enrichment.

PRACTICALLY SPEAKING

In your role as classroom teacher, do you:

Allow "exploratory talk" during reading and writing time?

Model positive oral communication attributes?

Help make oral communication safe and comfortable for students?

Include and encourage everyone to participate in the communication process?

Recognize and attend to the signs of communication and receiver apprehension?

Classroom environment shapes student perceptions of oral communication—what oral communication is, and why oral communication skills are important. Classroom environment can also shape student perceptions about the identity of communicators—who they are as people, and why their ideas and messages are important. For these reasons, establishing a communication-friendly classroom is an important step in sending realistic, positive messages to students about their behavior as communicators. A communication-friendly classroom can help foster healthy attitudes toward self and others.

What are the characteristics of a communication-friendly classroom? A "kinder, gentler" classroom is not all that is meant by "communication-friendly." Rather, a communication-friendly classroom uses oral communication in authentic ways to help children learn and develop literacy. Such a classroom also allows students to develop oral communication skills in a variety of settings. And a communication-friendly classroom helps students feel safe and able to take healthy risks necessary for effective interpersonal, small-group, and public communication.

EXPLORATORY TALK IN THE CLASSROOM

First, a communication-friendly classroom uses oral communication in authentic ways to help children learn and develop literacy. Barnes (1992) stresses the value of exploratory talk in the development of literacy. When allowed to talk through a problem, to sound out words, ideas, and sentences without fear of correction—students are better able to comprehend new information and to build on their previous knowledge. O'Keefe (1995) cited scholarly research linking oral communication proficiency to academic achievement in reading and writing, to capacity for abstract and higher-order thought, and to the construction of knowledge.

Booth and Thornley-Hall (1991a) collected case studies from teachers in the Peel (Ontario) Board of Education TALK project and observed that children made meaning from reading and writing by discussing their reactions to what they had read, holding peer conferences about their own writing, dramatizing plays and literature, and learning to tell and retell stories. Barnes and Todd (1995) continued along these lines by proposing that "students be given more control of their learning and therefore more responsibility for how they go about it" (p. 16).

One way of promoting exploratory talk without sacrificing too much classroom control is to include cooperative learning activities in the language arts. Cooperative (also known as collaborative) learning activities provide purpose, context, and structure for exploratory talk. Cooperative learning occurs when small groups of students work together in a self-guided fashion to complete a task that involves listening, recall of previous knowledge and information, critical thinking skills, and usually some attention to detail. The teacher is a facilitator and monitor but plays only a minimal role in correcting and guiding learning. Examples of cooperative learning activities include peer conferences to prepare, edit, and revise writing; peer tutoring; planning and rehearsing plays and puppet shows; small-group discussion and problem solving; and group presentations.

One challenge in allowing greater levels of exploratory talk and cooperative learning in the classroom is fear of losing control of the class. Teachers can set the stage for cooperative learning and allow students to earn responsibility and choice in their own learning through early training in observing classroom rules and procedures.

Ground Rules

Establish a set of general ground rules for classroom activities and explain to the class what those rules are and why you have chosen them. Claire Staab (1992) observes that ground rules are most effective when they are simple, direct, phrased in the positive, and essential (relevant) for learning. She advocates establishing a handful of classroom rules and procedures; practicing, enforcing, and reinforcing the rules until the class is close to self-regulating; and then gradually "loaning" control to the students, revoking it as necessary to preserve discipline. This sequence allows teachers to build trust in students and allows students to develop self-control and responsibility. Students may then work in pairs and in small groups without constant direction from the teacher. Examples of general classroom ground rules include:

- Listen when others are speaking.
- Everyone takes turns in speaking.
- Show respect for your classmates.
- Encourage each other to participate.

Project-specific ground rules may also be worthwhile for cooperative learning activities. MacGillivray and Hawes (1994) reported that ground rules are necessary for some kinds of peer coaching and conferencing. In their study of first-graders teamed in reading partnerships, some students used the opportunity to assert dominance and control over less accomplished partners. MacGillivray and Hawes suggest that teachers prepare for activities such as reading partnerships by creating guidelines for positive partner feedback. Students can role play (practice) assisting a partner in learning to read. The authors stress that in multiethnic classrooms, nonverbal communication might also be a topic of discussion in order to raise awareness of how nonverbal communication can be interpreted differently across cultures (p. 216).

In addition to setting general and project-specific ground rules, the risk of losing classroom control can be minimized by observing students as they participate in discussion and making adjustments in the composition of small groups to foster discipline and equity. Take note of any patterns that might be generally disruptive or damaging to the development of students in the class. Consider grouping students with others whom they like and with whom they feel comfortable. Such groupings help reduce apprehension about working in groups and provide a more supportive environment for quiet or shy children as they learn to assert themselves. On the other hand, you may wish to partition excessively noisy or uncooperative groups as necessary to maintain order.

The physical arrangement of a room can help create a sense of openness and trust

Physically arranging the classroom to promote small-group and individual learning can also be helpful in managing a class filled with exploratory talk. To allow healthy whole-class discussion while maintaining a sense of control and security, consider arranging desks or chairs in a semicircle; seating students on the floor in a circle; or seating yourself in a chair near the class (as opposed to behind a desk). Standing and walking among students (especially if desks are shaped in clusters for small-group work) makes it easy to intervene in a personal, subtle, and tactful manner should students become disruptive or demonstrate otherwise inappropriate behavior.

MODELING ORAL COMMUNICATION ATTRIBUTES

A communication-friendly classroom is a place where constructive oral communication is studied and modeled for the benefit of everyone. Just as teachers represent a "literate other" to students who are developing literacy skills, teachers also serve as a "communicative other" by modeling oral communication skills.

Teacher as Facilitator

Successfully initiating and facilitating active classroom discussion is one of the most important strategies a teacher can use to model oral communication skills. In acting as a discussion facilitator, a teacher models important speaking and listening skills, while providing students with a powerful learning tool. Experimental evidence supports the viewpoint that students learn as well, if not better, through discussion than through lecture (Klopf & Cambra 1991). By actively engaging in the learning process, students sharpen skills such as listening, speaking, responding, critical thinking, and conflict management.

Successful discussions don't just happen on their own, however. Teachers must be active participants, having carefully planned the discussion, facilitating it with the use of probing questions and consistent, constructive feedback about the discussion process. Although the length and sophistication of classroom discussion will depend on factors such as the age, maturity, and literacy levels of students, teachers can foster and guide classroom discussions by creating a climate conducive to discussion and participation; laying the groundwork through planning and preparation; and using open-ended questioning and response techniques to keep the discussion focused and productive.

Conducive Climate

An accepting climate can be established with icebreaker activities or warm, inclusive stories during reading hour. Students need to feel that their contributions are welcome and will be valued. One useful technique for beginning a discussion is to situate the class in a circle, then begin the discussion with a provocative question. Evoke a response from each member of the circle by name, continuing around the circle until everyone has had a chance to participate. More talkative learners will realize they are expected to listen to the contributions of others.

A safe climate for discussion can be established with the help of ground rules, as discussed earlier in this chapter. Even if learners believe that a teacher values their contributions, fear of ridicule by peers, or of "being wrong," can discourage participation. A technique that can be used with middle school students is to emphasize the *quality* of contributions over the *quantity* of contributions. Spend some time with the class outlining the meaning of a "quality" contribution. Invite the class to participate in defining the characteristics of a quality contribution. You may condense their suggestions into a set of manageable guidelines, such as:

- *Relate*—new ideas to what we have learned so far
- *Encourage*—someone quiet to elaborate on their ideas
- *Ask*—an insightful question that leads to new contributions by others
- *Think*—about what you are going to say before you say it
- *Listen*—to others before you respond

Ground rules can help reduce fear of ridicule or interruption, but teachers can also promote objectivity during disagreement by focusing on the ideas that are at issue, rather than the individuals raising or challenging the ideas. Teachers can ask other learners to comment, "Who else has a different opinion?" or "What other thoughts does someone have about this topic?" Another technique for focusing attention on ideas rather than individuals is to invite students to compare and contrast. "How is this idea similar to what we talked about yesterday? How is it different?" From time to time, it may be necessary to remind students of the ground rules.

Planning and Preparation

A discussion format can be formal, such as a panel discussion, or informal, such as a small-group discussion. The format should, however, empower all classroom members—that is, encourage all classroom members to feel that they can contribute and that their contributions are valuable. A discussion format that appears to favor only the more assertive students, for instance, is not empowering for those students who are shy, have learning disabilities, are English-language learners, or who have different cultural and ethnic backgrounds. Efforts should focus on ensuring opportunity for quality contribution and quality feedback.

As part of an effort to involve as many students as possible, stress to them the benefit of helping and teaching one another. Make learning by discussion a team effort. Point out how different experiences and perspectives can increase everyone's knowledge. Then, plan the discussion around readings, topics of study, films, or videos familiar to all students. Review vocabulary and define any new terms or ideas to provide a common background for the discussion. Every student needs to feel competent to follow along and contribute to a discussion on the subject matter.

An easy way to think about planning a discussion is to conceptualize three stages:

> *The Introduction.* Begin the discussion with an age-appropriate, attention-getting device of some sort. This could be a picture from a book, a puppet or stuffed animal, an interesting object, a provocative question—your imagination is the only limit. Then, spend a moment establishing the worthwhileness of the topic. Relating the topic to a student's life or recent learning experience is often a good tactic.

> *The Body.* Next, plan a series of questions with which to explore new ideas, compare and contrast those ideas with perviously learned concepts, solve a problem, make a decision, and so forth.

> *The Conclusion.* Finally, summarize major themes or ideas that arose during the discussion, draw conclusions, and pose questions for future thought.

Questioning and Response Techniques

Open-ended questioning and response techniques encourage learner participation. A teacher facilitates discussion by maintaining a probing atmosphere (for example: "Who else has a thought to share?") and encouraging difference of opinion ("Does anyone interpret the story differently?").

Be sure to follow up exchanges with mini-summaries and clarification so that students understand concrete ideas. Avoid student–teacher dialogues—keep the major focus on students learning to respond to and facilitate one another's ideas and reactions. Try to turn around questions directed to the teacher with responses such as "Good question. Who can respond to that?" This technique teaches students to elicit responses from one another.

The teacher as discussion facilitator should correct inaccurate information in a constructive manner and ask provocative questions in the spirit of critical thinking. It is also important to provide immediate and constructive feedback (we discuss this in detail in Chapter 5), and encourage the practice of other general interpersonal skills.

Experiencing the Oral Communication Process

Classrooms that feature a wide variety of speaking and listening activities are more likely to help students. As we have seen in Chapter 1, oral communicators send and receive verbal and nonverbal messages with a variety of different purposes and in a variety of different contexts (Speech Communication Association 1988). Lessons that explore different communication purposes and contexts teach students about the true breadth and depth of oral communication skills. An accurate view of oral communication competence shapes student expectations for performance and helps undermine the popular myth that, "I talk, therefore I communicate." A communication-friendly classroom might explore:

- *Informing*—Communicators send and receive messages containing new information.
- *Empathizing*—Communicators send and receive messages that express and respond to feelings.
- *Imagining*—Communicators send and receive messages that speculate, theorize, or otherwise involve imagination.
- *Socializing*—Communicators send and receive messages that build and maintain relationships and facilitate interaction.
- *Persuading*—Communicators send and receive messages that convince others.

In a communication-friendly classroom, students develop understanding of the oral communication process by experiencing these communication purposes. Students learn that all aspects of the process are necessary and worthwhile; that listening is as valuable as speaking; and that listeners are as valuable as speakers.

Experiencing Authentic Challenges to Oral Communication

Students benefit from realistic study and practice in recognizing and overcoming attitudinal barriers to communication. Like writing, oral communication is a process that facilitates the sharing of meaning between two or more people; but can be a much more personal, and certainly a more immediate, means of communication. People are challenged to communicate in spite of psychological and emotional barriers. In a communication-friendly classroom, students learn that:

- Communicators are people who come from different backgrounds, with different experiences, beliefs, and experiences.
- Communicators can overcome hostility, fear, and misunderstanding by choosing to use a variety of interpersonal and conflict-resolution skills.
- Sometimes oral communication is scary; but some fear and nervousness is normal, and lots of people experience it.

Sharing Respect

In a communication-friendly classroom, oral communicators treat each other with respect. They communicate truthfully and ethically. They are concerned with the well-being of others and with creating understanding. In this setting, students learn that:

- Communicators are open to new ideas and perspectives. They seek to understand and appreciate difference.
- Oral communicators are ethical in their presentation of information and in their attempts to persuade others.
- Oral communicators use interpersonal and conflict-resolution skills to express disagreement in a respectful and constructive manner.
- Oral communicators value and build trust with each other.

Developing Positive Attitudes About Communication

Finally, a communication-friendly classroom helps students develop positive attitudes toward oral communication. They begin to value the skills that can enrich their personal, academic, and workplace relationships. In a communication-friendly classroom, students learn that:

- People share new aesthetic experiences through oral communication.
- Oral communication skills can help reduce the negative impact of sad or hurtful events in life.
- Oral communication is a way for people to solve problems and create new things together.

A communication-friendly environment thus sends positive, constructive, and accurate messages about communication to students.

MAKING COMMUNICATION SAFE

Although some nervousness is normal and to be expected, a positive, psychologically safe environment, where children can take risks without fear of ridicule or criticism, will encourage students to respond creatively to communication challenges.

Preparation of a communication-friendly environment requires effort to identify and ameliorate sources of student anxiety about speaking and interacting with others. Sources of student anxiety may include competition among classmates, fear of negative evaluation by the teacher or by peers, fear of ridicule, or fear of laughter at imperfect English. In a mainstreamed classroom, students with physical disabilities or speech impediments may be fearful of standing in front of the class or may be fearful that peers or teachers will negatively evaluate their communication because of the appearance of disability.

You can use a number of strategies to increase the level of comfort and security in the classroom.

- Develop a manageable set of ground rules (as discussed earlier in this chapter).
- Encourage students who do not normally allow others to participate to do so by placing a premium on listening skills. Devise a way to validate listening efforts in a way that is meaningful to such students.
- Strike a balance in your correction efforts between form and function. Recognize that students who are learning to become competent oral communicators may need some freedom to make mistakes in form (i.e., mistakes in grammar, syntax, or pronunciation) so that they can build confidence in expressing the content of their thoughts. Students who are interrupted too often by a teacher in the interest of correcting form may feel that their ideas are not being heard and understood or, worse, that ideas do not matter to the teacher, only proper form.
- Choose a variety of fun, informal communication exercises and activities. Make a deliberate effort to build a sense of trust and community among students with icebreakers, cooperative learning, short oral presentations, and whole-class discussion.
- Be honest with students. Acknowledge their feelings about scary or unpleasant communication. Suggest ways of coping with those feelings by relating them to real world experiences. Share stories and personal examples from your own experience when appropriate. Let students feel that you trust them and want to relate to them.

The Inclusive Classroom

Classroom environment may also be affected by how comfortable children feel when reading, writing, and talking about the issues or topics that are presented for their reflection. Oral communication is a medium through which relationships between people, founded on perceptions of self and others, are established and maintained. Teachers can constructively direct the course of such relationships by monitoring the nature of material that is used as a springboard for classroom discussion.

In making a deliberate effort to use gender and interculturally sensitive communication, teachers model positive oral communication attributes and attitudes. Gender- and interculturally sensitive communicators strive to:

- Refrain from stereotyping another based on gender or culture
- Know the terms and symbols used in a specific culture when interacting with people from that culture
- Appear comfortable in a new and culturally different situation
- Adapt to communication differences that can lead to misunderstanding
- Choose words and language that are inclusive of gender and culture

Conversely, barriers to communication arise when stereotypes based on gender and culture are used to misinterpret, evaluate, control, and dismiss the contributions of another person in a communication event.

Gender

With respect to gender, studies have reported that boys are praised and challenged more by teachers in the classroom, while girls are more often ignored, complimented on appearance and demeanor, or discouraged by intimidating communication behaviors. These effects occur at the hands of teachers, parents, and peers alike. (American Association of University Women, 1992; Gilligan, Lyons, & Hammer 1990; Sadker & Sadker 1994). Members of minority cultures share similar experiences (Henkin 1995).

In a communication-friendly classroom, students can learn to recognize and refrain from using gender stereotypes when discussing activities, occupations, emotional characteristics, and relationship norms. Many students will be able to share examples from their personal or family lives that counter traditional stereotypes of gender. Students can learn to use gender-inclusive language. Training in active listening (see Chapter 4) will also assist students in identifying communication behaviors that might discourage girls from fully participating in group discussions, conferences, and conversations. Students may point out that males are also stereotyped unfairly. A discussion of how stereotypes impact each gender may help clarify why women tend to experience more discrimination as a whole, however.

Multiculturalism and Intercultural Communication

According to Flores (1993), intercultural communicators collaborate to build meaning. Collaboration occurs when the source and the receiver give each other additional information or offer appropriate verbal and nonverbal feedback. The extra information helps the other person redefine, or reinterpret, the original message. Two important forms of feedback are (1) paraphrasing how the message has been interpreted, so that the speaker has an opportunity to redefine the message; and (2) providing follow-up information, if necessary, to indicate confusion or a lack of understanding.

In addition to valuing difference in culture, a communication-friendly classroom allows opportunity for cultural collaboration. Exhibit 2.1 provides a closer look at the cultural collaboration and redefinition process. You will notice that it uses elements of the SMCR model (source–message–channel–receiver) introduced in Chapter 1.

Exhibit 2.1   Cultural Collaboration and Redefinition Process

Context. The appropriate words, grammar, examples, and actions that are expected because of the occasion, time, place, and relationship of the participants in the interaction. In intercultural communication situations, factors such as cultural norms and fields of experience may be key to determining context.

Source. The person or group that originates the message or speech. In intercultural communication, the source makes an initial effort to define a meaningful message by using four communication skills:

1. Thinking/feeling to determine the purpose of the communication
2. Selecting symbols to use in sending the message
3. Analyzing and adapting to the receiver
4. Sending the message

Message. The intended message is the set of verbal and nonverbal symbols used by the source to further the purpose of the communication. Often, however, the source may send unintentional messages that may impede understanding. This problem may occur frequently in intercultural communication, where symbol meanings, cultural norms, and field of experience are likely to differ greatly. Other communication barriers arising from various forms of interference (described below) can also obscure the meaning of an intended message.

When a source recognizes that the receiver has not understood the intended message, he or she must redefine, or clarify, the message using the following three communication skills:

1. Use ideas and beliefs that are likely to mean something to the receiver.
2. Use an arrangement of examples, reasons, grammar, pronunciation, and nonverbal behavior that will be perceived as logical by the receiver.
3. Adjust the message as necessary by alternating symbols for ideas and feelings.

Channel. The different ways a verbal or nonverbal message can be sent to the receiver. By sight (nonverbal) and by sound (verbal).

(continued)

Exhibit 2.1 *Continued*

Receiver. The person(s) for whom the message is intended. The receiver collaborates with the source to build and share meaning by:

1. Physically sensing the message (hearing and/or seeing).
2. Interpreting—making sense of the message.
3. Evaluating the message to determine a response. Based on the interpretation of the message, the receiver formulates a purpose in responding to the message.
4. Responding to the message.

In defining a response to a message, the receiver employs the same communication skills that are used by the source in defining the original message:

- using thoughts and feelings to determine the purpose of the communication
- selecting symbols to use in the message
- adapting the symbols so that they are meaningful to the other person, and then
- actually delivering the message.

If the source does not accept the response as leading to an understanding, the receiver must reinterpret the original message and redefine the response to that message. In doing so, the receiver uses the following skills:

- anticipating the ideas and beliefs that will be meaningful to the other person;
- using a logical arrangement of examples, reasons, grammar, pronunciation, and nonverbal behavior; and
- alternating symbols for ideas and feelings, as necessary, to build a shared understanding.

Interference. Barriers to interpretation of the intended message. There are three primary types of interference:

1. external interference—physical stimuli that draw the receiver's attention away from the message;
2. internal interference—psychological stimuli that distract the receiver, such as, mood; field of experience; and cultural beliefs, values, or attitudes; and
3. semantic interference—mispronunciation or inappropriate vocabulary.

Sometimes words or nonverbal behaviors can have a variety of meanings, which acts as interference.

Adapted and reprinted with permission of N. L. Flores (1993, p. 35).

Strategies for Gender and Multicultural Inclusiveness

Implementing the following strategies can help create an inclusive classroom environment.

- Seek ways to encourage intercultural equality within groups. Choose topics for class or small-group discussion that will appeal to both genders and to students with different cultural backgrounds.
- Celebrate holidays and customs from the different cultures of your students.
- Introduce native English speakers to words from other languages.
- If you notice that males dominate discussion, interrupt, or disparage the comments and contributions of girls during whole-class discussion, consider explaining to the class that you are interested in hearing from everyone and that everyone's questions and opinions are valuable and important. Then, make it a habit to deliberately elicit contributions from girls.
- Consider keeping track of the number of questions you ask and the number of times you accept answers from both genders; it is easy to acknowledge the first hand that is raised or the person who seems most impatient to answer. Sometimes, however, this practice occurs at the expense of quiet students who need to be coaxed into participation by the teacher or need to be validated when they do contribute. Such students often need more time to think about their answers or to gather the courage to say what they think. Allow them time; let them feel that they have your attention and support.
- Wherever possible, choose stories, plays, poems, and books that do not stereotype gender, race, or culture. Choose materials that depict members of underrepresented groups in favorable and provocative ways. Challenge students to recognize and rethink stereotypes.
- Choose materials that are authored by underrepresented groups.
- Choose materials for dramatization that allow girls and minorities to play significant, positive roles.
- Encourage the use of gender-inclusive language at all times.

The Benitez interview that follows describes the innovative and successful approaches taken by one elementary school with a multicultural student population. Exhibit 2.2 contains some exercises that can help create a safe and inclusive classroom. In addition to these selected exercises, many of those in Chapter 4 (listening) and Chapters 7 through 9 (exercises and activities for each level) are suitable for building a healthy classroom climate.

THE INTEGRATED LANGUAGE ARTS
IN A MULTICULTURAL SETTING

Interview with Mary Helen Benitez, Principal
Ezequiel A. Balderas Elementary School
Fresno, California

Balderas Elementary School exemplifies excellence in serving the learning needs of
Fresno's growing multicultural population. Most students attending Balderas are Asian,
Hispanic, and African American, with Asian students representing the majority of the
student body. Many students have a limited English proficiency, and the school has
successfully met this challenge by implementing several innovative and successful
approaches to the language arts. Principal Mary Helen Benitez describes some of these
innovative approaches and discusses the ways in which her school builds oral communication skills in a multicultural setting.

Q: *Could you describe the general language arts curriculum at Balderas?*

Our language arts curriculum is literature-based, integrating whole language
through activities such as storytelling, music chanting, poetry, and essay writing.
In kindergarten and first grade, we are primarily concerned with language devel
opment, since a large portion of our students are Hmong and have limited English
skills. We also have a Reading Recovery Program and an Early Literacy Program.
Later on, we integrate the language arts with content areas such as science and
math.

Q: *What kinds of cooperative learning activities do you use to integrate language with*
content areas?

First, you need to understand that our approach works in part because we are a
full-year, extended-day school. We have one extra hour, four days a week, during
which we implement some of our language development programs, such as the
Triad program. A triad is a group of three students from different grade levels,
working together as a team on homework and language skills. A triad consists of
either a sixth, fourth, and second grader or a fifth, third, and first grader. The older
students assist the younger students and serve as role models. We find that this
program is a wonderful opportunity for character development, especially among
the older students, in that it builds leadership and self-esteem.
    In the extended-day period, we also feature lessons taught by primary teachers
in students' primary languages. Teachers meet in advance to plan the content and
focus of these lessons. We also incorporate parents and college-student volunteers
into our learning activities during this extended time.

Q: *Your school is in many ways a model for cultural inclusiveness. How does your curriculum build language arts skills, particularly oral communication, in a multicultural setting?*

Well, as I mentioned, we have a literature-based program, and students learn language by reading and listening to stories about many topics, including cultural fairy tales. We also coordinate multicultural fairs, to which we invite parents and community members. An example of a multicultural fair is our month-long celebration of the Cambodian New Year. Students learn about the Cambodian culture through "potluck days" when parents and community members join the students for cooking in the classroom. Students learn about Cambodian foods; and foods from the cultures of other students in the class are also cooked and shared, although the primary emphasis would be on the culture that is celebrated at the time, such as Cambodian culture. In addition, students dress up and model their cultural costumes. Outdoors, they learn about traditional Cambodian games.

Our school has a closed-circuit television system that allows us to sponsor a student news team. Students create their own stories or poetry and read them over the closed circuit daily. During the multicultural fairs, we sponsor an essay contest, in which students write about their experiences coming to America from their homelands or write about their families. They later read these essays at an assembly for parents and over the closed-circuit television. The culminating assembly also features dances and songs by the children. I should note that our parent involvement is substantial. We hold monthly parent meetings in various primary languages, attended by roughly 150 to 250 parents. They share their ideas and concerns at these meetings.

Another example of our hands-on approach to learning is our science fairs. Students take field trips and develop projects for a science fair, at which they give oral presentations of their work in English and their primary languages.

Q: *Can you describe your portfolio assessment program?*

We have a portfolio assessment program that starts in kindergarten and features student work from the different content areas, such as language arts and the sciences. We collect student artwork, tapes of their language development, and items selected by the students themselves. The teacher keeps a separate folder of more personal information and work by the student. Teachers stay with students at our school for two years. The portfolio moves on with the students after that, and the new teachers will add or take out selections as necessary. We have two teachers with master's degrees in portfolio assessment who add a lot to our program.

Exhibit 2.2   Classroom Exercises

PERCEPTION ROLE-PLAY #1

Allow students to choose one of the following roles:

- A person of the opposite gender
- A person from another country who speaks a primary language other than English
- A person of another racial background
- A person who has a physical disability
- A person of another religion requiring strict adherence to its tenets

Instructions to students: Pretend you are a person who has the characteristic you have chosen from the list. How would you experience the following situations differently?

- Riding your regular school bus to school and back
- Playing with your friends during recess (participating in athletics)
- Reading a story that doesn't have any characters like you in it
- Reading a story where all the characters with your features are depicted as weak, immoral, or despised by others
- Participating in your class

What do these possible differences suggest to you about good communication?

PERCEPTION ROLE-PLAY #2

Divide the class up into pairs. Assign each pair one of the following roles:

- Two spies waiting to make contact with each other. Neither is sure that they have found the right person
- Two people who are angry with each other
- Two people who recognize each other but cannot remember where they met
- One person visiting the second person, who is sick in the hospital
- Two people who haven't seen each other in a long time
- Two people who just recently met and don't really know each other, but feel obligated to talk
- Two athletes who will be competing against each other tomorrow in a very important game/race/meet

Ask each pair to read the following dialogue with their partners, paying close attention to speech rate, pitch, tone, pauses, pronunciation, and articulation. Have each pair practice the dialogue and then perform it before the rest of the class.

Dialogue

A: Hi, how are you?
B: Fine, thank you. And you?
A: Just great. What have you been doing lately?
B: Oh, not much. But I've been keeping busy.
A: Well, it's been good to see you.
B: Yes, it has. Well, bye.
A: Goodbye.

Can the class guess what roles each pair was playing? What verbal or nonverbal clues led to the guess?

Exhibit 2.2 *Continued*

EYE CONTACT, PERSONAL SPACE, AND CULTURAL RULES

1. Divide students up into pairs. Ask them to stand facing each other while one person tells a story to the other person (about anything).
   - Students must maintain constant eye contact with each other for one minute. (Time them with a stop watch.)
   - Stop, repeat the exercise with the other person talking; this time, ask the students to stand one step closer to one another.
2. Ask the following questions:
   - What made you feel comfortable or uncomfortable?
   - What did you learn about eye contact? About personal space?
   - What are some cultural rules that you can infer from this experience about eye contact? About personal space?
   - What cultural rules do you think other cultures might have about eye contact? About personal space? (Discuss—it's helpful to offer examples from other cultures.)
3. Repeat exercise a final time with students standing back to back and having no eye contact at all.
   - What did you notice this time about your listening or communication habits?
   - What did you rely on to make sense of the communication?

FAMILY NARRATIVE

Students give a short (one-to-three–minute) speech focusing on a funny story that is always told when their family comes together at special occasions.

SOUND AND MOVEMENT CIRCLE

Everyone stands in a circle. One child makes a verbal noise (or says a short phrase) and combines this with a body movement. The whole circle repeats it. The person to the right (or left) makes a noise and body movement, and the whole circle repeats it. Move around the circle in this fashion quickly. This activity helps students lose their fear of looking silly in front of their classmates—everyone has to participate.

SELF-DISCLOSURE IMPROMPTUS

On a sheet of paper, write out a list of topics, such as the following:
- The movie I liked the best
- The person I admire the most
- My favorite pet
- My favorite story
- The vacation I liked the best
- My favorite thing to do for fun

Cut the paper up into strips with a topic on each strip. Allow students to draw a topic from a hat and to deliver a short (one-to-three–minute) speech about that topic. This should be a very informal, relaxed exercise. Students can stand at their desks to face the rest of the class; or have students form a standing or sitting circle.

(continued)

Exhibit 2.2   *Continued*

COMMUNICATION JOURNAL ASSIGNMENTS

Communication journals allow students to think and reflect on challenging interpersonal topics without having to engage in mass disclosure. Students should be informed that they are to write honestly and thoughtfully about the topics but that their writing is to be shared with the teacher and on occasion with the rest of the class. Suggested journal assignments are:

1. Perceptions and biases—Think about an occasion when your first impression of a person was absolutely wrong. What led you to make that first impression? What later caused the change in your perception?

2. Family communication—Think about a family event in which you were a good communicator and something positive happened as a result. What did you do that showed good speaking and listening skills? What happened as a result? What goals could you set for yourself in communicating at home?

3. Watch a television show with the sound turned off. Watch to see how the people in the show use nonverbal behavior to communicate with each other.
   - How do body posture and movement communicate a person's status and attitude toward others?
   - Can you identify some different ways in which people used eye contact to communicate?
   - What conclusions can you draw about nonverbal communication and working in groups at school?

4. People often develop personal biases when they live in one culture or another. Can you identify any biases that you have? How do you think these biases affect your communication with other people?

5. What do you like most about yourself as a communicator? What do you like least about yourself as a communicator? What are three communication goals you can set for yourself in class?

6. Have you ever been affected by stereotyping? If so, what happened? How did you feel? What can you do in your communication to avoid stereotyping other people?

7. How can we become better intercultural communicators?

8. Have you ever been the victim of a rumor? What happened? Do you share rumors with other people? What happens when people listen to rumors?

9. Locate a fairy tale, cartoon, television show, or movie that presents gender stereotypes. How are these stereotypes harmful to girls/boys?

10. Sheba has just come to our school from another galaxy. Sheba asks for your help in learning the rules of your culture. For example, Sheba doesn't know very much about the following four issues: (1) Is it okay to interrupt someone who is speaking and, if so, when? (2) How do you maintain a conversation with someone you have never met before? (3) How long do you maintain eye contact when talking with someone? How long do you maintain eye contact when listening to someone? (4) What do you do with your hands and feet when you are sitting in a chair and talking with someone? How do these rules differ depending on whether Sheba is a man or a woman? What advice can you give Sheba for dealing with these four situations?

COMMUNICATION AND RECEIVER APPREHENSION

Most people—whether children or adults—experience varying degrees of nervousness when speaking in public or other situations involving audience evaluation. Nervousness can also occur when a person is listening and anticipates evaluation. Trained speakers and listeners learn to recognize such anxiety as normal and can even learn how to channel their rush of adrenaline into positive energy that enhances their communication performance.

When anxiety levels are consistently severe enough to impede communication and interfere with social, academic, and life-management success, speech communication researchers use the terms *communication apprehension* and *receiver apprehension* to describe anxiety. Children and adults who have communication or receiver apprehension tend to avoid situations in which they experience the highest levels of anxiety. Consequently, the short-term effects of such apprehension may be to limit academic and social success among peers, but in the long term, communication apprehension can affect a person's choice of career and emotional and psychological satisfaction with self and social relationships.

Communication Apprehension

Communication apprehension may be defined as "a pattern of anxiety, established often in the elementary grades, which can profoundly affect much or all of a student's oral communication, social skills, and self-esteem" (Holbrook 1987, p. 1). According to several studies, at least 11 percent of elementary students experience severe communication apprehension and an additional 20 percent are affected by it to a lesser degree (Garrison & Garrison 1979; Harris 1980; Wheeless 1971). Students are not the only ones who experience communication apprehension—it has been reported among elementary and secondary school teachers as well (McCroskey, Andersen, Richmond & Wheeless 1981; McCroskey & Richmond 1991). McCroskey and Richmond (1991) found that as many as one in three teachers in the lower-elementary levels experience communication apprehension.

Different theories abound as to the cause of communication apprehension. Cooper (1995) cited four possible contributory factors: (1) a genetic predisposition to communication apprehension, which can be triggered by a child's social environment; (2) slow acquisition of communication skills, which may make the child feel different or isolated; (3) a tendency to model communicatively apprehensive parents or teachers who unconsciously send negative messages about communication; and (4) a lack of positive reinforcement during communication experiences, which causes the child to view communication as unpleasant, scary, or painful (pp. 244–45; see also Daly & Friedrich 1981).

Knowing what to look for when observing children can aid in identification of communication apprehension. Not all quiet or shy children are apprehensive, however; some may simply have quiet personality traits or may be members of a culture that values quietness and modesty. For these reasons, before any real action is taken toward suggesting treatment for a child suspected of having communication apprehension, it may be advisable to seek confirmation from independent observers and from those who specialize in recognizing speech and anxiety disorders. According to Cooper (1995), students with communication apprehension tend to exhibit the following attributes and behaviors:

> Generally, this student is withdrawn; has a hard time expressing self; is quiet, reserved, dissatisfied, easily annoyed, and strongly affected by emotions; lacks leadership; is a follower; is submissive; has a low task orientation; is restrained; avoids people and participation in groups; dislikes interaction; is shy; is an ineffective speaker; has little success in groups; is indecisive, tense, frustrated, and close-minded; has a low tolerance for ambiguous or uncertain situations, low need to achieve, and low self-esteem; chooses occupations requiring little communication; and sees others as controlling his life (p. 247).

McCroskey and Richmond (1991) developed three tools for classroom use that can indicate communication apprehension. First, the Shyness Scale asks students to agree or disagree with short descriptions of themselves, such as "I talk more in a small group (3–6) than others do" and "Other people think I am very quiet" (pp. 27–30). Based on responses to fourteen such questions, the Shyness Scale helps the user to interpret his or her own level of shyness. Teachers can use the Shyness Scale to evaluate younger children by reading the prompts to them out loud and recording their responses.

The second tool that may be used in the classroom to identify high levels of communication apprehension is the Personal Report of Communication Apprehension (PRCA). It uses a five-point scale to help students identify their degrees of personal experience with situations such as "Ordinarily, I am very tense and nervous in conversations" or "I am calm and relaxed when I am called upon to express an opinion at a meeting" (pp. 31–33). The PRCA is suitable for middle school students.

A third tool is the Personal Report of Communication Fear (PRCF). This tool is very similar to the PRCA. It consists of fourteen statements that focus specifically on fear rather than general anxiety. Questions are phrased using variations on the concept of fear, such as "I am scared to talk to people" or "Talking to teachers scares me" (pp. 41–43). The PRCF is suitable for use with younger children. Both the PRCA and the PRCF are available for in-classroom use from the publication department of the Speech Communication Association in Annandale, Virginia.

Receiver Apprehension

Receiver apprehension has been defined by Wheeless (1975) as "the fear of misinterpreting, inadequately processing, and/or not being able to adjust psychologically to messages sent by others" (p. 263). Ayres and associates (1995) found that a number of variables contributed to receiver apprehension, including a high *processing demand* (caused by a lack of cognitive structures that enable a person to understand complex messages), *motivation* (high motivation to perform; the student cares and wants to perform), and *evaluation* (the expectation that a person in authority will require the listener to demonstrate understanding of the message).

Considerably less is known about receiver apprehension than is known about communication apprehension. For instance, we don't yet know how often receiver apprehension occurs and among whom it most likely to occur. In the meantime, communication researchers have suggested that receiver apprehension may occur for some people only during certain listening experiences, such as during a group discussion or a lecture by someone in authority (Ayres et al. 1995, p. 234). When listeners experience receiver apprehension, they may not be able to concentrate, take efficient notes, or score well on objective tests (Cooper 1995, p. 255).

Classroom Climate and Apprehension

Once a student has been associated with communication apprehension or receiver apprehension, the classroom teacher may consult with a school counselor on a plan for treatment, perhaps one involving special stress-reducing exercises and sessions where students can focus on building self-esteem and confidence. When outside resources do not exist, however, a positive, communication-friendly environment can help prevent and minimize the occurrence of communication apprehension.

A lack of positive reinforcement about a student's spoken contributions in class has been linked to the onset of communication apprehension. Similarly, students who struggle when listening to difficult material may be more likely to suffer from receiver apprehension if their trials go unnoticed. These factors suggest that teachers who model positive attitudes toward communication and who allow students frequent opportunities to build communication skills are more likely to help prevent apprehension of both types. They are also more likely to help retrain apprehensive students to engage in speaking and listening with confidence.

SUMMARY

The study and practice of oral communication in grades K through 8 can be challenging for both student and teacher. A communication-friendly classroom helps shape student attitudes toward communication, self, and others. A positive classroom climate offers frequent opportunities for students to learn and practice oral communication skills in a variety of communication contexts, so that they recognize oral communication as a process, of which all aspects are useful and valuable. Exploratory talk allows students to use oral communication as a tool for developing literacy. Teachers can increase the responsibility that students have for their own learning by using ground rules that gradually establish trust. Guidelines for peer interaction can also be established to help maintain equity in the classroom.

Teachers model communication attitudes and skills when they interact with students. Indirectly, teachers shape understanding of oral communication in the way that they select oral communication activities and contexts; in the way they acknowledge and respect "real-world" communication; and the way in which they demonstrate positive attitudes toward oral communication.

A communication-friendly classroom is a psychologically safe environment where students can take healthy risks in self-disclosure. It is also an inclusive environment that fosters the self-esteem and positive self-concept of all students, encouraging them to become willing, proficient speakers and listeners, whether one-on-one, in small groups, or in front of a large audience. Some nervousness and apprehension should be expected in every classroom, but teachers should be on the lookout for students who may experience unusually high levels of anxiety when speaking and/or listening. Communication apprehension occurs when students experience unusually high levels of anxiety about interacting or speaking with others. It may be identified by considering a broad range of behaviors and attitudes and can be measured more precisely with three tools—the Shyness Scale, the Personal Report of Communication Apprehension, and the Personal Report of Communication Fear. Intensive counseling and relaxation techniques may be appropriate and available for some students, but building a communication-friendly classroom and attending to students' individual needs can help prevent and manage apprehension, especially in earlier grades.

REFERENCES

American Association of University Women. (1992). *The AAUW report: How schools shortchange girls.* Washington, DC: AAUW.

Ayres, J. A., Wilcox, A. K., & Ayres, D. M. (1995). Receiver apprehension: An explanatory model and accompanying research. *Communication Education, 44*(3), 223–235.

Barnes, D. (1992). *From communication to curriculum* (2nd ed.). Portsmouth, NH: Heinemann, Boynton/Cook Publishers.

Barnes, D., & Todd, F. (1995). *Communication and learning revisited.* Portsmouth, NH: Heinemann, Boynton/Cook Publishers.

Booth, D., & Thornley-Hall, C. (1991a). *Classroom talk.* Portsmouth, NH: Heinemann Educational Books.

——— . (1991b). *The talk curriculum.* Portsmouth, NH: Heinemann Educational Books.

Cooper, P. J. (1995). *Communication for the classroom teacher* (5th ed.). Scottsdale, AZ: Gorsuch Scarisbrick.

Daly, J. A., & Friedrich, G. (1981). The development of communication apprehension: A retrospective analysis of contributory correlates. *Communication Quarterly, 29,* 243–255.

Flores, N. L. (1994). Intercultural assessment of communication competency and English speaking skills: I ACCESS and user's manual. Paper presented at the Speech Communication Association summer conference on assessment, Alexandria, VA, August.

Garrison, J. P., & Garrison, K. R. (1979). Measurement of communication apprehension among children: A factor in the development of basic speech skills. *Communication Education, 28,* 119–128.

Gilligan, C., Lyons, N., & Hammer, T. J. (Eds.) (1990). *Making connections: The relational world of adolescent girls at Emma Willard School.* Cambridge: Harvard University Press.

Harris, K. R. (1980). The sustained effects of cognitive modification and informed teachers on children's communication apprehension. *Communication Quarterly, 28,* 47–56.

Henkin, R. (1995). Insiders and outsiders in first-grade writing workshops: Gender and equity issues. *Language Arts, 72,* 429–434.

Holbrook, H. T. (1987). Communication apprehension: The quiet student in your classroom. *ERIC Digest.* Bloomington, IN: ERIC Clearinghouse on Reading and Communication Skills.

Klopf, D. W., & Cambra, R. E. (1991). *Speaking skills for prospective teachers* (2nd ed.). Englewood, CO: Morton.

MacGillivray, L., & Hawes, S. (1994). I don't know what I'm doing—they all start with B: First graders negotiate peer reading interactions. *The Reading Teacher, 48*(3), 210–217.

McCroskey, J. C., Andersen, J., Richmond, V. P., & Wheeless, L. (1981). Communication apprehension of elementary and secondary students and teachers. *Communication Education, 30,* 122–132.

McCroskey, J. C., & Richmond, V. P. (1991). *Quiet children and the classroom teacher.* Urbana: ERIC Clearinghouse on Reading and Communication Skills.

O'Keefe, V. (1995). *Speaking to think, thinking to speak.* Portsmouth, NH: Heinemann, Boynton/Cook Publishers.

Sadker, M., & Sadker, D. (1994). *Failing at fairness.* New York: Charles Scribner's Sons.

Speech Communication Association. (1988). *Communication competencies for teachers.* Annandale, VA: Speech Communication Association.

Staab, C. (1992). *Oral language for today's classroom.* Markham, Ont.: Pippen Publishing.

Wheeless, L. R. (1971). Communication apprehension in the elementary school. *The Speech Teacher, 10,* 297–299.

———. (1975). An investigation of receiver apprehension and social context dimensions of communication apprehension. *The Speech Teacher, 24,* 261–268.

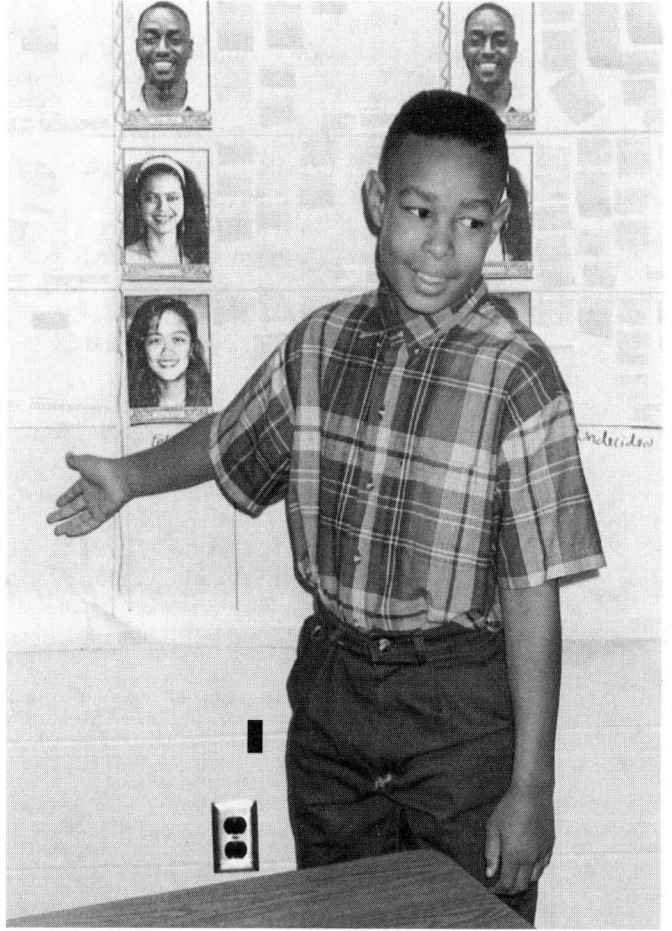

A formal presentation

3

Building Oral Communication Competency in a Variety of Contexts

In other words, children learn to read, write, speak, listen,
and think by having real opportunities to read, write,
speak, listen, and think. . . .
— J. DAVID COOPER

OVERVIEW

A competency-based approach to oral communication in the integrated language arts begins with determining an appropriate range of skills and attributes, or core competencies, around which authentic learning can be structured at age-appropriate levels. In this chapter, we will explore core competencies for a variety of speaking contexts (listening will be addressed in Chapter 4), based on widely accepted principles of speech communication for each context. These suggested core competencies are designed to serve as guidelines for lesson planning and may be adapted as necessary to target age-appropriate levels of proficiency.

PRACTICALLY SPEAKING

What specific learning opportunities are presented by the communication contexts of:

Debate
Public speaking
Conversation
Small-group discussion

Oral interpretation of literature
Plays and puppetry
Mass media

STUDYING COMMUNICATION CONTEXT

The Speech Communication Association (SCA) has recently released standards for speaking, listening, and media literacy in K through 12 curricula. According to the SCA (1996), the effective K through 12 speaker can demonstrate, in part:

- Knowledge and understanding of the relationships among the components of the speaking process across a variety of contexts;
- The ability to identify and use effective strategies for formal and informal speaking situations in public, group, work, and personal settings; and
- The ability to use language that clarifies, persuades, and/or inspires while respecting the listeners' backgrounds, including their culture, gender, and individual differences.

These standards suggest that speakers need both knowledge and ability to successfully build and share meaning with others.

In this chapter, we will focus on ways in which the study of different communication contexts can help students increase their oral communication knowledge, skills, and motivation. In particular, we will focus on speaking, dramatic performance, and mass media contexts. Listening contexts are discussed in Chapter 4. Appendix 3.1 outlines oral communication contexts and competencies taught in grades K through 8 and describes teaching approaches.

For practical purposes, we treat communication context as a type of communication activity characterized by *purpose, format*, and *participant needs and expectations.* In actuality, communication context is influenced by a myriad of personal, cultural, physical, and temporal variables that appear on a case-by-case basis. In examining purpose, format, and participant needs and expectations, however, we hope to encompass a number of these other situational variables.

Communication Purpose

The study of oral communication context begins with the communication purpose. The strategies employed by a speaker will differ according to the communication purpose the speaker hopes to achieve. Three communication purposes that are often pursued through speaking are (1) informing, (2) persuading, and (3) inspiring.

Informing.   A speaker's purpose is to inform when she seeks to share information useful in increasing another's understanding of a topic. An informative communication establishes its merit through timely, well-organized, viewpoint-balanced, interesting information.

Persuading. A speaker's purpose is to persuade when he seeks to convince another person to take a course of action or to adopt, maintain, or discontinue a set of beliefs, attitudes, or values. Persuasion can occur through logical arguments, emotional appeals, value appeals, and propaganda techniques (which some would distinguish from ethical persuasion).

Inspiring. A speaker's purpose is to inspire when she seeks to encourage or exhort another person. An inspiring communication frequently establishes its merit through a speaker's skillful use of imagery, word choice, rhythm, and delivery.

Each of these speaking purposes may occur independently of one another, but they may also overlap.

Communication Format

Oral communication context may also include a *format* for the communication activity. Format is the formal or informal structure of the activity and includes such factors as the time allotted for the event; the rules for who speaks, who listens, and for how long; and the physical characteristics of the event. For instance, the format of a public speech usually includes an individual speaker positioned in front of an audience, which in turn listens (usually without interrupting) until the end of the speech, or the speaker opens the floor for questions. In very formal speaking situations, a podium is usually made available for the speaker. A very different kind of format occurs with mediation. A mediator typically sits at a table between two (or more) participants. The mediator begins the session with an opening statement. Both sides then have a chance to explain their positions in the conflict, after which ideas are discussed between the participants facilitated by the mediator. When it appears necessary, the parties may break for private, one-on-one caucuses with the mediator, after which the parties reconvene and attempt to reach an agreement.

Participant Needs and Expectations

Finally, communication context always involves adaptation between *participants* as they interact with one another. The formality or informality of the communication, the occasion of the communication, and the demographic characteristics of the participants may determine what is considered to be appropriate speech and nonverbal behavior. In a presidential campaign speech, for instance, it is customary that the audience does not interrupt the speaker to ask questions until the speaker indicates a willingness to receive questions. In a small-group discussion, different members of the group may assume distinct leadership and supporting roles. Artistic license and emotional intensity are considered highly appropriate in dramatic performance, while those factors would likely be considered inappropriate in a job interview.

COMPETENCIES FOR SPECIFIC CONTEXTS

The factors influencing communication context can be very complex, as may be seen from the preceding examples. Because students learn to anticipate and adapt to context through experience, K through 8 curricula should include frequent opportunities for students to learn and practice oral communication in a variety of contexts. We'll concentrate now on several different communication contexts for which we have identified core competencies.

Debate

Formal debate is a highly structured form of argumentation between two or more speakers who advocate distinct (but not always opposite) sides of a claim. Debate is usually viewed as a way to exchange, critique, and defend ideas so as to enhance the quality of a decision-making process (Rieke & Sillars 1984). Debaters attempt to persuade the audience to agree with one side or the other through a clash of divergent ideas. If a compromise between the positions is desired, it is likely not to occur until after the debate has ended and another activity (such as a committee meeting) has begun. Even though their primary purpose is to persuade, debaters may also inform or inspire their audiences.

Format of the Debate

Debate formats differ according to the number of participants, time allotted for speeches and cross-examination (if any), and the rules for the particular style of debate. Teachers can experiment with format to create exercises that are easy to administer. Some general guidelines are as follows:

How much classroom time do you want to allocate to the debate?

How many students will participate?

How long will each student have to speak?

In what order will the speeches take place?

Will there be cross-examination? If so, when, for how long, and by whom?

Will there be rebuttal speeches?

How will you assign debate topics or decide which side students will take?

Will you use switch-side debating to maximize student critical thinking skills?

Will students work independently or in teams?

How will you decide which side wins (vote, large-group discussion, and so on)?

Will you use written critique as a critical thinking exercise?

Generally, more than two or three students per side on a debate is unwieldy and not to the advantage of the participants, who will have less time per person to speak and may have difficulty keeping track of the arguments. A debate symposium format, however, in which there are many individual speakers presenting multiple perspectives on an issue, may be feasible. Other potential whole-class debate formats include parliamentary debate or student congress formats, which mimic a legislative session and are facilitated by a speaker of the house or parliamentary chair, using rules of parliamentary procedure. For other examples of debate formats, see Chapter 10.

Building Arguments and Structuring Positions

Debaters structure their presentations so as to highlight the strongest arguments on their side of a topic. Throughout the debate, they vigorously defend their position while attempting to weaken the position of the opponent. Some forms of debate allow for cross-examination, while others allow questions from the audience. Parliamentary debate is one of the most familiar forms of debate. In parliamentary debate, the speakers follow established procedures to ensure orderly and (usually) respectful exchanges between debaters. Despite differences in format, all types of debate have one thing in common: the construction and defense of arguments.

The Toulmin Model of Argument.   The Toulmin model of argument (Toulmin, Rieke, & Janik, 1984) is a very useful way to help young learners understand how an argument is formed and how it can be attacked. The model features three elements—*claim, data,* and *warrant*—that are useful in explaining the most essential parts of an argument.

A claim is any statement or assertion of truth that a debater is defending, for example, "Our city should build a public park near the lake." The data is the information (evidence) used to support the claim, such as: "There are currently no public places in the city where people can gather outdoors. There is vacant land by the lake. People who jog and ride their bikes wish they could do so along the lake front." The warrant is the chain of reasoning and inferences (logic) that connects the data to the claim. For instance: "Since it doesn't seem to be any inconvenience to the city, and people would certainly use it if it were built, the city should build a public park near the lake."

Students can use a concept map to diagram an argument beginning with a shape for the claim; linked to one or two shapes that represent inferences or statements of reason; in turn, linked to shapes representing different pieces of data. A linear diagram could resemble the following:

Claim:	The city should build a public park next to the lake.
Evidence (Data):	1. There are currently no public places in the city where people can gather outdoors.
	2. There is a vacant plot of land by the lake.
	3. People who jog and bike wish they could do so along the lake front.

Logic (Warrant):   Since it doesn't seem to be an inconvenience, and people would certainly use it if it were built, the city should build a public park next to the lake.

Affirming or Defending a Position.   Once a student understands the elements of an argument and can diagram an argument using each of the three parts of the Toulmin model, the student will easily be able to put together a coherent affirmative or negative *position*. A debate revolves around one central *topic*, such as, "Should the city build a park by the lake?" but the topic is broad enough to encompass several different positions, each made up of individual *arguments*. "The city should build a public park by the lake" is an affirmative position in our example; but there is more than one way to argue in support of that position. A debater could also argue that a park might increase city revenue through metered parking, licenses to sell hot dogs, group access fees, and so on. Still another affirmative argument could be that "if the city were to build a park by the lake, crime in that area would be significantly reduced." When a debater puts a number of individual arguments together to support an affirmative position, we say that the debater is affirming the topic and has built an affirmative *case*.

Topic:	Should the city build a public park by the lake?
Affirmative position:	The city should build a public park by the lake.
Argument 1:	The city needs an outdoor recreational facility (supported by evidence and logic)
Argument 2:	A public park would increase city revenues (supported by evidence and logic)
Argument 3:	A public park would reduce crime in that area (supported by evidence and logic)

Negating (or Offering Alternatives to) the Affirmative.   In a debate with multiple speakers, each speaker presents a coherent position justifying his or her perspective on the topic. Our sample topic is phrased in a way that really only allows for two sides: Yes, the city should build a park; and No, the city should not build a park. However, a slight change in the way the topic is phrased could open the door for other advocates: "What should the city do to provide more recreational facilities for its residents?" Open-ended debate questions such as this are frequently heard on the floors of legislative discussions, during campaign stumping, and at public symposia.

When faced with a closed-ended topic such as "Should the city build a public park by the lake?," the responsibility of the negative speaker is to take the opposite side from the affirmative speaker and to undermine the affirmative case. When open-ended questions are used, multiple speakers attempt to make their positions appear the strongest, while undermining the positions of other speakers. Weaknesses in an opponent's position may be exposed through attacking the credibility of evidence and soundness of logic. Students who are familiar with the Toulmin model of argument will find the analytic skills it teaches to be especially helpful in identifying fallacies of logic and in comparing the strengths and weaknesses of evidence offered as support.

Types of Logic and Logical Fallacies. In the Toulmin model of argument, the warrant loosely represents the logical support, or "glue," that holds the evidence together with the claim. Debaters can use several different types of logic to attack and defend arguments. Likewise, debaters can learn to recognize logical fallacies employed by their opponents, and then construct arguments to attack such weaknesses. The forms of logic described in Exhibit 3.1 are also used in other kinds of persuasive activities such as formal persuasive writing.

Exhibit 3.1   Forms of Logic and Logical Fallacies

Deductive reasoning: Deductive reasoning starts with a general statement and then moves toward a specific conclusion.

    Example: The city has a recreational budget of $50,000. All the plans proposed today exceed that budget except for the plan of a public park.

    Therefore, the city should build a public park.

Inductive reasoning: Inductive reasoning starts with specific information and moves to a general conclusion. It is particularly subject to the fallacy of hasty generalization (discussed below).

    Example: Dayton Springs, Herndon, and Aurora, cities similar to ours in size and economy, all built parks last year and they are thriving.

    Our city will thrive also if we build a park.

Analogy: Reasoning by analogy compares similar events in an effort to predict a similar outcome. This kind of reasoning can be attacked by focusing on the ways in which the events are not similar, thus making any prediction uncertain.

    Example: This situation is a lot like a situation we faced as a community last year. Some people wanted to build a city swimming pool, but they were opposed by those who said people will never use it and it would turn out to be a waste of money. Well, they were wrong. The public really turned out to use the pool, and it made money for the city. The same thing will happen here. People will use the park and it will be successful.

Criteria: Criteria to application reasoning occurs when a speaker establishs a criteria and then uses is to measure all the other options to persuade that his or her option is the best available one.

    Example: The recreational budget criteria of $50,000 was met only by the plan to build a park. Other proposals exceeded the budget.

(continued)

Exhibit 3.1   *Continued*

Argument by Authority:	A type of logical fallacy in which a speaker tries to convince another person to agree by invoking fear or blind devotion to authority.
	Example: Your boss supports this plan to build a public park. You should, too.
Ad Hominem:	A type of logical fallacy that directs a personal attack on the speaker rather than an attack on the merits of the argument.
	Example: People who support a public park are selfish. They should be supporting a program to feed the hungry instead.
Hasty Generalization:	A type of fallacy in which a speaker draws a conclusion based on one of two things: (1) an unrepresentative example, or (2) so few examples that it is really impossible to accurately predict a result. In pointing out a hasty generalization made by a speaker, it is often very effective to offer a counter example to show the audience why it is dangerous to rely on an unrepresentative or inadequate set of examples.
	Example: Paris built the Louvre with the equivalent of $50,000. Today it is one of the world's most treasured and attended art museums.
	Our park is sure to become a popular attraction for tourists as well.

Evidence.   In addition to attacking and defending the use of logic, debaters attack and defend the use of evidence. Central to this task is the recognition that evidence is subject to differing degrees of credibility. The more credible the evidence, the stronger the support it provides for the argument. Newman and Newman (1969) outlined a number of factors affecting credibility. Among the considerations they suggest for evaluating the credibility of evidence are:

1. Is the source of the evidence careful not to make loose generalizations?
2. Is the source of the evidence a person of expertise or knowledge?
3. Is the source of the evidence fairly objective, not biased?
4. Is the source of the evidence a primary or secondary source?
5. Is the evidence recent?
6. Does the evidence offer genuine facts and information to support the claim, or is it merely someone else's opinion? (Is the evidence conclusory?)
7. Is there enough evidence to support the speaker's claim?

Keeping Track of the Debate

The colloquial term for taking notes during the debate is *flowing*, or *taking a flow of the debate*. At more advanced levels, debaters use shorthand to notate arguments in narrow columns on a horizontal legal pad, reserving some portions for affirmative argumentation and the other portion for negative argumentation. In grades K through 8, however, we recommend that note taking be kept as simple as possible. Students should keep an outline of each argument they will deliver in the debate, and then take notes of (1) the opponent's response to each argument, and (2) any new arguments raised by the opponent. Very young learners may not even need to take notes, especially if there is no opportunity for rebuttal.

The primary purpose of taking notes is to help a debater prepare cross-examination questions (if relevant to the debate format) and a rebuttal speech that strengthens the debater's position and highlights the weaknesses in an opponent's position.

Summary of Debate Competencies

In addition to basic vocal and physical delivery skills, which are discussed in the next section, a debater needs skills, knowledge, and attributes that enable her or him to:

- Recognize and understand the informative and persuasive purposes of debate
- Understand the difference between an affirmative and a negative approach to the debate topic
- Identify the elements of the Toulmin model of argument
- Understand the concept of credibility of evidence
- Recognize common forms and fallacies of logic
- Build strong individual arguments using the elements of claim, evidence, and logic
- Use several different arguments to support a position
- Listen to keep track of an opponent's arguments
- Listen critically to identify and counter weaknesses in an opponent's logic and evidence

Younger learners can debate (we know of some teachers who have taught second graders to debate), although their presentations tend to be mostly exchanges of claims and counterclaims, unsupported by evidence. Even at this rudimentary stage, there is no doubt that the activity sharpens critical-thinking skills and builds self-esteem and confidence. The competencies listed above, however, can be made age-appropriate by narrowing the list to focus on a smaller set of skills and by creating a very simple debate format, perhaps one that does not involve cross-examination and/or rebuttal speeches. More specific, practical information about implementing a debate exercise is contained in Chapter 10.

Public Speaking

Public speaking is the formal oral communication context most often explored in the elementary classroom, usually through the mechanism of an oral report. Here we explore a more challenging version of the speech, which will serve students well in a variety of situations. In delivering an original composition, a public speaker needs knowledge, skills, and attributes that enable him or her to:

- Determine an appropriate topic and purpose for the discourse
- Determine appropriate main points and organization according to the purpose of the speech
- Develop main points with relevant, credible supporting materials
- Create an effective introduction and conclusion
- Use language and vocabulary that appeal to the audience
- Use nonverbal delivery to maintain interest and personal credibility
- Use vocal delivery to maintain interest and personal credibility

Public-speaking formats vary according to both the purpose of the speaker and the manner of delivery. In this section we will review basic speech organization and content, and briefly explain how the content might change according to the three purposes of informing, persuading, and inspiring. After that, we will explain different methods of delivery and make suggestions as to which delivery skills are essential for students to learn in K through 8. At the end, we will use a ceremonial speech assignment and evaluation form to illustrate these concepts.

Organizing the Content of a Speech

Topic and Purpose.   The first step in organizing the content of a speech is to narrow the *topic* to a manageable scope. In K through 8, teachers can assist greatly in this process by assigning topics in the form of simple questions or by asking students to limit speeches to two or three main ideas focused around a central concept. After the topic has been narrowed, if the speaker's purpose is not already apparent from the wording of the topic, the speaker should decide on a purpose. For example:

Topic: Dolphins

Purpose: To inform my audience about dolphins

Main Points and Organization.   We teach our students to prepare the introduction and conclusion of the speech after the body has been carefully planned and written. It is often easier then to develop a preview statement for the introduction and summary statement for the conclusion. Limit the body of the speech to between one and five main points; limit the body to one or two points for younger children. Good main points are separate and distinct, relevant and significant. Children often have trouble distinguishing between main points and subpoints, however, so a discussion of outlining accompanied by a speech outline assignment is usually very worthwhile.

Main points are organized differently for persuasive and informative speeches. A persuasive speech must present the main points in a logical order that appeals to the audience. One example of a persuasive organizational pattern is the problem–solution format. A problem–solution format simply organizes those main points that describe the problem (the nature of the problem and its significance to the audience) into the first portion of the speech, and those main points that describe the potential solution into the second half of the speech (what the solution is; how it will work; whether it is feasible).

Common informative organizational formats include time–sequence (when describing a process or timeline, citing main points in order of occurrence); topical (a collection of concepts generally related to the topic); and spatial (when describing a physical object, connecting main points to the object in a way that helps the audience visualize and remember the points). The purpose of developing an organizational format is to assist the audience in following the speech and in remembering the main ideas.

Supporting Material.   Persuasive speakers use a combination of reasoning and evidence to support their ideas. Informative speakers also use supporting materials to explain and develop their points. There are several different types of supporting materials (evidence) suitable for public speaking:

Testimony	Eyewitness or fact-based opinions
Empirical examples	Descriptions of historical events or artifacts
Hypothetical situations	Used to help make abstract concepts more concrete and meaningful to the listener
Statistics	Numbers or percentages that describe the probability or occurrence of events
Scholarly research	Studies or essays that offer theories or explanations

Transitions.   Transitions between main points help the audience recognize when the speaker is shifting focus from one point to the next.

Introduction and Conclusion.   Once the content of the speech is organized, an effective introduction and conclusion can be developed. An effective introduction at the eighth-grade exit level would optimally include the following elements:

1. Attention-getting device (interesting quote, surprising statistic, anecdote, humorous riddle, question for the audience)
2. A clear statement of the topic, connecting it to the audience
3. A preview statement of the main points

An effective conclusion at the eighth-grade exit level would optimally include the following elements:

1. A clear transition into the end of the speech (preferably something other than "In conclusion")
2. A summary of the main points or ideas in the speech
3. A final thought for the audience to consider

Introductions are critical to stimulating audience interest in the speech. It is much harder to generate or recapture the audience's attention later. Similarly, the conclusion is the last part of the speech the audience will hear and is generally remembered the most. If the conclusion whimpers off or is too abrupt, a favorable impression of the speech as a whole may be affected. Keep in mind, also, that the introduction and conclusion should each comprise only about 15 percent of the speech. The real emphasis should be on the content of the speech. Students have a tendency to get carried away telling stories in the introduction or, conversely, telling stories in the conclusion. Guide them into an understanding of the functions of each section.

Delivery

Choice of Language and Audience Adaptation.   High standards of grammar and syntax, combined with a thoughtful choice of words, are appropriate for public speaking. At the eighth-grade exit level, students should be aware of gender and cultural inclusiveness as well, choosing words that demonstrate respect for, and interest in, the audience. Students can also adapt to their audience by using supporting materials that the audience will understand and appreciate. Inspirational and persuasive speeches often use vivid, descriptive words and take advantage of rhetorical devices such as metaphors, alliteration, dramatic pauses, and so on.

Use of Voice.   Vocal characteristics can be used to express feelings and to place emphasis on important points. Rate (pace of speech), volume (loudness or softness), pitch (relative highness or lowness), silence (as in dramatic pauses), and vocal variety (mixture of all these factors to keep the audience interested) are important.

Vocalized Pauses.   These "fillers" are distracting if they are heard too often. Vocalized pauses include nonwords such as "umm," "uhh," "er," and "ah" and words such as "like," "y'know," "okay," and other trendy speech mannerisms.

Physical (Nonverbal) Delivery.   As tempting as it is to use a podium in teaching students to speak in public, it may be undesirable for several reasons: (1) students do not learn to handle minimal notes and to give strong eye contact with the audience; (2) students do not develop awareness and comfort with their bodies in front of an audience, because they can "hide" behind the podium; and (3) students tend to use the podium as a crutch for their arms and hands. The most important reason, however, for teaching public speaking without a podium is that it is an authentic context. A great many formal speaking situations in the real world do not feature podiums.

Posture, gestures, and facial expressions are all important mechanisms for communicating meaning to the audience. Posture should be straight (though not rigid), with head up, shoulders back. Watch for twisting at the waist and bending and crossing the legs; resting weight on one leg and splaying the other out at an angle. Correct these habits early—doing so sends a message that you believe each student is capable of giving a dynamic, credible, effective presentation. Students who want to learn more about gestures can practice in front of a full-length mirror and can watch themselves on videotape.

Direct, sustained, friendly eye contact is one of the most effective forms of nonverbal communication. If your students can write well enough to use large index cards, these are preferable to loose sheets of paper. Students can write an outline of the speech on cards and are less tempted to read verbatim from their notes. Index cards are neater, less visually distracting, and less likely to make sounds when they are shuffled.

Manuscript Delivery.   In this style of delivery, the speech is completely written out and is read verbatim. It is a technique that is appropriate for highly formal events such as eulogies, award ceremonies, political appearances, and situations in which there is a high degree of stress or pressure.

Extemporaneous Delivery.   This style of delivery offers great flexibility. The speaker prepares a detailed outline of the speech and rehearses from that detailed outline, going over the speech again and again until the major concepts, the organization, the supporting materials, and the language and audience-adaptation techniques are familiar. After the speaker becomes comfortable with the speech, he or she condenses the full outline into what is known as a *speaker's outline*. A speaker's outline is written on note cards and contains key words and phrases that trigger memory of the introduction, main points, supporting materials, and conclusion. Some speakers write cues about delivery to themselves on the card, such as "eye contact," "slow down," "relax," and so on.

Impromptu Delivery.   This type of delivery affords a speaker the least amount of preparation. Many speakers find that after mastering the topic–purpose model they are able to identify and speak about an aspect of their topic without notes in a matter of minutes. Impromptu delivery is frequently found in informal contexts and in the workplace.

Writing the Speech

The writing of the speech itself involves a number of issues, including topic, purpose, audience, organization, content, and choice of language. Even young children are capable of mastering these skills if the topic is simple and the number of main ideas is small. Exercise 3.1 is an sample special-occasion speech that is flexible enough to be used at different proficiency levels. The evaluation form (Exhibit 3.2) is also flexible in its statement of criteria.

EXERCISE 3.1   A SPECIAL-OCCASION SPEAKING ASSIGNMENT

Length: About five minutes

Objectives: 1. To inform and inspire the audience through a speech paying
                     tribute to a person you admire
                  2. To practice basic organizational and delivery skills
                  3. To practice adapting a speech to an audience and situation

Instructions: Using the speechwriting principles we have discussed in class, create
                  a speech in which you pay tribute to a famous person you admire.
                  (It can be someone from history or someone currently living.) Pretend
                  you will give this speech at a dinner honoring this person's accom-
                  plishments. Give the audience (imagine who they are likely to be)
                  information about the person and their achievements to celebrate
                  this occasion.

When you have finished planning your speech, practice it from an outline on notecards.
This speech does not need to be memorized, but you do need to practice using an outline.

Conversation

According to Hazelton and Metts (1994), conversation differs from debate and
formal speaking events in that (1) conversations do not have a predetermined
length or speaker order, (2) people connect speaking and listening turns with very
little time in between, and (3) people begin their turns almost immediately after
another person stops speaking, yet are able to avoid interrupting each other. Conversation is an important means by which we inform, persuade, and inspire/en-
tertain others on a daily basis.

To maintain a meaningful conversation, a communicator needs skills and attributes that enable her to:

- Know when to start and stop a conversation
- Take turns speaking and listening
- Ask questions or make follow-up statements to maintain the conversation
- Share meaningful, relevant information

Knowing when to start and stop a conversation.   Shafer (1993) points out that
young people need to recognize and interpret the nonverbal messages that
indicate when a person might or might not be receptive to conversation, such
as eye contact and smiling. Location, time, and occasion might also have
bearing on whether or not conversation is appropriate.

Taking turns.   Conversationalists take turns speaking and listening. The
speaker offers information, or asks a question, and the listener then takes a
turn, responding both verbally and nonverbally.

Exhibit 3.2   Evaluation Form for Special-Occasion Speech

Speaker:

Topic:

Rating scale: 4 = Excellent   3 = Very good   2 = Satisfactory   1 = Needs improvement

CRITERIA	4	3	2	1
Content/Organization				
Adapted to imaginary situation and audience	_____	_____	_____	_____
Referred to occasion and situation	_____	_____	_____	_____
Clear organization	_____	_____	_____	_____
Used interesting words and phrases	_____	_____	_____	_____
Used supporting material	_____	_____	_____	_____
Strong introduction and conclusion	_____	_____	_____	_____
Delivery				
Vocal qualities and expression	_____	_____	_____	_____
Gestures	_____	_____	_____	_____
Confidence, poise	_____	_____	_____	_____
Extemporaneous delivery	_____	_____	_____	_____
Attitude toward assignment	_____	_____	_____	_____
Speech Outlines				
Preparation outline	_____	_____	_____	_____
Speaker's outline	_____	_____	_____	_____
Overall impression	_____	_____	_____	_____

Comments:

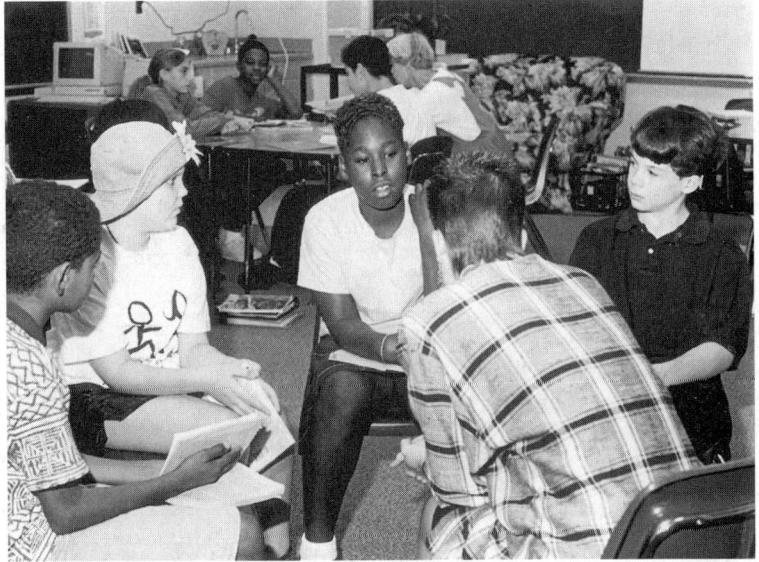

Small-group discussion

A conversationalist shows respect for his or her partner by trying not to interrupt and learning to wait for his or her turn.

Asking questions or making follow-up statements to maintain the conversation. Conversations can lapse when one speaker is only interested in talking about herself or himself or personal interests. Conversations can also lapse when one person remains silent and does not respond to the other person.

Sharing meaningful, relevant information. Conversationalists share information that means something to the other speaker, advances the topic of conversation, or that changes the topic to another mutually acceptable topic.

Small-Group Discussion

Small-group discussion is generally an informal context for communication, although the topics, issues, and problems discussed in small groups are frequently very significant and are accompanied by argumentation and persuasion on the part of group participants. Self-guided discussions are a form of authentic learning because they often occur in that manner in the real word (Smagorinsky & Fly 1993).

Small-group participants must have knowledge, skills, and attributes enabling them to:

- Play different roles (leadership/support/facilitator) within the group to help the group achieve its purpose
- Help maintain a positive group climate so that all members feel valued and are encouraged to participate

- Assist the members of the group in accomplishing group tasks by doing a fair share of the workload
- Find ways to reach consensus when necessary
- Discuss and debate ideas freely, respecting the contributions and ideas of other members

Exercise 3.2 is a sample highly structured, small-group, problem-solving activity that requires students to demonstrate these core competencies. Students work together in small groups to solve the problem; peer- and self-evaluations then provide students with feedback on their participation.

Oral Interpretation of Literature

Dramatic performance entertains, inspires, and broadens our intellectual horizons. For the integrated language arts classroom, oral interpretation, plays, and puppetry provide an exciting way to "get into" the literature and to think about composition. The communication purpose of these activities is generally to inspire and/or entertain.

The oral interpretation of literature is distinguished from dramatic acting in that the interpreter primarily emphasizes vocal, rather than physical, delivery. In stories with multiple characters, the oral interpreter may even adopt different voices and communication styles. Oral interpreters must be able to:

- Select material appropriate for the occasion and the audience
- Make an effective "cutting" that conveys an interesting scene or narrative
- Creatively interpret the piece in an artistic fashion for an audience using voice and appropriate nonverbal expression
- Display poise and presence before the audience

Material suitable for oral interpretation can be in the form of prose or poetry. In Chapter 10, we have reprinted, with permission, guidelines developed by the National Forensic League, which sponsors middle school and high school competitions in the categories of dramatic interpretation, humorous interpretation, prose, and poetry.

Storytelling is related to oral interpretation. One of the finest resources available on storytelling, with numerous practical examples suitable for all age levels, is *Look What Happened to Frog* (Cooper & Collins 1995).

Plays, Skits, and Puppetry

Plays and skits are another way of learning verbal and nonverbal forms of expression. They challenge students to use higher-order thinking skills and have been linked to increases in reading comprehension (Hoyt 1992) and writing skills (Coty 1993). Plays and skits can be created by small groups or can be acted out from a published work. Puppetry has an additional advantage of serving as an interper-

EXERCISE 3.2   GROUP PROBLEM SOLVING: CREATING A VOLUNTEER ORGANIZATION

Objectives:	1. To practice group brainstorming skills
	2. To practice group leadership and facilitation skills

Description of the Exercise: Students will create a volunteer organization that meets a specific need in a community. They will develop a skeleton of how the organization will work and give a polished presentation on it to the class.

Procedures:

1. Divide students into small groups. Each group brainstorms to create a volunteer organization, using the following questions as food for thought:
   - What needs could this organization meet?
   - How would it recruit and train volunteers?
   - How would it obtain funding?
   - How would it publicize its services to people who need them?
   - What would be the name of the organization?

2. Students prepare written materials and artwork:
   - A name and logo that conveys the essence of the organization
   - A company handbook that outlines the goals of the organization and the responsibilities or requirements of volunteers, such as rules, qualifications, benefits of being a volunteer, and so on.
   - Examples of promotional materials to recruit volunteers, raise funds, and publicize the organization

3. Students deliver a group presentation to the class about their organization that reflects the creativity of the group and shows command of basic organizational skills.
   - Each member should speak two to three minutes, for a group time of about 15 minutes.
   - Students should cite sources for any research they may have conducted in developing their organization.
   - Emphasis should be on explanation of the organization and its strategy, not on the visual aids.
   - Content, clarity, and creativity should be important elements of this assignment.

PEER GROUP PROJECT EVALUATION

Rate each person in your group on a scale of one to ten and give a two- or three-sentence explanation for the rating. If you are having trouble rating your peers, consider the following issues that are related to working effectively in groups. You only need to address one or two of the issues.

Make sure you put your name and the name of the group member you are evaluating at the top of your paper.

EXERCISE 3.2 *Continued*

Did the group member have a good attitude about participating in the group?

Did the group member put effort into his or her portion of the assignment?

Did the group member practice his or her presentation effectively?

Would you want to work with that member again?

What did you like best about working with that group member?

What would you do differently if you were that group member?

SELF-EVALUATION: GROUP PROJECT

In writing, discuss the following questions. Turn in your evaluation on the day after your group presentation.

1. What were the strengths of your group's process and presentation?
2. What were the weaknesses of your group's process and presentation?
3. What were the strengths of your individual performance in the group?
4. What were the weaknesses of your individual performance in the group?
5. What do you think you will do differently next time when you are a member of a group and have to work together with others to solve a problem?

---

sonal communication medium for younger children. We've described a few ideas in Chapters 4 and 7 as to how young students can tell stories and demonstrate empathic listening skills with puppets.

Mass Media

Students benefit from study of the mass media because it is a source of informative and persuasive messages. As mass media consumers, students listen to and observe (hopefully in a critical manner) media messages. As creators of mass media products, students practice audience analysis, organization, composition, physical and verbal delivery. Mass media projects also tend to be fun and interesting for students. There is a certain mystique about "being on the radio" or "being on TV."

The Speech Communication Association (1996) standards for K through 12 curricula state that the effective media participant can demonstrate:

- The effects of the various types of electronic audio and visual media, including television, radio, the telephone, the Internet, computers, electronic conferencing, and film, on media consumers, and;
- The ability to identify and use skills necessary for competent participation in communication across various types of electronic audio and visual media.

One of the interesting communication aspects of mass media is that each form of media is a channel for messages shared between speaker and listener. This role as a channel or "mediator" of messages poses a unique challenge to the listener. A speaker's subjective purpose to persuade or manipulate may be masked by the entertaining qualities of a particular media format. For instance, television commercials feature common propaganda techniques, such as *glittering generalities* (sweeping statements about the benefits of a product); and the *bandwagon effect* (urging listeners to keep up with the Joneses—everybody's doing it, so you should, too).

Accordingly, we suggest here that students creating or responding to mass media messages need to acquire knowledge, skills, and attributes enabling them to:

- Know the difference between persuasion and propaganda
- Identify mediated persuasion and propaganda
- Critique mediated persuasion and propaganda
- Analyze an audience
- Organize a clear, concise, interesting radio or television message
- Effectively deliver a radio or television message using voice and/or nonverbal communication
- Distinguish fact from opinion
- Distinguish reality from fantasy

Exercise 3.4 encourages students to think critically about messages conveyed through mass media. Other suggested mass media exercises appear in Chapters 7 through 9.

DEVELOPMENTALLY APPROPRIATE CURRICULAR GUIDELINES FOR K THROUGH 8

What is the impact of development on K through 8 proficiency levels in oral communication? Until a greater research effort is made to test theories on this matter, there is no straightforward answer. Perhaps it is best that teachers and curriculum specialists collaborate to develop guidelines that fit their own communities of learners.

Toward that end, in addition to its standards for speaking, listening, and media literacy in K through 12 curricula (1996), the Speech Communication Association (1991) has also developed guidelines for oral communication curricula in grades K through 12 by combining competencies identified by the District of Columbia public schools (1988) and communication educators. Examples of competencies from those guidelines for grades K through 8 appear as Appendices 3.2 through 3.10. Bear in mind that they are just examples and, in several cases, focus only on one or two communication contexts.

EXERCISE 3.4   THINKING CRITICALLY ABOUT THE MEDIA

Objectives: To practice evaluative listening skills in identifying propaganda techniques and persuasive strategies as used in mass media, including:

- exaggeration
- "weasel words"
- manipulative imagery
- omitting negative information, or omitting positive information about an alternative to the product/campaign
- emotional appeals
- false reasoning

Set-up: This exercise can work in one of several ways: (1) select a series of full-page magazine advertisements that rely on many of the concepts listed above and mount them on construction paper for use in small groups; (2) video tape television commercials with the same characteristics for use with the whole class; (3) have students conduct a search on the Internet for advertisements or political messages.

Procedures: Students read (in small groups) or watch and listen to the ad (whole class). Ask students to collaborate in their groups, or discuss as a whole class,the reasons that a consumer might have for not trusting the advertiser's message. Ask the class to name as many reasons as they can about why the ad or commercial might be misleading.

Tips for Teacher Preparation: 1. This exercise should follow a unit on propaganda and persuasive strategies that introduces students to specific propaganda techniques (such as those listed above).

2. Suggested probes if discussion lags:

Does the ad exaggerate the benefits of the product or exaggerate the consumer's satisfaction with the product? How?

Does the commercial use ambiguous or deceptive words that are confusing? (i.e., "weasel words," small, fine-print restrictions or disclaimers, or quickly spoken submessages such as, "X sold separately. Batteries not included.")

Does the ad rely on images to imply that the product will do something it won't? (Make the consumer happier, more popular, more muscular, and so forth.)

Does the ad omit negative information about the product?

Does the ad rely on appeals to emotional needs, such as happiness, security, or fear?

Does the ad use faulty reasoning, such as claiming false cause and effect relationships?

Does the ad present accurate information about available alternatives?

SUMMARY

A competency-based approach to oral communication within the integrated language arts is possible through careful consideration of the knowledge, skills, and attributes that students are expected to achieve at designated exit levels. Competencies may be identified for a wide variety of formal and informal speaking and listening contexts, including dramatic performance and mass media. Learning activities that integrate reading and writing may be structured around core competencies to target age-appropriate proficiency levels. Activities such as debate and public speaking offer unique opportunities to learn about the components of arguments and the credibility of evidence. More informal speaking contexts, such as conversation and small-group discussion, help students learn to take turns and to develop problem-solving, role-playing, and general interpersonal skills. The oral interpretation of literature, plays, and puppetry helps students develop an appreciation for dramatic performance. The task of making a "cutting" for oral interpretation also helps students think critically and imaginatively about literature. Finally, students should be critical consumers of all forms of mass media.

REFERENCES

Cooper, P. J., & Collins, R. (1995). *Look what happened to frog: Storytelling in education.* Scottsdale, AZ: Gorsuch Scarisbrick.

Coty, S. P. (1993, January). Writers all: Drama in the middle. *English Journal,* pp. 48–52.

District of Columbia Public Schools. (1988). *English language arts oral communication elementary level competency-based curriculum.* Washington, DC: District of Columbia Public Schools.

Hazelton, V., & Metts, S. (1994). Verbal messages. In M. E. Comadena and W. D. Semla (Eds.), *Introduction to speech communication.* Prospect Heights, IL: Waveland Press.

Hoyt, L. (1992). Many ways of knowing: Using drama, oral interactions, and the visual arts to enhance reading comprehension. *The Reading Teacher, 45*(8), 580–584.

Newman, R., & Newman, D. (1969). *Evidence.* Boston: Houghton Mifflin.

Rieke, R. D., & Sillars, M. O. (1984). *Argumentation and the decision-making process* (2nd ed.). Glenview, IL: Scott, Foresman.

Shafer, K. (1993, January). Talk in the middle: Two conversational skills for friendship. *English Journal,* pp. 53–55.

Smagorinsky, P., & Fly, P. K. (1993). The social environment of the classroom: A Vygotskian perspective on the small group process. *Communication Education, 42,* 160–171.

Speech Communication Association. (1991). *Guidelines for developing oral communication curricula in kindergarten through twelfth grade.* Annandale, VA: Speech Communication Association.

Speech Communication Association. (1996). *Speaking, listening, and media literacy standards for K through 12 education.* Annandale, VA: Speech Communication Association.

Toulmin, S., Rieke, R., & Janik, A. (1984). *An introduction to reasoning* (2nd ed.). New York: Macmillan.

ADDITIONAL RESOURCES

Cooper, M., & Nothstine, W. (1992). *Power persuasion: Moving an ancient art into the media age.* Greenwood, IN: Educational Video Group.

Grice, G., & Skinner, J. (1995). *Mastering public speaking* (2nd ed.). Boston: Allyn and Bacon.

Larson, C. (1992). *Persuasion: reception and responsibility* (6th ed.). Belmont, CA: Wadsworth Publishers.

Lucas, S. (1995). *The art of public speaking* (5th ed.). New York: McGraw-Hill.

Pratkanis, A. (1992). *Age of propaganda: The everyday use and abuse of persuasion.* New York: W. H. Freeman.

Speech Communication Association. (1994). *Speaking and listening competencies for elementary school students.* Annandale, VA: Speech Communication Association.

Speech Communication Association. (Forthcoming). *Activities for teaching speaking, listening, and media literacy standards.* Annandale, VA: Speech Communication Association.

Sprague, J., & Stuart, D. (1992). *The speaker's handbook* (3rd ed.). San Diego: Harcourt Brace Jovanovich.

Tupper, M. (1995, October). Writing for radio. *Teaching K–8,* pp. 62–63.

APPENDIX 3.1
Oral Communication Contexts and Competencies
Taught by K through 8 Teachers:
Responses to Survey Questions

Question: *What oral communication contexts do you teach?*

Conflict resolution (peer mediation)

Debate
- analysis of research articles and formulation of points for effective debating
- questioning skills in debate

Discussion
- predicting results of a problem
- discussing results of group projects

Drama
- multicultural fairy tales
- musicals
- plays
- puppetry
- skits

Listening skills

Music

Reading aloud
- echo reading
- taping reading (using the same passage and comparing at least three times per year) of stories and poems

Speaking
- announcements
- conversation
- entertaining speeches
- expressing and supporting opinions
- giving directions
- informative speaking
- interviews
- oral presentations of research information
- oral reading of all creative writing assignments
- persuasive speaking
- presentation skills (general: posture, pronunciation, enunciation, projection, use of notes, relaxation techniques)
- voice/speech techniques

Storytelling
- anecdote
- author's teas
- creating drama to go with a story

APPENDIX 3.1 *Continued*

Question: *How do you incorporate oral communication contexts into your lesson plan?*

Drama:
"Skits and plays are performed by students to demonstrate understanding of social studies or science topics—examples: act out the Boston Tea Party, plays about being on a wagon train, weather reports, act out trials of various historical figures, debates, etc."

"In a dramatics workshop, I use exercises which range from pantomime to playing a part in a skit or play. Students work through activities which require communication of emotions and activities through facial expressions, body language, voice, and character interpretation."

"Acting out emotions as identified on task cards."

" 'Sculpture and sculptor,' whereby one student will have to manipulate the 'clay' of another student and fix arms and legs in a hardened position. Students then reverse roles."

"Students form letters of the alphabet and are photographed in place for spelling out names and titles."

"Choral readings."

"Role playing."

Listening:
"Writing a response to something heard; following directions, or note taking."

"We do exercises on being a good listener or good audience and learn to rate each other accordingly."

"I teach listening skills with tapes of recorded short stories. We study styles of authors and then listen to recorded tapes to see if we can hear words for style and mood established. We use passages and change the words to see the effect of word choice on the meaning of the message. In writing areas, we read aloud our work in groups and the group responds to choices of words and questions and responds to those choices to reflect the writer's meaning."

Reading
and discussion:
"In a Junior Great Books seminar, I incorporate oral communication skills as an essential part of the inquiry/strategy/discussion phase of the program. Students prepare ahead for a round-robin discussion in which they must support their views as they are interpreted from the selection. Students find that they must be able to communicate their opinions (interpretations) clearly to the rest of the group of readers."

"Students take leadership roles in holding an interpretive discussion about a story the group has been reading and studying; leaders must keep a seating chart of participants, what they contribute to the discussion, and how well they agree or disagree in their opinions with other members of their group."

"Use the P–M–I chart (plus–minus–interesting) to discuss all aspects of an issue."

"In writing groups, students must read all writings to a partner. The listener must evaluate his messages, the language used to convey his message, and his skills in presenting the message."

(continued)

APPENDIX 3.1   *Continued*

	"If I am using [a lesson about] descriptive language, I often use selected paragraphs from the works of Willa Cather. Her works are good examples of places and people described so that we often diagram or draw the pictures, e.g., one passage from *My Antonia*."
	"Round-robin oral review is done as students add and expand on information for test review or literature discussion and interpretation."
Reading and writing:	"For three years, I've been introducing my students (eighth graders) to Plato's dialogues, then having them write a dialogue of their own. I also use a copy of a modern dialogue."
Speaking:	"We discuss characteristics of a good speaker (i.e., eye contact, clear diction, posture, etc.), and the children are eventually evaluated on these elements after practice."
	"I model a persuasive speech; we look at persuasive writings; we incorporate oral communication with library research skills; I teach outlining and note taking; critiquing skills."
	"I've found success in using Patricia Sternberg's book, *Guidelines to Effective Speaking,* as outlined for student use in note form."
	"We do forensics in all language arts classes with a school and county contest."
	"I (1) use discussion about what constitutes effective communication skills, (2) consciously model effective communication skills, and (3) have students analyze sample lessons for effective communication skills."
	"We film our kids and let them view themselves. Then we throw their images on our computers and enhance with programs their performances."
	"Another exercise I've done is have the students write instructions for how to do or make something. Then they turn it into a three-to-five–minute 'how-to' speech and demonstration."
	"Radio project: I had two guest speakers first: one a radio producer and the other a d.j. Then I created a 'WOHS' radio station and had each of my three sections of eighth graders take responsibility for one-third of a simulated day in the life of WOHS radio programming. They further divided up into pairs of disk jockeys and wrote their own twenty- to-thirty–minute shows. They recorded them, with music, and played them for the entire class." (See Tupper 1995.)
	"I make an attempt to videotape my students each year either doing a presentation of information they have researched; debating; or reading an essay, poem, etc., they have written."
	"Student makes a mobile of six symbols; gives presentation explaining the symbols."
	"Questioning is often done in informal groups with students presenting the questions to their peers."

APPENDIX 3.2
Examples of Kindergarten Oral Communication Competencies

Listening
1. Identify his or her full name when he or she hears it.
2. Identify classroom sounds.
3. Identify environmental sounds.
4. Demonstrate the ability to reproduce sounds.
5. Describe differences in pitch (loud/soft, higher/lower).
6. Identify source of sounds.

Speaking
1. Identify concrete objects.
2. Identify pictures objects.
3. Name body parts.
4. Name activities in the environment.
5. Demonstrate the ability to repeat spoken words.
6. Demonstrate the ability to imitate correct speech patterns.
7. Demonstrate the ability to speak in unison.
8. Demonstrate the ability to speak clearly and distinctly.
9. Describe objects according to shape and color.

Creative drama
1. Demonstrate the ability to pantomime nursery rhymes and stories.
2. Demonstrate the ability to pantomime sensory awareness and daily activity.
3. Demonstrate the ability to orally share information and experiences.
4. Construct an original story orally.

Nonverbal communication
1. Demonstrate the ability to interpret nonverbal messages through pictures.
2. Identify body movements as a means of nonverbal communication.

Reprinted with permission of the Speech Communication Association (1991, p. 17).

APPENDIX 3.3
Examples of First-Grade Oral Communication Competencies

Listening
1. Identify initial consonant sounds.
2. Identify words which sound alike at the beginning.
3. Name rhyming words.
4. Identify rhyming pictures.
5. Name descriptive sounds.
6. Identify a complete thought.

Speaking
1. Describe ideas relative to the subject.
2. Order ideas in sequence.

Creative drama
1. Demonstrate the ability to tell a familiar story.
2. Demonstrate the ability to dramatize a fairy tale.
3. Demonstrate the ability to role play realistic situations.

Nonverbal communication
1. Identify meanings conveyed by facial expressions.
2. Identify messages conveyed by signs.

Reprinted with permission of the Speech Communication Association (1991, p. 18).

APPENDIX 3.4
Examples of Second-Grade Oral Communication Competencies

Listening
1. Identify the main idea.
2. Identify descriptive words and phrases.

Speaking
1. Describe familiar helpers in their environment.
2. Demonstrate the ability to make simple introductions and greetings.
3. Demonstrate the use of inflectional tone to convey an emotion.

Creative drama
1. Demonstrate the ability to role-play events in a story.
2. Construct and dramatize a puppet story.
3. Construct and tell a flannel board story.
4. Demonstrate the ability to read a story orally.

Nonverbal communication
1. Demonstrate the ability to orally summarize the meanings conveyed by nonverbal symbols.
2. Identify specific nonverbal actions which reinforce or detract from a verbal statement.

Reprinted with permission of the Speech Communication Association (1991, p. 19).

APPENDIX 3.5
Examples of Third-Grade Oral Communication Competencies

Listening
    1. Identify compound words.

Speaking
    1. Demonstrate the use of inflectional tone to convey an emotion.
    2. Demonstrate the use of the telephone for business and social calls.
    3. Construct a summary for a story.

Creative drama
    1. Demonstrate the ability to dramatize a story.
    2. Construct and dramatize a story ending from a story starter.

Nonverbal communication
    1. Demonstrate the use of pantomime as a means of nonverbal communication.
    2. Identify how alternative nonverbal actions increase the clarity or more effectively reinforce a verbal message.

Reprinted with permission of the Speech Communication Association (1991, p. 20).

Appendix 3.6
Examples of Fourth-Grade Oral Communication Competencies

Listening
    1. Use pitch to reflect changes in meaning and feelings.

Speaking
    1. Demonstrate the use of figurative language.
    2. Identify the standards for good speaking.

Creative drama
    1. Construct and dramatize a story.
    2. Demonstrate the ability to give an oral report.
    3. Construct and deliver an informative speech.

Nonverbal communication
    1. Demonstrate the use of a signal systems as a means of nonverbal communication.
    2. Emphasize meanings in conversations, discussions, and oral presentations by use of pauses, gestures, and facial expressions.

Mass media
    1. Identify major types of mass media.
    2. Explain how measures differ when conveyed by different media.

Reprinted with permission of the Speech Communication Association (1991, p. 21).

APPENDIX 3.7
Examples of Fifth-Grade Oral Communication Competencies

Listening
1. Describe inferred meaning taken from context.
2. Identify the standards of a good listener.

Speaking
1. Apply the rules for conducting interviews.
2. Demonstrate role playing techniques.
3. Apply the rules for conducting discussions.

Creative drama
1. Construct and deliver an inspirational speech.
2. Construct and dramatize a two-character scene.

Nonverbal communication
1. Demonstrate the use of pictorial representations to recount main ideas and information.
2. Demonstrate appropriate use of eye contact, nonverbal, expression, and adjustment of rate, pace, and volume in face-to-face communication with a number of different people of different ages.

Mass media
1. Identify the audience to be attracted by mass media.
2. Distinguish between fact and opinion.
3. Distinguish among the four types of propaganda.
4. Identify an effective advertisement.

Reprinted with permission of the Speech Communication Association (1991, p. 22).

APPENDIX 3.8
Examples of Sixth-Grade Oral Communication Competencies

Listening
1. Distinguish between hearing and listening.
2. Identify the significance and functions of listening in the communication process.
3. Identify the different types and levels of listening.
4. Identify barriers to effective listening.
5. Identify and apply techniques for effective listening.

Speaking
1. Demonstrate good discussion techniques in terms of listening.
2. Apply the rules for making an oral report and be able to identify these rules as a listener.
3. Demonstrate the ability to organize a two-minute talk using effective speaking techniques and be able to identify these techniques as a listener.

Creative drama
1. Demonstrate the ability to perform quality improvisations and identify the qualties of improvisation as a listener.
2. Based on the anticipated reactions of others derived from the role of a listener, construct and dramatize an original play.
3. Construct and deliver a persuasive speech and be able to identify persuasive techniques as a listener.

Nonverbal communication
1. Identify nonverbal modes of communication which impede effective listening.
2. Identify and employ nonverbal modes of communication which promote effective listening.

Mass media
1. Identify factual claims in a 30-second television and/or radio commercial.
2. Identify verbal and nonverbal acts in a 30-second television and/or radio commercial which can be understood in two or more ways.

APPENDIX 3.9
Examples of Seventh-Grade Interpersonal, Nonverbal, and Small-Group Communication Competencies

Interpersonal communication
1. Identify and explain the major purposes of interpersonal communication.
2. Identify and explain the functions of the major variables in any communication process.
3. Identify and explain the major variables related to the accuracy of interpersonal perception.
4. Explain the concept of effectiveness in interpersonal communication.
5. Identify, explain, and provide examples of concepts associated with interpersonal communication, such as empathy, supportiveness, trust, equality, expressiveness, self-monitoring and other-orientation.

Self and self-awareness
1. Define and explain the usefulness of the following concepts of self in interpersonal communication: open self, blind self, hidden self, and unknown self.
2. Define self-disclosure and identify the major factors affecting self-disclosure.
3. Identify major guidelines recommended for responding to the disclosure of others.
4. Distinguish and illustrate the differences among apprehension, aggressiveness, assertiveness, and nonassertiveness.

Understanding perception
1. Explain the influence of the perceiver, the person perceived, and the situation on the process of perception.
2. Name aspects of the object perceived that affect perception.
3. Name aspects inside the perceiver that can influence perception.
4. Describe the use of categories in organizing perceptions.
5. Identify and explain major factors which clarify perception and can solve communication problems.

Language and meaning
1. Define language and identify its major social functions.
2. List and define the major characteristics of a language.
3. Define meaning in terms of denotative and connotative language.
4. Explain the concept of language subtitles.
5. Define and identify examples of the use of racism and sexism in popular language.

Relationships
1. Identify and define the major characteristics of an interpersonal relationship.
2. Identify and explain the major functions of communication in relationships.
3. Explain why relationships develop and identify stages which account for the evolution of interpersonal relationships.
4. Identify the major factors people judge to be attractive in a potential partner.
5. Explain how similarity and complementarity affect interpersonal communication.
6. Identify major sources and types of power which influence interpersonal communication and how power functions in interpersonal communication.
7. Distinguish, identify, and define major types of friendship and love.

APPENDIX 3.9   *Continued*

Conflict
1. Define interpersonal conflict.
2. Explain the differences between content and relationship conflict.
3. Identify positive and negative aspects of conflict in interpersonal communication.

Nonverbal communication
1. Define nonverbal communication and identify its functions in human relations.
2. Identify and define the major kinds of nonverbal communication people use.
3. Explain how verbal and nonverbal communication influence each other (e.g., repeat, contradict, substitute for, complement, accent, regulate) to enhance and hamper effective human communication.
4. Explain how the meaning of nonverbal communication can change from one situation to another (e.g., classroom, courtship, televised politics, etc.).
5. Explain how children acquire or learn specific nonverbal behaviors.
6. Explain how environmental factors such as setting, personal space, and territory affect human communication.

Group communication
1. Identify and define the primary characteristics of a group.
2. Describe the primary functions of small groups in society.
3. Identify and define several major types of small groups.
4. Describe the factors which unify and divide group members.
5. Identify the functions of feedback in the small-group communication process.
6. Identify the range of roles and functions of each of these roles in the small-group communication process.
7. Identify and describe the major forms of leadership style.
8. Describe the relationships between task and social functions within small groups.
9. Describe several communication patterns or styles common to small groups.
10. Observe a group situation and diagram its interaction pattern.

Problem solving through group communication
1. Name and explain the steps used in problem solving.
2. Explain the relationships between the problem-solving steps and thinking.
3. Observe several small groups and identify group fantasies which dominate each group.
4. Identify the relationships between problem-solving decisions and small-group fantasies.
5. Explain the purpose of public discussions.

Participating in parliamentary groups
1. Explain the purpose of parliamentary procedure.
2. List the basic principles of parliamentary procedure.
3. Describe the responsibilities of the president in conducting meetings.
4. Explain the major classes of motions.
5. List the precedence of motions.

APPENDIX 3.10
Examples of Eighth-Grade International and Intercultural Communication Competencies

1. Identify verbal and nonverbal communication cues distinguishing one's own and others' cultural environments and heritage.

2. Identify verbal and nonverbal communication patterns which are shared by distinct cultural systems.

3. Identify social institutions and historical experiences which distinguish and are commonly used by cultural systems.

4. Develop a sensitivity to and appreciation for the diverse ways in which experiences can be articulated verbally and nonverbally.

5. Develop an awareness of one's own desires, assumptions, and beliefs in order to experiment more freely in new patterns of behavior.

6. Communicate effectively in alternative cultural systems (e.g., adjust to different environments) without losing one's basic values.

7. Develop a self-concept which fosters trust, ego strength, open-mindedness, and the ability to accept ambiguity and diversity among people.

Reprinted with permission of the Speech Communication Association (1991, p. 30).

4

Focus on Listening

OVERVIEW

Listening is often the most overlooked component of the oral communication process. This chapter takes a closer look at four listening functions that are important for academic, work, and life-management success and suggests beginning, intermediate, and advanced competencies for each function. The remaining portion of the chapter describes some activities and assessments.

PRACTICALLY SPEAKING

What is listening?
Why is listening instruction important?
What are the major listening functions?
What are some functional listening skills and attributes for grades K through 8?
What are some innovative ways to teach and assess listening?

WHAT IS LISTENING?

Listening has been defined as a four-step process that includes elements of receiving, interpreting, evaluating, and responding (Galvin 1985). Listening has also been defined to involve attending, and assigning meaning, to aural stimuli (Wolvin & Coakley 1988). These definitions are helpful, but what exactly does it mean to "receive," or to "attend," to "aural stimuli"? Most definitions of listening encompass both physical and mental aspects. When we "receive" (hear) or "attend to" (pay attention to; think about) "aural stimuli" (sounds that we recognize as meaningful), we are using sensory, cognitive, and affective attributes.

In plainer language, listening is the portion of the oral communication process that involves

1. Hearing aural symbols;
2. Storing and interpreting aural symbols in order to comprehend them (using short-term memory during a period of suspension or waiting while the listener gathers more information from the speaker); and
3. Responding with verbal and nonverbal feedback to facilitate the communication process.

Above all, listening is active rather than passive; good listeners devote considerable physical and mental energy to the process of listening.

Hearing Aural Symbols

Hearing is a physical, or sensory, activity that refers generally to the action of soundwaves in stimulating the eardrum and the mechanisms of the inner ear. The mental activity of listening occurs when sounds are perceived as meaningful. Over time, listeners attach meaning to sounds such as language, sounds occurring in nature, or sounds that are mechanically produced. These sounds with attached meaning become recognized by the listener as aural symbols. Silence is also an important aural symbol, often used to convey meaning, even though it is not itself a sound.

Storing and Interpreting Symbols to Comprehend Meaning

Attending
One of the key features of listening is a period of suspension, or waiting, in which aural symbols are received and interpreted. Storing and interpreting symbols may or may not occur in a linear fashion. That is, listeners are capable of suspending the interpretation and evaluation of information for a period of time in order to pay attention to the speaker. This process is sometimes called *attending*. Good listeners recognize when they are not attending—when they are ignoring a speaker or reacting uncritically to a speaker's message—and are willing and able to subsequently adjust their listening behavior.

Short-Term Memory
In general, memory is the function of the human brain that stores information derived from sensory intake and from thought. Short-term memory is limited and stores only that information the mind perceives as necessary for only the amount of time perceived as necessary. Good listeners can improve their ability to retain information through short-term memory by focusing on information-intake strategies.

Responding to Facilitate the Communication Process

Responding
Listening usually involves some kind of verbal or nonverbal response to a speaker's message. Typical verbal responses include sounds indicating emotional reaction ("Oh my goodness!," "You must be joking," "I'm sorry to hear that," "Wow!") and sounds indicating understanding or processing of information ("Uh huh," "Yes," "Hmm," "I don't get it," "What did you say?"). Nonverbal responses include the whole panoply of facial expressions, gestures, posture, and so on.

Facilitating Communication
For trained listeners, the purpose of responding with verbal and nonverbal feedback is to facilitate the communication process—to build and share meaning, to enhance understanding. Feedback assists the speaker in adjusting his or her message to better reach the listener. The word *facilitate* conveys the affective or attitudinal component of listening. Trained listeners devote energy to responding with appropriate feedback because they believe that communication is important and that communication is the joint responsibility of both speakers and listeners. Good listeners are willing to devote effort to listening.

WHY IS LISTENING INSTRUCTION IMPORTANT?

Listening has traditionally received only minimal attention in the K through 8 language arts curriculum for a number of reasons. First, listening has been severely undervalued in general education as a human activity worthy of pedagogical emphasis. Second, listening has been seen as involving primarily behavioral rather than cognitive and affective components (though, as we shall see, it is often the cognitive and affective components that are most important in facilitating good communication). Third, daily practice in "paying attention" has often been the primary focus of listening instruction. In reality, there is a fairly broad scope of important listening skills that require instruction and practice. Like reading and writing, listening skills can be taught, and do not "naturally" evolve to levels of proficiency.

The Value of Listening as a Human Activity

According to the International Listening Association, we spend more time listening at home, in school, in the workplace, and with friends than we do involved in any of the other traditional strands of the language arts. We spend 53 percent of our time listening, 16 percent of our time speaking, 17 percent of our time reading, and 14 percent of our time writing (Hunsacker 1989, p. 27). Other studies suggest similar breakdowns in time and usage. In spite of the dominance of listening activity in our daily lives, however, the average listener is very inefficient, retaining only about 20 percent of what he or she hears (Cooper 1995), even though studies suggest that we can listen to speech at a rate three times faster than the average rate, without losing significant meaning (Nichols & Lewis 1954).

Inefficient listening does not merely refer to short- and long-term memory of speech. Inefficient listening occurs because of a lack of cognitive skills and affective attributes that enable a listener to concentrate on understanding aural symbols and to give feedback that reinforces and clarifies that understanding. When all three elements of the listening process are working well together—hearing the symbols, storing and interpreting them, and then responding to the speaker—listeners retain more information.

Listening also holds value as a critical life-management skill that strengthens an individual's or a group's decision-making process. Listening enables people to provide emotional relief to one another. Ultimately, listening increases the quality of our lives by enhancing our enjoyment of aesthetic experiences. We will talk more about the functions of listening later in this chapter.

Listening Involves Cognitive Skills and Affective Attributes

For many years in the elementary classroom, to listen was to "pay attention to the teacher." Even with an integrated curriculum, cooperative learning, and emphasis on performance assessment, it's only natural that we bring similar expectations to the classroom and to our personal interaction with children. We want them to pay attention so that they will learn from, and remember, their classroom experiences.

Paying attention, however, is only one facet of good listening. Good listening involves critical thinking skills and positive attitudes toward communication. It requires conscious choices about how to respond to a speaker, and it requires self-awareness on the part of the listener. For example, listeners need courage to solve interpersonal conflicts without threats and violence. Listeners must have the will to continue conflict-resolution dialogue when the other side just won't "play fair." And listeners must have knowledge of conflict-resolution concepts and strategies to craft an agreement with which everyone can live.

Communication contexts, such as debate, persuasive speaking, and group problem solving, challenge listeners not only to "pay attention," but in particular, they challenge listeners to use a variety of higher-order thinking skills.

Listening Skills Require Instruction and Practice

Kindergarten teachers will be the first to report that children need help in learning to pay attention, and efforts to help children learn to concentrate continue throughout their education. Similarly, other listening skills, such as summarizing, recognizing "body language," identifying supporting material, and distinguishing fact from opinion, also benefit from instruction. In the absence of instruction, children tend to learn only indirectly about listening through the modeling of their parents, teachers, and peers. These sources of information may not be sufficient to help a child become a proficient and active listener.

Barriers to effective listening exist at both a physical and psychological level. Physical barriers to listening may arise when we are tired or busy, when we can't hear well, when we are too warm or too cold and don't feel like concentrating. Psychological barriers to listening include value judgments about the speaker, personal like or dislike of the topic, strong emotions such as anger or fear, or simple lack of interest and apathy. Instruction and frequent opportunities to practice listening skills can help students overcome these barriers to listening at a very early age. Instruction need not, however, always be formal. Informal listening activities can be very effective in introducing a wider scope of listening competencies.

WHAT ARE THE MAJOR LISTENING FUNCTIONS?

We listen to accomplish four specific purposes that correspond to four specific purposes of speakers. The four listening functions are *discriminative* listening, *evaluative* listening, *empathic* listening, and *appreciative* listening (Wolff et al. 1983). The four listening functions are not mutually exclusive; communicators may easily shift in and out of each depending on the communication situation. All four functions are appropriate for K through 8 instruction.

The Discriminative Function

Listeners use the discriminative function of listening in order to gather, understand, and retain useful information from an oral message. Discriminative listening and appreciative listening (discussed further below) are probably the most predominant listening functions taught in the K through 8 classroom.

The discriminative function is so named because listeners decide which information is most important or useful in a speaker's informative message. This selective gathering of information allows a listener to comprehend a complex message without becoming overwhelmed. Rather, a discriminative listener concentrates on the facts or details most necessary to gain maximum benefit from a message. The longer and more complex an informative message, the more important efficient discriminative listening becomes.

When do elementary students use the discriminative listening function? Students listen discriminatively in school to the teacher, to announcements over the public address system, to educational films, and to their peers. They listen discriminatively to school health workers, bus drivers, and athletic coaches. At home, students listen discriminatively to television and radio news reports, to their parents and adult caretakers, and to their friends.

Discriminative Listening Competencies

Beginning students:
- Perceive and distinguish among sounds in the environment
- Perceive and distinguish among sounds in words
- Describe differences in pitch
- Identify the source of sounds
- Recognize and infer meaning from aural symbols (such as words and nonverbal behavior)
- Understand and follow directions
- Recall important ideas in an oral message
- Recall details in an oral message
- Identify a complete thought in an oral message

Intermediate students:
- Describe the difference between hearing and listening
- Identify main points in an oral message—learn to
  - Distinguish main points from subpoints
  - Distingush supporting materials (facts and illustrations) from subpoints
  - Follow clues about main points from previews, transitions, and summaries

- Identify the organizational pattern of main points in an oral message
  - Identify main points organized to show a chronological sequence (usually in explanations of processes and historical accounts)
    Example:
    A. Diamonds start out as lumps of coal buried deep in the ground.
    B. The pressure of the heavy earth forces the lumps of coal to become stones.
    C. People build mines and search for these special stones underneath the ground.
    D. Then a jeweler uses special tools to cut away the rough surface of the stone, revealing the beautiful diamond inside.

  - Identify main points organized around a central topic or theme
    Example:
    A. One genre of literature is the poem.
    B. A second genre of literature is the play.
    C. A third genre of literature is the short story.
    D. A fourth genre of literature is the novel.

  - Identify main points organized to show a problem–solution or cause–effect pattern
    Example:
    A. First I will explain to you some of the diseases that often strike young babies and children.

      B. Then I will explain how early vaccination programs can help prevent these diseases.

- Identify main points organized to show their spatial relationship to one another
Example:
      A. The top of the Sears building in Chicago, Illinois, has large lightning rods that keep the lightning from damaging the rest of the building when it strikes.
      B. The middle of the Sears building holds offices and special luxury apartments, called penthouses.
      C. Inside the Sears building is a set of two special, high-speed elevators that can go up and down the building in about ninety seconds.
      D. The bottom of the Sears building holds shops and a large mechanical sculpture by a famous artist, Alexander Calder.

Advanced students:
- Give helpful verbal and nonverbal feedback to the speaker
  - Demonstrate awareness of facial expressions and body posture
  - Recognize different messages that facial expressions and body posture communicate to the speaker
    * Direct eye contact versus indirect or no eye contact
    * Open posture (uncrossed arms; leaning slightly forward) versus closed posture (crossed arms; tapping feet)
    * Relaxed and open hands versus tightly clenched fists or playing with objects
    * Smiling and nodding the head versus scowling and rolling the eyes
  - Adopt facial expressions that help the speaker clarify and adjust the message
  - Develop and ask questions when possible to help the speaker clarify and adjust the message

- Prepare for listening
  - Cease distracting activities in order to give full attention to the speaker
  - Choose to be open-minded about the speaker and the message; look for reasons to value listening in each situation
  - Sit in a location and posture that indicates alertness to the speaker and allows the listener to remain alert
  - Prepare for longer listening sessions by reading a little bit about the topic beforehand

- Take notes in an efficient, useful manner
  - Demonstrate various ways to record important points and concepts (such as outlining a presentation or taking notes during a meeting)
  - Edit and review notes to refresh the memory
  - Organize notes so that they are easily accessible for later use (such as a notebook or a file)

The Evaluative Function

Listeners use the evaluative function of listening in order to evaluate the merits of a persuasive message. Persuasion is essential to most decision making. It is okay, and even desirable, to accept ethical, responsible persuasion if the result is consistent with the listener's best interests (Larson 1992). Thus, evaluative listeners learn to monitor persuasion and weigh both its potential benefits and drawbacks. Evaluative listeners understand their own self-concept and recognize how it affects their response to persuasion. Finally, evaluative listeners learn to recognize their own selective perception bias.

Ethical, responsible persuasion.   On one hand, evaluative listeners recognize that not all persuasion comes from sources who have the best interests of the listener in mind. Sometimes persuaders use tactics and strategies that trick or manipulate listeners. On the other hand, evaluative listeners also recognize that persuasion can serve the best interests of the listener. In other cases, the shared interests of persuader and listener would be mutually enhanced. Accordingly, evaluative listeners learn to investigate the goals and tactics of the persuader and to compare those against their own best interests.

Self-concept.   A listener's response to persuasion is often affected by his or her self-concept, which plays an important role in shaping psychological needs and motivations. Persuaders often use emotional and value appeals that are carefully targeted to stimulate a listener's self-concept. Understanding one's own values, emotional needs, or desires can help evaluative listeners distance themselves from a message in order to objectively critique its merits.

Selective perception.   Evaluative listeners learn to recognize and better monitor selective perception. Because we hear so many different sounds at once, humans have a filtering process known as selective perception. Selective perception allows us to focus our physical and mental energies on those aural symbols to which we attach the most importance, and to block out those sounds that are less efficient to process. The limitations of our short-term memory make selective perception an important defensive mechanism.

Listeners lose the benefits of good communication, however, when they engage in selective perception habits that are too restrictive—when selective perception becomes a filter not just to protect the mind and body from an onslaught of aural stimulation, but a filter to immediately evaluate, construe, or dismiss aural symbols in situations when it might not be beneficial or appropriate to do so. Good evaluative listeners learn to recognize their own selective perception habits and strive to refrain from uncritically dismissing or reacting to information.

When do elementary students use the evaluative listening function? Although evaluative listening offers important opportunities to employ higher-order critical thinking skills, it is not as frequently taught and practiced among elementary students as is the discriminative function. And yet, students would benefit from more instruction in evaluative listening because of the unique challenges posed by oral communication—the immediacy and impermanency of speech (described in Chapter 1). Children who can "think on their feet" when faced with an aural persuasive message will be better prepared than others for academic, work, and life-management success.

In the classroom, elementary students can benefit from evaluative listening when discussing literature in the language arts class or when talking about history, law, and society in other areas of the curriculum. With respect to life management, particularly in the middle school years, students can benefit from strong evaluative listening skills when facing peer pressure to engage in potentially harmful activities; when facing unethical persuaders who might otherwise take advantage of their youth and inexperience; when facing a barrage of media images and messages proclaiming whom they are to admire, what they are to buy, and how they are to spend their time.

Evaluative Listening Competencies

Beginning students:
- Distinguish a persuasive from an informative message
- Identify a persuasive message in a story
- Identify a persuasive message communicated by a friend or sibling
- Explain the persuasive purpose of an advertisement
- Identify a claim made in an advertisement

Intermediate students:
- Identify a speaker's purpose in sending a persuasive message
- Distinguish fact from opinion
- Describe some ways that speakers use vocal pitch and facial expressions to persuade
- Identify emotional or value appeals in a persuasive message
- Identify some common persuasive tactics
  - Identify logical fallacies and propaganda techniques such as the hasty generalization, weasel words, glittering generalities, and bandwagon effect (these logical fallacies are discussed in Chapter 3)
  - Identify exaggeration or distortion of information
  - Identify the underlying bias or assumptions in the speaker's message

Advanced students:
- Identify a logical argument made by a speaker
- Predict the logical implications of arguments made by the speaker
- Identify inconsistencies between the speaker's verbal and nonverbal messages
- Identify situations in which a person might want to avoid making an "impulse decision"
- Describe a time when persuasion targeted your personal feelings
- Identify and compare the pros and cons of solutions to a social problem

The Empathic Function

Listeners use the empathic function of listening in order to help a speaker express emotions. An empathic listener recognizes situations in which a speaker needs to express emotion and needs to feel understood. An empathic listener provides relief and shows understanding by mastering a set of verbal and nonverbal skills. Most of these skills are also helpful in resolving conflict and, in general, they are helpful in facilitating effective interpersonal communication.

Advanced empathic listening skills include summarizing and reflecting. Summarizing consists of gently restating the speaker's main idea so that the speaker can either agree (and feel understood), or clarify (and feel respected and cared for; for example, "Your friends did not invite you to the party and you really wanted to go." Reflecting occurs when a listener names the feeling itself: "You seem frightened and upset" or "You're hurt because your friends did not invite you to the party and you really wanted to go." Listeners can also give simpler empathic verbal feedback such as "I see," "Mmmm," "Yes."

When do elementary students use the empathic listening function? At a very young age, children learn to recognize and express their feelings. As they begin to recognize the expressed feelings of others, children may naturally demonstrate desire to provide relief. Children naturally incorporate "feeling talk" into their play time with puppets, dolls, and stuffed animals. As children grow older, specific empathic listening strategies may be learned and practiced. Children as young as first grade have learned some of these skills when taught as part of a comprehensive peer-mediation program. At the middle school level, empathic listening skills become critically important for successful life management. Empathic listening training can help build a healthy self-concept as well as respect for others.

One example of a context involving empathic listening is peer mediation. Hazelwood Elementary School in Louisville, Kentucky, implemented a successful peer-mediation program involving fourth and fifth graders, according to Dorothy Logan (1995), a counselor at the school. At Hazelwood, teachers and administrators chose a number of students to participate in the program as peer mediators. The students who were chosen as mediators were not necessarily the most academically talented or the most likely to be leaders; some students were chosen because they appeared to have trouble getting along with others. Using the book *Creating the Peaceable School* (Bodine et al. 1994), teachers designed a fifty-hour training curriculum of role-playing and modeling. Peer mediators learned the importance of ground rules in conflict management, such as respect for the individual and the self, the importance of only one person speaking at a time, and how to record an agreement between participants. At Hazelwood, teachers were amazed at how students learned to value peaceful, constructive communication in a community facing many serious challenges to the self-esteem and academic achievement of its students (Logan 1995).

Empathic Listening Competencies

Beginning students:
- Identify feelings of a character in a story
- Using a puppet or a stuffed animal, show how the character might have expressed feelings with words or actions or, using details in the story itself, recall how a character expressed feelings

Example:

Juan has a new baby sister who cries a lot. The baby stays upstairs in a special crib. One day when Juan's parents went out to dinner, the baby started to cry very loudly. Alicia, the babysitter, did not hear the baby. Juan thought something was wrong. Perhaps the baby was hungry. Juan ran downstairs right away and told Alicia the baby was crying.

Do you think Juan cared about his baby sister? Why or why not?

- Identify your own feelings
- Tell how you express your feelings with words and actions
- Tell who listens to you when you express your feelings and how that person shows you they understand how you feel

Intermediate students:
- Listen to a speaker finish his or her thoughts without interrupting
- Explain why speakers who are having strong feelings might need more time than others to express their thoughts
- Give the speaker direct eye contact; concentrate on the speaker
- Identify and practice facial expressions that are open and friendly
- Identify and practice body language that is open (see Exhibit 4.1)
- Use silence to help a speaker gather his or her thoughts
- Distinguish between open-ended questions and closed-ended questions
  - Use an open-ended question to help a speaker feel understood and respected
  - Use an open-ended question to ask for clarification of a speaker's thoughts

    Examples:

    "How did that make you feel?"

    "And then what happened?"

    "What do you mean when you said that _____?"

Exhibit 4.1   Behaviors That Say "I'll Listen!"

Open Behaviors:	*Closed Behaviors:*
direct eye contact	stare
touching	fake yawn
smiling	looking away
nods	nervous habits, fidgeting
eyes wide open	shakes head negatively
forward lean	moves away from speaker
positive facial expression	negative facial expression

Advanced students:

- Describe communication situations in which summarizing might be an appropriate form of support
  - Use summarizing to help a speaker feel understood and respected
    Examples:
    "It sounds as if you have mixed feelings about going to the party and you're apprehensive about making a decision" (Snively 1987).
    "What I hear you saying is that the coach won't let you play more than ten minutes in a game and you'd really like to play longer."
- Describe communication situations in which feeling–reflecting might be an appropriate form of support
  - Use reflecting to help a speaker feel understood and respected
    Examples:
    "You sound sad to me."
    "You're angry because you waited a long time to get a swing and then, just when you got one, recess was over."
- Describe the concept of *judging* (making a comment that shows you disapprove of a person or her actions) and how it might hurt empathic communication
  - Listen empathically without judging the speaker
    Examples of judgmental comments:
    "You're acting like a baby."
    "It's all your fault."
    Examples of nonjudgmental comments:
    "I see."
    "Go on."
    "How did you feel after that?"

The Appreciative Function

Listeners use the appreciative function of listening in order to increase the quality of their life through some pleasurable or inspirational listening experience. The hallmarks of appreciative listening are an open mind toward new sounds and new information; willingness to look for interesting and rewarding information in a new listening experience; and willingness to spend time seeking out new listening opportunities.

When do elementary students use the appreciative listening function? Appreciative listening is encouraged in elementary school through experiences such as storytelling, drama, special speakers at school assemblies, pep rallies, poetry reading, and musical performances.

Appreciative listening assists in building positive attitudes and values toward literature. In early grades at schools with whole-language curricula, children read

Middle school students listen appreciatively at a pep rally

stories and retell the stories back to the teacher. Listening to cultural fairy tales or to the oral history of a culture can build positive attitudes toward reading, literature, diversity, and studying history (see the Benitez interview in Chapter 2).

Appreciative Listening Competencies

Beginning students:
- Identify sources of pleasurable and interesting sounds
- Describe how you feel when you listen to different kinds of music
- State something new that you learned from listening to a story
- Name your favorite TV program or bedtime story and explain why you like to watch or listen to it

Intermediate and advanced students:
- Identify the kinds of listening experiences that are most important to you
  - Set goals for participating in more of your priority listening attributes
- Identify similarities between new appreciative listening experiences and previous listening experiences
- Identify differences between new appreciative listening experiences and previous listening experiences
- Explain how new listening experiences have the potential to increase your self-knowledge and knowledge of the world
- Choose to spend time participating in new listening experiences

WHAT ARE SOME INNOVATIVE WAYS TO TEACH AND ASSESS LISTENING?

The following exercises represent a variety of ways to approach all four listening functions (see summary in Exhibit 4.2). Additional listening exercises are described in Chapters 7 through 9.

1. If you lecture, try this: speak for fifteen or twenty minutes, break for five minutes and let students stretch. Then divide students into groups and have them summarize the main lecture points. While in the groups, students may discover they have genuine questions about the content.

2. Include a factual error in something you say and notify students beforehand that you are going to do this. After a reasonable period of time, break into groups and identify the error. As a whole class, discuss ways in which students were able to identify the error or why they were not able to find it. Be certain to correct the error!

Exhibit 4.2   Summary: The Four Functions of Listening

Function	Purpose	Typical Skills and Attributes
Discriminative	• To gather, understand, and retain useful information • Used when the speaker's purpose is to inform	• Prepare to listen, if possible, by becoming familiar with the speaker's topic beforehand • Concentrate on identifying the most important points, usually main points. • Take notes if necessary to help retain information • Consciously give feedback that helps the speaker know if you understand or do not understand the message. • Ask questions; write them down for later research if there will be no question-and-answer session. • Bored? Make a commitment to find something interesting in the message

Evaluative	• To evaluate a persuasive message on its merits
	• Used when the speaker's purpose is to persuade
		• All the skills of a discriminative listener, plus:
		  – Look for fallacies in reasoning
		  – Identify emotional and value appeals
		  – Recognize your own emotional response to a message
		  – Is someone else pressuring you to make a major decision? Give yourself at least a day or two before taking a position
		  – Be open-minded and objective
		  – Weigh the credibility of the evidence used to support a persuasive message

Empathic	• To help another speaker express emotions • Used when the speaker's purpose is to express emotions	• Identify feelings and how they are expressed • Give speakers time to express their thoughts and feelings • Show understanding by summarizing main ideas • Show understanding by reflecting the speaker's feelings • Show understanding by refraining from judgmental comments • Use open-ended questions to help speakers fully express themselves and to achieve clarity
Appreciative	• To increase the quality of life through pleasurable or inspirational listening experience • Used when the speaker's purpose is to entertain or inspire; or when the listener is in contact with sounds of music, nature, or other nonverbal source of sound	• Listen with an open mind • Identify similarities and differences between new listening experiences and previous knowledge • Identify personal listening preferences • Set goals and invest time in listening

3. Play listening scavenger hunt. At the beginning of a unit, give students five to ten questions whose answers will be revealed at some point during the unit. Divide students up into teams of three or four and give a prize or extra points to teams that correctly obtain and write down the answers to all the questions.

Alternatively, tell students that at the end of the unit you will ask five to ten questions, the answers to which will be revealed at some point during the unit, and reward teams who can recall or review the information in their notes to come up with the correct answers.

4. Help students improve their note-taking skills:
- Pass out a set of notes on an oral presentation or group session that meets your expectations for student performance. Students can then use your notes as a model.
- Pass out a partial outline of a guest speaker's presentation or a film, and have students fill in the rest of the outline using the completed part as a model.
- Create a class notebook. Each student in the class is responsible for taking notes for one day. Keep the notebook on reserve as a reference manual.

5. Ask students to summarize a lesson or unit. At the end of a lesson or at the conclusion of a larger unit, call on a student or a group to give a short summary of the main ideas of the lesson or unit. You can make this an overnight assignment and have the group report at the beginning of the next class.

6. Have students keep listening journals, in which they write about listening experiences they have had at school, at home, or with their peers. The purpose of the journal should be to challenge students to recognize and apply listening concepts they have learned in class to other contexts. You can stimulate writing by asking students to react to assigned questions. Examples follow.

For beginning students:
If children are not yet able to write, in a private time with the teacher, they can answer questions like these orally; the teacher writes the answers in the journal for them.

This week, I listened to a story about _____ .

The people in the story were _____ and _____ .

I learned that _____ .

My favorite song to listen to is _____ .

I like it when we take a field trip and I can hear the sounds of _____ .

When I hear the sounds of _____ , I feel _____ .

For intermediate students:

What kinds of nature sounds did you hear this week? Were those sounds similar to or different from other sounds you have heard?

Describe a person who is a good listener. What does that person do or say that makes them a good listener?

For advanced students:

Describe an experience you had this week involving persuasion. What listening skills did you use? What happened when you used those skills? Is there anything you would do differently next time?

Describe a conversation you had with another person who needed someone to listen to them. What listening skills did you use? What happened when you used those skills? Did anything happen that surprised you? Is there anything you would do differently next time?

7. Assign a controversial current event report to each of several groups. Have the groups prepare a written report using newspaper accounts. After the groups make their reports, ask them to spend a day asking people outside the classroom (peers, family members, neighbors) what they have heard about the event. Discuss any factual differences and the variety of opinion differences.

8. If you teach advanced students, try this summarizing exercise.

- Divide students up into groups of four to six. One person is the referee.

- Assign an appropriate controversial question to the group, perhaps based on a recent unit, such as "Which is more important: saving endangered plants and animals or using the environment to provide things that people need?"

- Each person in the group (other than the referee) should discuss the question, but the key is that each participant must first summarize, in their own words and without notes, the views expressed by the prior speaker. If anyone else in the group feels the summary is incomplete or inaccurate, the group makes a decision about what the accurate summary is before the next person can speak. The referee's responsibility is to intervene and help clear up any misunderstanding.

- After the summary is acceptable to the group, the listener takes a turn as a speaker, and the summary cycle continues until the first person who spoke finishes the exercise by summarizing the last speaker's description.

- Discuss questions as a whole class:

  How easy was it to stick to the rules and summarize what the person before you had said before you started on your own description?

  Did members of your group feel frustrated at times? If so, how did they show their frustration?

Was there a tendency for participants to learn to make shorter and more clear statements?

What other changes did you notice in the way people talked in this situation compared with normal give-and-take conversations? Does that say anything about whether we are really listening to each other in normal situations?

Are there any features of this exercise you might want to use in every-day communication?

9. This summarizing exercise is appropriate for beginning students.
   - Read a passage from an interesting story at an appropriate literacy level.
   - Divide students into pairs and ask one student to retell the passage in their own words to the other student.
   - Can the second student find any other details to add?
   - Read a second passage and take turns.

10. This exercise in empathic role playing works well with beginning students.
    - Children sit in a circle on the floor. Tell students they are going to play the game, "How Am I Feeling Today?"
    - With pictures mounted on construction paper, talk about different feelings that people may have and how they might show those feelings using words and body language. Select five or six feelings (such as

Empathic listening with assistance from a stuffed bear

happy, sad, surprised, afraid, sleepy, proud, caring) and use the felt board or pictures to illustrate how people might show those feelings.

- Each child takes a turn holding a stuffed animal or a puppet. Tell each student to pretend that the stuffed animal/puppet feels a certain way. Ask the child to use the stuffed animal/puppet to act out the feeling or to say words that give clues about the feeling.

- Ask the other children in the circle to guess the feeling and say why they guessed that feeling. If the guess is wrong, keep going. If the guess is right, talk about the similarities and differences between ways of expressing different feelings.

11. This empathic/persuasive role-playing exercise is for intermediate/advanced students:

- Divide students up into groups of three. One person will play the role of the listener, a second person will play the role of the speaker, and a third person will observe the speaker and listener as they interact.

- Give the speaker a sheet of paper or an index card with this role (or one you have prepared) written on it:

Speaker: The Customer

You are the parent of a small child. Yesterday you spent $50 on a toy that your child had wanted very badly. The toy is called the Super Sonic Thingamajig. It broke as soon as you gave it to your child, who became very upset and cried for a long time. You are very angry because you paid lot of money for the toy and believe that it should work. You have come to tell the store manager what happened and about how angry you are. You want the store to give you a refund or exchange the toy for another one.

- Give the listener a sheet of paper or an index card with this role (or one you have prepared):

Listener: The Store Manager

You are the manager of a toy store. It is your job to make sure that all your customers are happy. Sometimes customers get angry when toys they buy do not work. You exchange the toys for another one, or you give them their money back. When a customer is angry, you try to make them feel that you understand why they are angry and then you try to make them feel better by offering to exchange the toy or refund their money.

When a customer comes to you, you always begin by saying, "Hello, I'm the store manager. How can I help you?"

- Tell the role-playing students that their responsibility is to act out the roles as sincerely as they can. They should show their emotions with their faces, posture, hands and arms, voices, and words.

- The third person in the group watches and carefully listens to each person.

- After about ten minutes, stop the interaction. Ask:

  What techniques did the listener (store manager) use to show that he or she was listening? Did the person who was observing the role-play notice those techniques?

  Did the speaker (customer) feel that the store manager listened to the problem and wanted to help?

  Did speaker and listener use vocal expression in trying to communicate with the other person?

  Did the speaker and listener use facial or body expressions in trying to communicate with the other person?

12. Teach students about using body language with these exercises:

    Beginning students:

    - Use a hand puppet to show someone nodding his head when another person is talking. Ask: "What does it mean when a person nods her head up and down?"
    - Use a hand puppet to show someone shaking his head from side to side when another person is talking. Ask: "What does it mean when a person shakes his head from side to side?"
    - Pantomime a story you read in class. Try to show what happened by using your facial expressions and body.

    Intermediate/advanced students:

    Pantomime the following scenarios (or ones that you prepare) in small groups:

    - A small group of people trying to move a very heavy grand piano up several flights of stairs
    - Two people trying to decide who gets the last piece of pie
    - People walking through the park or playing outdoors and getting caught in the rain without raincoats or umbrellas
    - Someone scratching off the numbers on a lottery or scratch-and-win game piece
    - People watching a sporting event, frustrated and angry because their team is losing

13. Have intermediate students practice identifying body language. Provide students with a collection of old magazines. Give students a list of the following emotions and ask them to find pictures in the magazines that match the emotions. Make an interesting collage with the pictures during art class.

angry	concerned	proud
anxious	determined	sad
apathetic	excited	scared
bored	happy	thankful
calm	joyous	wishful

14. Provide intermediate/advanced students with practice in using open-ended questions. In small groups, ask them to think about ways that they could ask open-ended questions to help the following speakers feel better. Or, you can use statements made by characters in literature the class has read recently. The point of the exercise is to work out different options for an empathic listening response.

"I tripped and fell on the playground in front of lots of people."

"Someone I care about is very ill and in the hospital."

"I received some money from one of my relatives on my birthday. I have to decide whether to spend it on one or two things I really need or one big thing I really want."

"My best friend is angry with me."

"I'm lost. This is not my neighborhood."

15. Self-Assessment #1 (Intermediate Students)

Do I find that it is hard to listen to conversations or talks on topics that I am not interested in?

What topics or subjects are boring to me?

Do I react emotionally to certain words and ideas? What are these?

Do I daydream while people are speaking to me? What causes me to do this?

Do I want people to listen to me when I am speaking? Why?

16. Self-Assessment #2 (Advanced Students)—see Exhibit 4.3

17. Self-Assessment #3 (Intermediate/Advanced Students)—see Exhibit 4.4.

18. Create a persuasion concept web with intermediate/advanced students. Show students a short film or videotape with a persuasive message. A sixty-second advertisement will usually do. Ask students to diagram the main concepts and appeals in the advertisement, drawing lines between the concepts to show the relationship between ideas. Give one point for every valid concept or emotional/value appeal; give one additional point for each valid relationship indicated between concepts and appeals.

Exhibit 4.3   How Well Do You Listen?

Circle the number that best describes your listening habits.
Be honest! This is a learning exercise.

1. I get distracted by other things when I should be listening to someone else.
   5 (Almost never)   4 (Rarely)   3 (Sometimes)   2 (Usually)   1 (Almost always)

2. I give up on trying to listen when the material seems difficult or complicated.
   5 (Almost never)   4 (Rarely)   3 (Sometimes)   2 (Usually)   1 (Almost always)

3. I would rather listen for the facts, rather than the main ideas of the speaker.
   5 (Almost never)   4 (Rarely)   3 (Sometimes)   2 (Usually)   1 (Almost always)

4. I do not listen to speakers with whom I disagree.
   5 (Almost never)   4 (Rarely)   3 (Sometimes)   2 (Usually)   1 (Almost always)

5. When a speaker goes too slowly, I try to predict what they are going to say, rather than listening to what is said.
   5 (Almost never)   4 (Rarely)   3 (Sometimes)   2 (Usually)   1 (Almost always)

6. I interrupt people before they have a chance to finish what they are saying.
   5 (Almost never)   4 (Rarely)   3 (Sometimes)   2 (Usually)   1 (Almost always)

7. I have a hard time concentrating on what other people are saying.
   5 (Almost never)   4 (Rarely)   3 (Sometimes)   2 (Usually)   1 (Almost always)

8. If a person tries to tell me how I can do something better the next time and it hurts my feelings to hear their suggestion, I stop listening and fake attention instead.
   5 (Almost never)   4 (Rarely)   3 (Sometimes)   2 (Usually)   1 (Almost always)

9. I make fun of a speaker's clothing and looks, rather than listening to what is said.
   5 (Almost never)   4 (Rarely)   3 (Sometimes)   2 (Usually)   1 (Almost always)

10. Whenever I enter a room, I try to sit in the back.
    5 (Almost never)   4 (Rarely)   3 (Sometimes)   2 (Usually)   1 (Almost always)

Reprinted with permission of Mike Cronin, Director of Oral Communication Program, Radford University (year unknown).

Exhibit 4.4   Are You a Good Listener?

Circle *Y* for "Yes" or *N* for "No" after each question about
your listening habits and attitudes.

1. Do you like to listen to other people?	Y	N
2. Do you encourage other people to talk?	Y	N
3. Do you listen even if you do not like the person who is talking?	Y	N
4. Do you treat all people the same when you listen to them—whether or not they are friends, family, adults, children, male, female, or from a different country than you?	Y	N
5. Do you stop what you are doing so that you can give your full attention to a speaker?	Y	N
6. Do you look at the speaker?	Y	N
7. Do you smile and nod your head?	Y	N
8. Do you think about what a speaker is saying?	Y	N
9. Do you try to figure out what the speaker means?	Y	N
10. Do you let the speaker finish what he or she has to say?	Y	N
11. Do you encourage shy or quiet people to talk?	Y	N
12. Do you sometimes repeat back to the speaker what they said to see if you got it right?	Y	N
13. Do you ask questions if you don't understand an idea very well the first time?	Y	N
14. Do you ask the speaker to explain any words you've never heard before?	Y	N
15. Do you wait for speakers to finish their thoughts before you criticize what they have said?	Y	N

SUMMARY

Listening is the process of hearing aural symbols, storing and interpreting their meaning, and giving feedback to the speaker that helps facilitate the communication process. Listening is an active process that requires physical and mental energy, unlike hearing, which is mainly a physiological, passive process in which sound waves provide sensory data to the eardrum.

Listening instruction is important because listening is a frequently used strand of the language arts that is necessary for further academic, work, and life-management success. Instruction and frequent practice need not be formal to be effective, but should cover a broad range of listening competencies representing all four of the listening functions.

The four listening functions are discriminative (listening to informative messages for the purpose of gathering and understanding information); evaluative (listening to persuasive messages in order to evaluate the message on its merits); empathic (listening to a speaker in order to provide emotional relief); and appreciative (listening to experience pleasure and increase the quality of life).

REFERENCES

Bodine, R., Crawford, D., & Scrumpf, F. (1994). *Creating the peaceable school: A comprehensive program for teaching conflict resolution.* Champaign, IL: Research Press.

Cooper, P. (1995). *Communication for the classroom teacher* (5th ed.). Scottsdale, AZ: Gorsuch Scarisbrick.

Cronin, M. (Year unknown). Listening assessment. Radford, VA: Radford University, The Oral Communication Program.

Galvin, K. (1985). *Listening by doing.* Lincolnwood, IL: National Textbook.

Hunsaker, R. (1989). What listening skills should be taught to teachers and students? In P. Cooper and K. Galvin (Eds.), *The future of speech communication education.* (pp. 27–30). Annandale, VA: Speech Communication Association.

Larson, C. U. (1992). *Persuasion: Reception and responsibility* (5th ed.). Belmont, CA: Wadsworth Publishers.

Logan, D. (1995, September). Telephone interview.

Nichols, R., & Lewis, T. (1954). *Listening and speaking: A guide to effective oral communication.* Dubuque, IA: William C. Brown.

Snively, M. (1987). Techniques for teaching types of listening to high school students. Paper presented at the Speech Communication Association Annual Convention, Boston.

Wolff, F., Marsnik, N., Tacey, W., & Nichols, R. (1983). *Perceptive listening.* New York: Holt, Rinehart, and Winston.

Wolvin, A., & Coakley, C. (1988). *Listening* (3rd ed.). Dubuque, IA: William C. Brown.

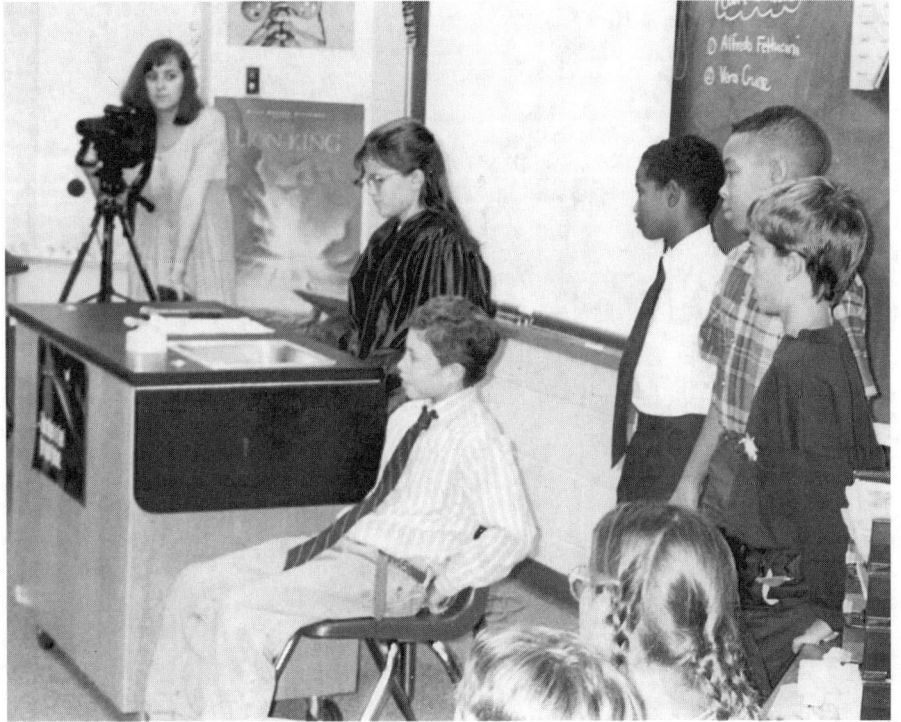

Videotaping a moot court simulation for a portfolio

5

Authentic Performance Assessment
Evaluating Oral Communication Competency

*Just as we learned that red markings all over a child's
writing inhibit writing, red marking a child's speech
has the same deleterious effect. Even more personal
than writing, speaking performance is treated as an
object to be graded, forgetting the red-faced child
standing behind those words. These two practices
in the average classroom devalue both speaking
and the student speaker.*
—*VIRGINIA O'KEEFE*
SPEAKING TO THINK, THINKING TO SPEAK

OVERVIEW

"I suppose that one of the greatest challenges in teaching oral communication,"
remarked a colleague in another discipline, "is that it is untestable. How do you
really know for sure when a student has really learned a new skill, or even improved on an old one?" The question raises an interesting point: Just how do educators evaluate a student's progress as both a learner and user of oral communication skills? This chapter discusses assessment as it pertains to oral communication
and provides examples of various approaches to performance assessment across
communication contexts.

PRACTICALLY SPEAKING

What does it mean to *assess?*
What are some different approaches to assessment?
What are the major issues in oral communication assessment?
What are some guidelines for formal and informal assessment?

EXPLORING THE CONCEPT OF ASSESSMENT

Assessment is the formal or informal evaluation of a learner's work so as to measure a learner's progress toward some predetermined set of goals or learning objectives. In most cases, assessment involves the evaluation of some product (created from the learner's mix of cognitive and affective attributes) and performance
(springing from the learner's behavior) (Goulden 1992). Assessment is the evaluation of a learner's work; the work is an artifact representing the learner's actual
abilities and actual progress. In the case of oral communication, a student's artifacts or performances in an assignment allow us to observe only part of a whole
range of knowledge, skills, and attributes and skills that in the real world function
together as part of a process. For this reason it is important to carefully consider —
as painstaking as it may be—the methods and objectives by which we evaluate a
learner's progress.

Assessment has become such a familiar term in American education that we
sometimes bandy it about without real reflection on how it impacts learners and
the learning process. Douglas Barnes (1992) illustrates this impact in his discussion of what he calls the *assessment* function of teaching. Barnes notes that both a
reply and an assessment function are essential to teaching. The reply function is
served when teacher feedback affirms student efforts to make sense of the world
and represents a collaborative relationship between the teacher and student. The
assessment function, in contrast, compares student efforts to make sense of the
world against an adult view of what that understanding ought to be:

> When a teacher assesses what his [sic] pupils say he distances himself
> from their views, and allies himself with external standards which may
> implicitly devalue what the learner himself has constructed. . . . [A]ssess-
> ment is turned towards the public standards against which pupils must
> eventually measure themselves. . . . (p. 111)

Too much emphasis on meeting such external standards can thus lead to undesirable effects on the learning process:

> If a teacher stresses the assessment function at the expense of the reply
> function, this will urge his pupils toward externally acceptable perfor-
> mances, rather than towards trying to relate new knowledge to the old
> (p. 111).

Why, then, do we assess? As imperfect as it is, assessment is necessary to help us determine whether learners are increasing their knowledge in areas we think are important—and whether they are learning to do the things we think they ought to be able to do. Effective assessment also helps the learner build self-concept. From yet another perspective, assessment sheds light on the efficacy of our teaching practices (Backlund 1983). We assess to develop an appropriate range of criteria for our students and school that helps us ensure consistency in our evaluation of their learning. At the same time, however, consistently low achievement by a significant number of learners could indicate that there are weaknesses in our teaching methods or that they lack overall relevance to the learner.

When, and how frequently, we assess oral communication may bear on our success in charting student progress. Standardized reading achievement tests are administered statewide and nationally at least once every school year. Presumably, they measure progress made in the classroom over a period of months, bolstered by a locally developed curriculum that targets national, state, and locally recognized standards. Speaking and listening, however, are generally not assessed on a national level, in large part because of the technical difficulties in developing a valid, reliable, and feasible standardized performance measure. State departments of education may mandate minimum standards of speaking and listening proficiency, but in general it is left to school districts and individual teachers to determine when and how often students will be assessed.

Virginia O'Keefe (1995) suggests that an appropriate schema of assessment for speaking and listening would consist of many individual assignments—rather than one single speaking or listening event.

> Instead of one assignment fulfilling multiple criteria, we could have several assignments each fulfilling a separate criteria, with perhaps the final one encompassing all. Records of these talks would become part of the child's portfolio, with comments and responses by peers, teachers, and the child about the experiences. When a dozen or more assignments are involved, we would hope that the child would be able to pick topics close to her interest and experience as she would with writing. We would also hope that the frequency and informality of the talks would increase both her competency and fluency (p. 159).

A study of teachers in Kentucky's Instructional Results Information System revealed, however, that even though teachers have a positive view of broad-based performance assessment, a lack of familiarity with how to administer such assessments, and a belief that assessments could not be adequately implemented within classroom time constraints, prevented teachers from actually moving forward in a meaningful way (Guskey 1994). These views are certainly shared by teachers elsewhere in the country who face pressures to "do more and teach more." With these very real concerns in mind, we turn to a discussion of oral communication assessment.

APPROACHES TO AUTHENTIC PERFORMANCE ASSESSMENT

Performance-Based Assessment

There are a variety of approaches to the assessment of oral communication. Because oral communication skills are exhibited through observable behavior, attempts to measure them have always been categorized as *performance-based*. According to Doris Bergen (1993, p. 99), "A performance assessment requires children to demonstrate not only what they know, but also what they can do." Traditional performance assessments, however, have been limited to such familiar activities as pencil-and-paper listening comprehension tests, audiotaped pronunciation drills, and the ubiquitous oral report.

Authentic Assessment

Traditional performance assessments, such as the examples described above, are limited in their usefulness. Pencil-and-paper tests and rote "drill-and-skill" exercises simply do not provide an accurate profile of a learner's communication competency across contexts. To elicit more complete information about a learner's progress in oral communication, a performance assessment must be *authentic* (sometimes called *alternative*). An authentic performance assessment is an opportunity for a child to apply her knowledge and skills during an actual or simulated real-world event. The best authentic assessments, according to Bergen (1993), share three primary qualities: (1) they are integrative; (2) they are applied; and (3) they are often group-based.

An authentic assessment is *integrative* if it measures a number of characteristics simultaneously in the event. For example, an integrative discussion assessment might measure specific skills required to express a point of view; to clarify and achieve shared understanding; and to actively listen to comprehend another speaker's message.

An authentic assessment is *applied* if it allows the student to make choices about how to adapt to situational factors and demonstrates the student's flexibility in using different skills to achieve a communication purpose. An applied discussion assessment might ask students to reach a decision as a group about how their school could recycle waste products. Students demonstrate the skills of discussion in a particular context (small group) with a particular communication purpose (determining a solution to the problem of recycling).

Authentic assessment is often *group-based*—although it may be individual. Group-based performance assessments create a stake in both individual performance and in group performance — the individual must perform well to contribute to the overall success of the group in achieving its purpose.

Assessment Approaches and Scoring Methods

Developing a performance assessment involves identifying the purpose of the assessment and the specific competencies to be evaluated, choosing an "authentic" communication context for the assessment, and selecting a method of evaluating the learner's performance. This section focuses on two general approaches to evaluation—holistic and atomistic—and four specific types of scoring methods.

Goulden (1992) describes the relationship between assessment approaches and individual scoring methods. The holistic approach to assessment focuses on evaluation of the performance as a whole, while the atomistic approach focuses on evaluating the individual parts of a performance, without any concern for obtaining an overall rating.

The Holistic Approach

The holistic approach is represented by three primary scoring methods: the holistic method, the general impression method, and the analytic method.

The Holistic Method of Scoring.   Although the term can be used in a number of different ways, Goulden (1992) describes a holistic method of scoring as having three main features: (1) the evaluator is assessing the performance as a whole, (2) the evaluator records only one score, and (3) criteria or scoring guides based on the parts of the whole are used indirectly to help determine the single score. For instance, a holistic scoring method for a public speech might include a predetermined criteria (Table 5.1) that is indirectly used to reach a general evaluation and score (Table 5.2). In using a holistic scoring method, the teacher is not limited to that pre-

TABLE 5.1   A Holistic Scoring Criteria for Seventh- or Eighth-Grade Oral Presentations

A good presentation:
1. Falls within the assigned time limit (or is reasonably close)
2. Has a clearly identifiable speech purpose and a thesis statement
3. Has an introduction, body, and conclusion
4. Shows a basic understanding of effective verbal and nonverbal delivery
5. Shows respect for the audience

An excellent presentation, in addition to meeting the above criteria:
1. Deals with an interesting and challenging topic (if student was allowed to choose topic)
2. Includes both a strong introduction and conclusion that achieve all their major functions
3. Is well organized
4. Develops points with appropriate supporting materials (relevant, credible)
5. Is skillfully delivered (verbal and nonverbal delivery)

A superior presentation meets all of the above criteria, and:
1. Uses clear, appropriate, and vivid oral language
2. Is delivered fluently and in a polished manner
3. Is interesting and well adapted to the audience
4. Supports points with provocative and compelling supporting material
5. Constitutes a genuine contribution to the knowledge and/or beliefs of the audience

A fair presentation meets some, but not all, of the grading criteria for a good presentation.

A poor presentation meets almost none of the requirements for a good presentation.

TABLE 5.2   Holistic Evaluation of a Formal Speech

Speaker's Name: Suzy Berman

Speech Topic: Visiting the Botanical Gardens

Speech Score: Excellent

Suzy, what an interesting speech! I had no idea that there were so many different kinds of plants and trees in the botanical gardens here in Baltimore. You did a very nice job of explaining the difference between the major types of trees found in the gardens here and in Chicago. You used your voice well to keep our attention and to emphasize important points. In particular, you spoke loudly and clearly; we could hear and understand each word, even at the back of the room. Your voice revealed a lot of enthusiasm for the topic, which made us all want to learn more about it.

For the next time, work on building a stronger conclusion. I know you were nervous and probably a little bit anxious about getting back to your seat, but remember what we talked about in class: that a conclusion is the last part of the speech an audience hears, and so it is also the last part of the speech they are likely to remember. To help the audience have a strong memory of your speech, then, you have to summarize the main points in the conclusion and give them an interesting thought to emphasize the importance of your topic. This time when you concluded your speech, you said, "In conclusion, thank you for listening, and I hope you will visit the botanical gardens soon." How would you change your conclusion if you were to give this speech again, to a new audience?

Overall, this was excellent. We are all looking forward to your next speech!

---

determined criteria and is not obligated to weight each part equally. The criteria serve only as a general guide in forming an overall impression of the performance.

The General Impression Method of Scoring.   In contrast to the holistic method of scoring, the general impression method uses criteria that may have been formalized at some point but which are unique to the scorer. The criteria are not so specific as to break down the performance into individual parts or competencies. Each teacher may choose to weight different aspects of the performance differently. Goulden (1992) suggests that competitive speech and debate events are a concrete example of the general impression method:

> [General impression] is the method used in forensics competition when each judge has a blank sheet of paper with instructions to write comments and record a rank and/or rating for each competitor. Although the conventions of public speaking form some general boundaries, individual judges make different choices as to which elements are most important in forming the successful whole; also, individual judges are free to ignore the components that are considered crucial by other judges (p. 263).

An example of a general impression evaluation form is reprinted here as Exhibit 5.1.

Exhibit 5.1   A General Impression Evaluation for an Oral Presentation

Judge's Ballot   National Forensics League

ORIGINAL ORATORY

Round _____   Section _____

Order	Contestant	Title	Rank
1			
2			
3			
4			
5			
6			

Reprinted with permission of the National Forensics League (1995).

The Analytic Method of Scoring.   The analytic method of scoring identifies a set of traits or competencies that together comprise the whole (Exhibit 5.2). The teacher then evaluates each individual competency and assigns a rating to that competency; the subscores are totaled to reach an overall score.

The Atomistic Approach
In an atomistic approach to assessment, there is no attempt to form an overall impression of the performance; rather, the focus is on the individual parts of the performance. A teacher may use either the analytic method of scoring (see previous discussion) or the atomistic scoring method. The analytic method (Exhibit 5.2) may be used to evaluate individual competencies without attempting to form an overall impression of the performance. The atomistic scoring method (Exhibit 5.3), like the analytic method, focuses on the individual parts of a performance.

Unlike the analytic method, however, an atomistic method is more likely simply to identify positive or negative parts of a performance and to count the number of times those traits were displayed. The atomistic scoring method places less emphasis on evaluating the individual parts of a performance, and more emphasis on determining whether or not those parts actually occurred during the performance.

Assessment Approaches and Scoring Methods Summary
There are two primary assessment approaches: holistic and atomistic. The holistic approach is used to reach an overall evaluation of an oral communication perfor-

Exhibit 5.2   An Analytic Scoring Evaluation for an Oral Presentation

Speaker's Name: _____   Topic: _____

CONTENT	Superior	Excellent	Good	Fair	Poor
Introduction					
Caught attention; stated topic and purpose of speech; previewed main points	5	4	3	2	1
Body					
Main points were clear, distinct, and supported the purpose of the speech	5	4	3	2	1
Organization was clear and consistent throughout	5	4	3	2	1
Logic and analysis (if a persuasive speech) were strong	5	4	3	2	1
Supporting materials were credible, useful, appropriately cited, and adequate for each main point	5	4	3	2	1
Language choice was interesting, appropriate for the occasion and audience, with appropriate grammar	5	4	3	2	1
Conclusion					
Concluded with psychological impact, summarized main points, brought closure to the speech	5	4	3	2	1
DELIVERY					
Audience Adaptation:					
Adapted to the physical characteristics of the speaking situation	5	4	3	2	1
Adapted to the background and perspective of the audience	5	4	3	2	1
Chose words and language that were meaningful to, and demonstrated respect for, the audience	5	4	3	2	1
Vocal Delivery:					
Appropriate volume, rate, pitch, and variety of expression	5	4	3	2	1
Avoided too many non-fluencies (e.g., "uh," "um," "like," "okay," "y'know")	5	4	3	2	1
Used pauses and silences effectively (if a speech that lends itself to drama)	5	4	3	2	1
Physical Delivery:					
Good posture; absence of nervous shifting of body weight, twisting at the waist, leaning on podium, etc.	5	4	3	2	1
Gestures and facial expressions were well-timed, natural, expressive	5	4	3	2	1
Eye contact was direct, sustained, inclusive	5	4	3	2	1

Additional comments:

Total Score: _____ (out of a possible 80 points)

Exhibit 5.3   An Atomistic Scoring Evaluation for Part of an Oral Presentation

Vocalized Pauses: Includes "um," "uh," "er," etc.; "like," "y'know," "okay," "right," and other types of fillers and nonfunctional syntax

5	Speech is free of vocalized pauses
4	Occasionally a vocalized pause, but speech is generally clear
3	Scattered vocalized pauses
2	Pervasive vocalized pauses
1	Meaning in speech is completely obscured by vocalized pauses

---

Reprinted with permission of Chaney and Burk (1997).

---

mance. The atomistic approach is used to reach an evaluation of the parts of a performance, without regard for an overall score.

Each of the two assessment approaches spawns a set of evaluation methods. The holistic approach may manifest itself in three evaluation methods: the holistic method (a general criteria used indirectly in evaluation of the whole), the general impression method (a general or specific criterion which may be used differently by different raters), and the analytic method (specific competencies are itemized and scored; the subscores are added together to produce a total score for the whole).

Finally, the atomistic approach to oral communication assessment includes two primary evaluation methods: the analytic method (as used in the holistic approach, but with no attempt to link scores on individual competencies into a score for the whole); and the atomistic method (merely recording the existence and prevalence of competencies or traits without any attempt to evaluate them or to reach a composite score for the whole).

Portfolios

Portfolios can be used to systematically document a learner's progress over time, and usually contain student work, teacher observations, and self- and peer-assessments. Evaluation methods such as those described above may be flexibly employed to record and document student progress in a variety of communication contexts, including listening activities, small-group discussions, oral interpretations and drama, and debate. Familiarity with different types of evaluation methods may assist teachers in developing efficient ways to record and document an oral communicator's progress over time, especially the progress of more advanced learners. Without scoring rubrics or evaluation instruments, frequent, systematic assessment of speaking and listening can be a daunting process. We have found that one type of portfolio—a *speech folder* containing a student's written products, such as speech outlines, texts, and written evaluations—is very helpful in reminding us of our own feedback to the student before he or she is evaluated on the next performance. We can look back over the work in the speech folder and recall better what we asked the student to work on for next time.

Portfolio documentation can include many different kinds of observations and information. Viechnicki and associates (1993) studied the use of performance-based portfolios in uncovering early signs of giftedness. In their study, the Early Assessment of Exceptional Potential Project, portfolios included anecdotal records of a minimum of one per child per week; observations of six sample lessons; a peer/self questionnaire; a home–community survey; and examples of work produced by the child. Teachers used the information gathered for the portfolios to redesign their primary curriculum and classroom environments.

Grace (1992) suggests that portfolios include documentation in the form of a child's writing, artwork, journals, videos or photographs of large projects, and audio recordings of children reading or telling stories. Forms of teacher observation can include anecdotal notes of a child's activities in the classroom and at play (holistic; general impression or holistic evaluation); a skill checklist or inventory used to monitor regular activities (atomistic evaluation); rating scales for complex behaviors (analytic evaluation); open-ended questions and requests (holistic or general impression evaluation); and screening tests that take stock of a child's initial skills, attributes, and knowledge to be used as a foundation for later comparison (atomistic or analytic evaluation).

Although there are a variety of approaches to portfolio assessment, a common thread is how they are used in evaluation of the learner's progress:

> Appropriate evaluation always compares the child's current work to her earlier work. This evaluation should indicate the child's progress toward a standard of performance that is consistent with the teacher's curriculum and appropriate developmental expectations. Portfolios are not meant to be used for comparing children to each other. They are used to document individual children's progress over time. The teacher's conclusions about a child's achievement, abilities, strengths, weaknesses, and needs should be based on the full range of that child's development, as documented by the data in the portfolio, and on the teacher's knowledge of curriculum and stages of development (Grace 1992, p. 2).

An example of how content standards and applied performances have been linked to comprehensive portfolio assessment (Exhibit 5.4) and report cards is found in the Rochester City School District (1995) language arts curriculum (see Slattery interview). Developmentally appropriate content standards and stage descriptors (an atomistic method) are used as one means of systematically documenting the progress of students. Rochester's report cards use stage descriptors to provide information for parents about the student's progress (see Chapter 1).

DEVELOPING A COMPREHENSIVE ASSESSMENT PROGRAM

Interview with Dr. Jean Slattery
Supervising Director, Curriculum Development and Support
Rochester City School District, Rochester, New York

Q: *How did the Rochester City School District develop its language arts content standards and stage descriptors?*

We were working on portfolios, and I was very concerned that portfolios would be floating out there as patchwork collections of student work without being grounded. In formulating the content standards we drew from a variety of sources—principally, the New York State Language Arts Framework, the New Standards Project,[1] California's Framework and "English in the National Curriculum" for England and Wales. We were also very impressed with the literacy profiles from Victoria, Australia. We talked about their usefulness as a way to chart development in student progress in literacy. One of the reasons I liked the Australian work was that it was based on five years of student and classroom research. With Victoria's permission, we worked with our own teachers to create a district version of their developmental stages. These became the backbone of our language arts portfolios.

Q: *Your report card system is linked to your portfolios. How does that work?*

Our report cards indicate the developmental stages a student is working in, so that it is patently clear to students, parents, as well as district evaluators, what literacy really means. The portfolio contains concrete evidence of a student's accomplishment, so there is documentation that a student has actually become a better reader, a better writer, a better speaker and listener. We also mandate portfolio conferences with parents to help them understand more precisely what their child really knows and is able to do.

Q: *Describe how your teachers are trained to use the speaking and listening curricula.*

First of all, it's important to understand that a number of teachers assisted directly in the development and piloting of our content standards and stage descriptors. Those teachers then became a core group of teachers that started to implement the work in schools. We run summer institutes every year and we've kept them focused on developing content standards, stages, and portfolios. In addition,

---

1. Funded by support from the Pew and McArthur Foundations, the New Standards project is a partnership between the National Center on Education and the Economy (directed by Marc Tucker) and the Pittsburgh Learning Research and Development Corporation (directed by Lauren Resnick).

we have city-wide early-dismissal Wednesdays once a month and at least one superintendent's conference day a year that we can use for professional development.

Q: *What manner of text(s) do language arts teachers use in implementing the Rochester curriculum?*

In the fall of 1989, we went from one districtwide basal reading text to allowing schools to choose between five unranked texts. We had lots of conversations and dialogues within the district about the integrated language arts and whole language. For a good number of years we have offered ELIC and Frameworks courses for teachers on a volunteer basis.[2] Unfortunately, one message some teachers took from whole language was that phonics no longer needed to be taught, and although on an administrative level we were expecting that phonics would be taught in context, in some cases it wasn't being taught at all. For that reason, we are investigating options for a new language arts text to be implemented in the fall of 1996.

Q: *Describe how the Rochester portfolio program works and how speaking and listening activities are incorporated into the portfolio.*

The portfolio grew up from kindergarten teachers in the district who wanted to use the portfolios for five-year-olds as a way of avoiding inappropriate standardized tests. Portfolios are useful in helping students value and feel a sense of ownership in their work. Portfolios allow the student to reflect on the greater question of "Who am I as a learner?" But as I mentioned earlier, I was worried that portfolios might float out there like an untethered zeppelin—so what we did was to set forth our own content standards and examples of applied learning. Keeping in mind that school-to-work notion, we first established overarching goals and related expectations for learners.

Unfortunately the portfolios are weakest in the area of oral language—it's harder to capture students' proficiency in that area. We did develop a rubric for oral presentations that can be adapted for grades 3 through 12. We've since added portfolio requirements that address speaking and listening for grades 3 through 5 and are experimenting with audio and video taping. The ultimate solution will be electronic portfolios.

---

2. Early Literacy Inservice Course © Education Department of South Australia 1984, 190; Frameworks © 1991 Illawarra Technology Corp., University of Wollongong, NSW, Australia and Wayne-Finger Lahn BOCES, Stanley, NY.

Exhibit 5.4 Rochester City School District Portfolio Guidelines: The Portfolio as a Portrait of a Learner

PRE-K
REQUIRED

- Cover Sheet
- Summary of Observation based on ongoing Anecdotal Observations (1x/year-end or when transferring)
- Writing Samples—scribbles, marks, forms, shapes, "temporary spelling" (minimum of two)
- Story Dictated to Teacher (Goal—to write verbatim child's own words and thoughts)
- Draw-a-Person (3x/year)
- Art Samples (child's original work/non-directed)
- Language Arts Developmental Stage Cards (ongoing)

RECOMMENDED

- Photographs
- Documentation per Teacher Choice
- Social Growth and Development Profiles
- Math Portfolio
- Pre-Stage A Cards (for children not yet on Stage A)

KINDERGARTEN
REQUIRED

- Cover Sheet
- Summary of Observations (1x/year-end when transferring)
- Anecdotal Observations (2x/year)
- K Screening Report (1x/year)
- Independent Writing: writing samples (child's original phrases or sentences/journal pieces; printing name, numbers, and letters from memory
- Comprehension Assessment (for example, art depiction of a story with teacher's comments on student performance)
- Self-Portrait
- Language Arts Developmental Stage Cards—Speaking and Listening, Reading, Writing (ongoing)

RECOMMENDED

- Photographs
- Tape of Language Samples/Example of Dictated Stories
- Documentation per Teacher Choice
- Summary—Major Parent Conferences

GRADE 1
REQUIRED

- Cover Sheet
- Summary of Observations (June)
- Anecdotal Notes (ongoing)
- Independent Writing Samples (3x/year); at least one sample will include a rough draft and final copy
- Comprehension Assessment (2x/year); add teacher comments on student's performance: oral, reading
- Letter/Sound Assessment (3x/year)
- Language Arts Developmental Stage Cards—Speaking and Listening, Reading, Writing (ongoing)

RECOMMENDED

- Self-Evaluation
- Reading Logs
- Photographs
- Documentation per Teacher Choice
- Reading Survey
- Oral Reading Summary

GRADE 2
REQUIRED

- Cover Sheet
- Summary of Observations (June)
- Anecdotal Observations (ongoing)
- Independent Writing Samples (3x/year); label pieces as rough draft and final copies
- Comprehension Assessment (2x/year); add teacher comments on student's performance
- Letter/Sound Assessment (3x/year)
- Reading Log (ongoing or month-long report)
- Self-Evaluation (2x/year)
- Language Arts Developmental Stage Cards—Speaking and Listening, Reading, Writing (ongoing)
- DRP Label (June)

RECOMMENDED

- Oral Reading Assessment
- Photographs
- Documentation per Teacher Choice
- Art/Self-Portrait

(continued)

Exhibit 5.4   *Continued*

GRADE 3
REQUIRED

- Table of Contents
- Reading Response Log (ongoing)
- Baseline Piece (first writing sample of the year; many teachers recommend that this be autobiographical in nature)
- Descriptive Piece plus two other genre pieces (i.e., personal narration or story, process (how to . . .), persuasive)
- Comprehension Assessments (2x/year)
- Retelling
- Self-Evaluation (end of year)
- Oral Presentation on Topic of Student's Choice
- Response to an Oral Presentation
- Student Self-Reflections
- Developmental Stage Cards

RECOMMENDED

- Letter/Sound Assessment (3x/year)
- Teacher/Parent Letter
- Student Letter to Family (an example of a descriptive piece)
- Parent Input
- Performance Task Samples
- Best Piece (student choice)
- Running record
- Audio Tape of Child Reading
- Anecdotal Records
- Reading Response Journal

GRADE 4
REQUIRED

- Table of Contents
- Baseline Piece (first writing sample of the year; many teachers recommend that this be autobiographical in nature)
- Reading Response Log (ongoing)
- Process Piece (how to . . .) plus two other genre pieces (i.e., narration or story, descriptive, persuasive)
- Comprehension Assessments (2x/year)
- Retelling
- Group Oral Presentation
- Response to an Oral Presentation
- Student Self-Reflections
- Self-Evaluation (end of year)
- Developmental Stage Cards

RECOMMENDED

- Teacher/Parent Letter
- Parent Input
- Performance Task Samples
- Best Piece (student choice)
- Audio Tape of Child Reading
- Anecdotal Records
- Reading Response Journal

GRADE 5
REQUIRED

- Table of Contents
- Baseline Piece (first writing sample of the year; many teachers recommend that this be autobiographical in nature (i.e., describing a significant incident, or a photograph of the student engaged in an activity)
- Reading Response Log
- Persuasive Piece plus two other genre pieces (i.e., personal narration or story, process (how to . . .), descriptive)
- Comprehension Assessments (2x/year)
- Retelling
- Extemporaneous Presentation
- Response to an Oral Presentation
- Student Self-Reflections

GRADE 6
REQUIRED

- Table of Contents
- Letter of Introduction/Self-Evaluation
- Baseline Piece
- Growth Piece (twice a year) (i.e., 2 narrative essays)
- Free Choice Entry (student choice)
- Content Area Piece
- Reader Response to Literature—fictional novel
- Reading Log
- Genre Pieces (Friendly Letter or Personal Narrative plus one of the following: Business Letter, Persuasive Essay, Research Paper)
- Language Arts Developmental Stage Cards

GRADE 5
REQUIRED *(cont.)*

- Self-Evaluation (end of year)
- Language Arts
  Developmental Stage
  Cards

RECOMMENDED

- Teacher/Parent Letter
- Parent Input
- Performance Task Samples
- Best Piece (student choice)
- Audio Tape of Child Reading
- Anecdotal Records
- Reading Response Journal

GRADE 6

RECOMMENDED

- Reading Process Piece
- Listening and Speaking Piece—"How to . . ."
  (Demonstration on an area of interest)

GRADE 7
REQUIRED

- Table of Contents
- Letter of Introduction/Self-Evaluation
- Baseline Piece
- Growth Piece (twice a year) (i.e., 2 narrative essays)
- Free Choice Entry (student choice)
- Content Area Piece
- Reader Response to Literature—Biography or Historical Fiction
- Reading Log
- Genre Pieces (Business Letter or Persuasive Essay plus one of the following: Business Letter, Research Paper, Friendly Letter, Personal Narrative)
- Language Arts Developmental Stage Cards

RECOMMENDED

- Reading Process Piece
- Listening and Speaking Piece—Mini-Lesson (specific to class work)

GRADE 8
REQUIRED

- Table of Contents
- Letter of Introduction/Self-Evaluation
- Baseline Piece
- Growth Piece (twice a year) (i.e., 2 narrative essays)
- Free Choice Entry (student choice)
- Content Area Piece
- Reader Response to Literature—Nonfiction
- Reading Log
- Genre Pieces (Research Paper plus one of the following: Business Letter, Friendly Letter, Personal Narrative, Persuasive Essay)
- Language Arts Developmental Stage Cards

RECOMMENDED

- Reading Process Piece
- Listening and Speaking Piece—Demonstration Out of Class (i.e., to younger students)

ISSUES IN AUTHENTIC ASSESSMENT
OF ORAL COMMUNICATION

> Due to the unique nature of communication, assessment of speaking
> and listening performance encounters certain limits and problems. Oral
> communication is an interactive process. Thus, its correctness is based
> on the situation. . . . Both nonverbal and verbal aspects of communica-
> tion must be defined, criteria of competence that take cultural and sit-
> uational differences into account must be identified, and methods that
> assess performance consistently and accurately must be developed
> (Backlund 1983, pp. 60–61).

Validity and Reliability

There is always going to be some subjectivity in the assessment of oral communication. Just as in any audience-oriented performance, such as theater, music, creative writing, and dance, a performer's style is directly observed or otherwise
identified by the audience and may figure substantially in its overall evaluation of
the performance. Even though the speaker and listener are participating together
in a communicative act, their nonverbal behaviors, appearance, and demeanor are
nonetheless directly observed by the teacher and may be weighted more or less
heavily depending on that particular teacher's view of what constitutes *good* oral
communication.

All this is not to say that oral communication cannot be assessed in a meaningful and constructive manner. In fact, questions about subjectivity and bias per-
meate discussions about most testing and assessment instruments, across disciplines. We would be hard pressed to find an assessment technique or instrument
that was entirely value-free in either its development or administration. Before we
go on to discuss some safeguards against undue subjectivity, it may be helpful to
put the problem in its proper perspective.

Imagine for a moment that we are all on one panel observing student participation in a debate activity. Although there would be some variation among our
perceptions of specific communication skills or attributes as demonstrated by different students, if we were to rank the performances of ten debaters, we would
probably all agree on which students as a subgroup were most advanced, which
were least advanced, and which were in the middle. Precision in ranking students
within each subgroup, however, is the aspect of rating that is most difficult to
achieve among raters because of the different weights that people ascribe to various communication skills and attributes.

Two principles that help avoid undue subjectivity in assessment are the validity and the reliability of an assessment tool. In its most general sense, *validity* is "the ability of a test to measure that which we want it to assess, not something else" (Backlund 1983, p. 66). Assessment scoring guides used in the classroom have more validity if they are designed to measure progress toward core competencies at age-appropriate proficiency levels.

Reliability generally refers to "the consistency with which a test measures what it is supposed to measure" (Backlund 1983, p. 67). Authentic assessment scoring guides have more reliability if they can be applied consistently to the performances of all students.

Examples of rubrics with a high degree of reliability are the following small-group performance rubric for group development and cohesion and organizational communication rubric (see Table 5.3 on pages 134 and 135 and Table 5.4 on page 136). Dr. Pat Arneson (1994), associate professor of speech communication at the University of Northern Colorado, developed these rubrics and others for use in assessing small-group performance.

Although the rubric in Table 5.3 is appropriate only for Grades 13 through 16, we have included it to help show the degree of precision and reliability that it is possible to achieve with a rating scale for an oral communication activity. An interview with Dr. Arneson on developing performance assessments for small groups, in which she further discusses the concepts of validity and reliability, follows.

DEVELOPING PERFORMANCE ASSESSMENTS FOR SMALL GROUPS

Interview with Pat Arneson, Ph.D.
Associate Professor of Speech Communication
University of Northern Colorado, Greeley, Colorado

Q: *In general, how did you determine performance standards for your grades 13–16 small-group rubrics?*

The Department of Speech Communication at the University of Northern Colorado has identified a set of skill competencies, so I worked closely with that document. In developing these rubrics, I relied on small-group communication literature to identify characteristics that scholars recognize are important for effective small-group communication. Because I work at the university level, the next exit level for my students is the workplace—that means the rubrics and activities I design should emulate the workplace. Students need to be competent communicators after they leave the university. Good communication skills are essential for success in the workplace.

Q: *What have you found to be the most important variable in effective performance assessment?*

In my experience, I have found three key areas of importance:

1. The performance criteria should be clearly identified and introduced to students. Students need to understand what is expected of them. After all, that's usually the way of the work world. Most of us have a list of job performance expectations (or we know what they are, otherwise) and we strive to meet those expectations. Likewise, students should have no surprises in the criteria when we administer performance assessments.

2. Validity issues are also important. Validity means that the experience students engage in when we examine their skills should simulate a real-world test of their ability. Real-world tests are at the heart of the concept *authentic assessment.* We want to avoid assessing students in some contrived or unnatural situation.

3. The reliability of the instrument is another major concern. Reliability means that as teachers we are examining the same skills for each student. One way that I have checked reliability is to work with professional teacher-education students. These students may be using rubrics one day, so I work with them; and in doing so, I can see if the instrument is developing in a way that ensures consistency in application.

Another type of small-group evaluation is shown in Exhibit 5.5. It is one that can be applied in middle school settings.

Exhibit 5.5 Evaluation of the Group Participant

Name _____

Discussion Topic _____

Assign for each criterion one of the following ratings:

    5 = superior   4 = excellent   3 = average   2 = below average   1 = poor

Criteria	*Rating*
1. *Attitude.* Objective; open-minded; willing to modify views when presented with new evidence	_____
2. *Knowledge.* Understood the issue under discussion; showed skill in introducing information about the topic	_____
3. *Thinking.* Analyzed the issue for discussion well; able to develop relationships between ideas	_____
4. *Listening.* Kept track of the discussion and comments made by others; avoided obviously irrelevant or redundant contributions	_____
5. *Speaking.* Expresses ideas clearly; easily clarifies ambiguous points	_____
6. *Spontaneity.* Reacts to what is happening at the time; is not merely reciting "programmed" remarks	_____
7. *Consideration.* Is courteous of others; disagrees without being disagreeable; avoids monopolizing the discussion; interested in helping the group achieve its goal	_____

Additional comments:

TABLE 5.3 Small-Group Performance Rubric: Group Development and Cohesion

Advanced Standard	Proficient Standard	Essential Standard	In-Progress Standard
1. Integrates concern for group task and socioemotional aspects of group to expedite decision-making process. Exhibits flexibility, competence, and willingness to enact group roles.	1. Expresses concern for both task and socioemotional aspects of group process. Exhibits flexibility and willingness to enact group roles.	1. Identifies task and socioemotional aspects of group process. May emphasize one or the other but acknowledges both aspects of group work. Demonstrates some flexibility of roles.	1. Unconcerned with task and socioemotional aspects of group productivity; emphasizes one or the other. Does not demonstrate flexibility or competence in roles.
2. Accepts and supports group members: a. encourages members to feel valued; b. freely offers genuine praise; c. encourages group members to work within group rules/norms; d. encourages group members to excel	2. Accepts group members: a. encourages members to feel a sense of belonging; b. offers praise; c. encourages group members to work within group rules/norms; d. encourages group members to accomplish tasks.	2. Engages in minimal communication showing acceptance of group members. Encourages group members to get along with each other and to be compatible to group rules/norms. Exhibits a cooperative attitude.	2. Does not exhibit acceptance of group members. Does not encourage members to be compatible or follow group rules/norms. Does not exhibit a cooperative attitude.
3. Willingly cooperates with others to achieve ideal communication: a. seeks and offers verbal and nonverbal feedback; b. learns the interests of others; c. explains ideas in various ways to achieve understanding; d. asks others to explain ideas in various ways to achieve understanding; e. keeps an open mind.	3. Works with others to achieve good communication: a. seeks and offers verbal and nonverbal feedback; b. explains ideas in various ways when necessary to achieve understanding; c. asks others to explain ideas in various ways to achieve understanding; d. keeps an open mind.	3. Communicates with other group members: a. minimal exchange of verbal feedback; b. explains and elaborates ideas to achieve understanding; c. asks others to clarify their ideas; d. may come to the meeting with a predetermined position, but does not try to get the group to accept it.	3. Engages in minimal communication with other group members: a. does not seek or offer feedback to others; b. does not care about the interests of others; c. identifies ideas, but does not explain or elaborate on them fully; d. attends the meeting with a predetermined position and tries to get the group to accept it.

134

4. Initiates and encourages a positive social climate:
   a. shows solidarity by raising another's status, offering to help the group, volunteering, making personal sacrifice;
   b. tension release by laughing, smiling, joking;
   c. agreement with others.
5. Models cooperative attitude:
   a. willing to exchange information and communicate cooperatively for the good of all;
   b. discloses feelings;
   c. describes group process;
   d. develops trust.
   Helps group develop an attitude for process discussion.
6. Takes initiative and helps others. Assists in distributing the workload among group members, integrating each member's needs. Does fair share of the workload. Volunteers to be responsible for activities and assists others to make sure work is accomplished in the best way possible. Cares about the work of others as it affects the group.

4. Encourages a positive social climate:
   a. exhibits solidarity by raising another's status, offering to help the group, volunteering, making personal sacrifice;
   b. tension release by laughing, smiling, joking;
   c. agreement with others.
5. Demonstrates discussional attitude, willing to exchange information and communicate cooperatively for the good of all.
6. Assists others in distributing the workload among group members. Assists others to make sure work is accomplished in the best way possible. Does fair share of the workload. Cares about the work of others as it affects the group.

4. Supports a positive social climate:
   a. exhibits solidarity by raising another's status, offering to help the group, volunteering, making personal sacrifice;
   b. tension release by laughing, smiling, joking;
   c. agreement with others.
5. Exchanges information and works cooperatively to reach the best solution for all.
6. Does share of the workload as distributed. Concerned about the work of others as it affects the group.

4. Does not care about a positive social climate. Exhibits antagonism which makes others uncomfortable, does not discuss group tension, and disagrees unconstructively with others.
5. Hides information and uses technical language to protect status as an expert. Does not work cooperatively with others for the good of all, but for the good of self.
6. Does not do share of the workload. Waits for assignments. Does not care about the workload of others as it affects the group.

TABLE 5.4   Small-Group Performance Rubric: Organizational Communication

PROFICIENCY IN GROUP DEVELOPMENT AND COHESION	Advanced	Proficient	Essential	In Progress
Integrates concern for task and socioemotional aspects of group	4	3	2	1
Accepts *and supports* group members	4	3	2	1
Willingly cooperates with others	4	3	2	1
Initiates and encourages a positive social climate	4	3	2	1
Models a cooperative attitude	4	3	2	1
Takes initiative and helps others	4	3	2	1

Pre- and Post-Assessment

A carefully designed system of pre- and post-assessments can assist teachers in developing an approximate measure of a child's learning progress over the course of a particular unit. Effective pre- and post-assessments are based on one set of learning objectives and are administered in like manner to reduce the chance that a teacher's change in assessment method greatly distorts the results of the assessment. For instance, a pre-assessment for small groups involving a problem-solving activity would be matched with a postassessment also involving a problem-solving activity of the same level of difficulty.

The assessment tool in Exhibit 5.6, created by the Center for Gifted Education at the College of William and Mary (Van Tassel-Baska, Johnson & Boyce 1993), utilizes the concept map or web approach to scoring. In a concept map or web, students use circles or other shapes to represent concepts. Lines between the shapes represent relationships between ideas. In deciding whether concepts are related to one another, and in what fashion, students recall information gathered through listening and/or reading about the concepts.

Exhibit 5.6   Listening Pre- and Post-Assessment

Directions to the teacher: For each stage of the assessment, show a videotape of a 5- to 7-minute speech or presentation that clearly addresses 2 to 5 main points. Portions of a television news program or videotapes of an older student delivering a speech will work. Students may take notes during the video. Then hand out the worksheet below and give students ample time to respond to the following questions.

Name: _____

1. Explain each of the main points that were developed by the speaker.
2. Organize your information by using a graphic organizer such as a concept map or a web.

SCORING THE LISTENING
PRE- AND POST-ASSESSMENT

1. Student's task: Explain each of the main points that were developed by the speaker.

   Scoring: Assign points to student's response:
   5   All main points are clearly identified and explained in great detail
   4   All main points are clearly identified with some elaboration
       OR
       Some main points are identified along with detailed explanation
   3   All main points are identified with minimal or no explanation
   2   Some main points are identified, but description is incomplete
   1   Only random facts from speech cited; listing of phrases rather
         than summary
   0   No response

2. Student's task: Organize your information by using a graphic organizer such as a concept map or a web.

   Scoring: Read the concept map and identify any relationships that are not valid.
   - *Relationships:*   assign one point for each valid relationship (count the number of connectors between concepts).
   - *Levels of hierarchy:*   assign one point for each hierarchical level in the longest path of the map. Do not count words that have simply been strung together without clear subordinate relationships.
   - *Cross links:*   assign two points for each cross link showing a correct relationship between two concepts in different sections of the map.

Adapted with permission of Van Tassel-Baska, Johnson, and Boyce (1993, pp. 52–53).

GUIDELINES FOR FORMAL AND INFORMAL EVALUATION

Formal Grades

Both graded and ungraded evaluations can be used to measure progress and encourage accountability. Because oral communication performance can be a very personal and ego-identified event for the learner, however, grades can be a particular source of anxiety. For this reason, grading oral communication activities may not be the most effective way to encourage risk-taking in the classroom if it is the first time a class has engaged in formal self-disclosure of any sort if the activity is highly competitive; or if there is an unusual disparity in language ability among students.

We recommend, in general, that teachers who intend to grade oral communication activities do so as part of a comprehensive evaluation strategy that includes frequent opportunities to practice oral communication skills combined with ungraded, meaningful, and accurate feedback.

Informal Ungraded Feedback

The evaluation of oral communication activity should occur frequently in combination with structured oral communication activities.

Personal Conferences

Schedule a five- or ten-minute time to meet with each student during the week in a quiet, private area of the classroom. Try to arrange the setting so that the student feels comfortable meeting with you, and begin the conference by complimenting the student on something that he or she has done well in the last exercise. Ask open-ended questions about what the student has learned or enjoyed. How do they feel about themselves when they communicate orally in class? What types of activities do they like the best? Which ones do they like the least? Why? What goals will they set for the near future?

Videotapes

The videotape is an extremely useful tool for teachers who have access to a camera and a VCR for playback. It may be used with children of all ages and for a wide variety of activities, including drama, storytelling, group discussion, conflict resolution, and oral presentations.

Because students will have anxiety about speaking when they know that they will be videotaped and especially conscious of making mistakes, it is probably best to emphasize all the good things pertaining to the taped performance. Employ self-evaluation: ask the student to point out potential areas for improvement. Discuss strategies for improving that particular area, for example, "How would you use your voice next time to show that the character is feeling sad?," "How do you think you could explain that point better next time? What information would you include that you did not include here?"

One of the most effective uses of videotaping is to turn the tendency to be self-critical on its head by asking the student to identify pleasant characteristics that were surprises, for example, "You have a good delivery. Let's talk about it for a minute. What do you think your strengths are, after viewing this tape of your speech/discussion/negotiation?"

Video or Audiotape Portfolios

We recommend a system of creating and storing video or audio work products in conjunction with a speech folder containing written work products. Audiovisual work products include:

- an impromptu speech
- an interpersonal or conflict-management role-play exercise
- a small-group discussion
- a prepared speech
- practice sessions of the activities above as well as the final products

Written work products include:

- outlines of speeches
- notes or concept maps to demonstrate active listening
- essays about an oral communication experience
- teacher evaluations
- self- and peer evaluations

Another use of the videotape portfolio is to provide examples of a student's progress for parents. It may be important to explain to the parents what the student had learned prior to the assignment and what you were looking for in the assignment, so that they can place the activity they are viewing in its proper context.

Interviews and Constructed-Response Assessments

Exhibit 5.7 is an example of an assessment which uses the constructed-response method (Flores 1995). That is, the rater asks an open-ended question and then applies a uniform criteria to the listener's response, which is recorded as closely as possible on the evaluation.

Exhibit 5.7 Assessment of Oral Communication and Pronunciation Competency

Rating: 5 = effective   4 = proficient   3 = functional   2 = at-risk   1 = restricted

QUESTION	CRITERIA
1. What do you like most about this country, and why do you like that feature?	__ Is Audible __ Uses Standard Vowel and Consonant Sounds __ Explicitly Articulates Word Endings __ Conveys Meaning of Emphasized Syllables __ Communicates Message Function and Intention

Answer:

2. What is your favorite game to play and why do you like that game?	__ Is Audible __ Uses Standard Vowel and Consonant Sounds __ Explicitly Articulates Word Endings __ Conveys Meaning of Emphasized Syllables __ Communicates Message Function and Intention

Answer:

3. Give me an example of someone who doesn't understand you when you speak English. What happens when you try to speak with that person?	__ Is Audible __ Uses Standard Vowel and Consonant Sounds __ Explicitly Articulates Word Endings __ Conveys Meaning of Emphasized Syllables __ Communicates Message Function and Intention

Answer:

Total Score: _____ ÷ 3 = _____

Diagnostic: _____ Contrasted to: _____ Date: _____

Reprinted with permission of Flores (1995).

Self-Assessment

Speaker self-evaluation is often as important as being critiqued by others. Understanding one's own strengths and weaknesses is essential for effective improvement. The following activities and assignments encourage speaker self-evaluation. Consider using self-assessment to help students face their own fears about speaking in class.

- A self-evaluation form is similar to the extended critique written by a peer critic. The difference is that the speaker writes this critique to himself or herself (Exhibits 5.8 and 5.9). Just as the student would probably write in a supportive tone to a peer, the student should exhibit that same feeling when writing to himself or herself.
- Simple, open-ended self-assessments are especially effective with younger children. You may learn how they feel about their own performance, their classmates, or even your own interaction with them. You can design simple open-ended questionnaires for self-assessment that might look

---

Exhibit 5.8   Speaker Self-Analysis (Intermediate/Advanced)

Name:

Speech Topic:

Date of Presentation:

After thinking carefully about your speech/oral report, write a short paragraph about each question below:

1. What were your goals for this presentation? Did you meet them? Did you improve in the areas you wanted to improve? If not, what might have kept you from improving?

2. Do you feel as though you communicated your message clearly? Are there ways that the speech/oral report could have been better organized?

3. Were your arguments/points understood by the audience?

4. How did you like your use of voice, facial expressions, and body language in delivering this speech/oral report? How will you use these features differently next time?

5. What was the best feature of your performance? What do you think you most need to work on for next time?

Exhibit 5.9   Listening Self-Evaluation (Advanced)

How often do you find yourself relying on these ten bad listening habits? Check yourself carefully on each one.

Habit	Almost Always	Usually	Some-times	Seldom	Almost Never
1. Giving in to mental distractions	_____	_____	_____	_____	_____
2. Giving in to physical distractions	_____	_____	_____	_____	_____
3. Trying to recall everything a speaker says	_____	_____	_____	_____	_____
4. Rejecting a topic as uninteresting before hearing the speaker	_____	_____	_____	_____	_____
5. Faking listening	_____	_____	_____	_____	_____
6. Jumping to conclusions about a speaker's meaning	_____	_____	_____	_____	_____
7. Deciding a speaker is wrong before hearing everything she or he has to say	_____	_____	_____	_____	_____
8. Judging a speaker on personal evidence	_____	_____	_____	_____	_____
9. Not paying attention to a speaker's evidence	_____	_____	_____	_____	_____
10. Focusing on what the speaker looks and sounds like, rather than on the speaker's message	_____	_____	_____	_____	_____

Total: _____

How to score: Give yourself the following scores for every frequency checked

For every "almost always" —2   For every "usually" —4
For every "sometimes"   —6   For every "seldom" —8
For every "almost never" —10

Total score interpretation: Below 70   = You need a lot of training in listening
From   71–90 = You listen well
Above 90   = You listen exceptionally well

something like the following, and administer them orally to younger children:

Open-Ended Self-Assessment (Beginning/Intermediate)

1. When I talk about a book we are reading with my classmates, I feel . . .
2. Something I said in class this week that I feel very good about was . . .
3. The time I am most nervous or scared to speak in class is when . . .
   I feel scared during this time because . . .
4. The time I am most confident when I am speaking in class is when . . .
   I feel confident during this time because . . .

- Self-evaluations can be used to help students reshape their self-concept and performance expectations. Such evaluations are helpful in countering negative feelings or normal fears about speaking in front of an audience, as shown in Exhibit 5.10.

Exhibit 5.10   Reshaping Expectations (Beginning/Intermediate/Advanced)

When I talk in front of the class, I feel afraid that:	Some positive ways of thinking about that situation are:

- Instead of having students write their self-evaluations, you might give them the option of recording their critiques on video or audio tape. Some students open up more when not confronted by a blank piece of paper.
- An outgrowth of self-evaluation should be setting goals for improvement. Prior to a round of presentations, students should list specific goals they hope to achieve. (You can use a goal-setting form.) Afterward, they should ask themselves which goals were met, which were not accomplished, and what strategies might have helped achieve the goals that were not met.
- Students can keep a speaker's journal in which they write to you about their speaking and listening experiences in class. Assigning different topics to write about will help keep the journals focused, and you can write positive feedback and ask questions in the journals to let students know that you have read and respect their writing. An alternative approach to a journal assignment asks students to record and evaluate their involvement throughout the process of developing and delivering a public presentation. Assignments that focus on self-analysis of communication apprehension, the research and writing process, and performance are all productive learning exercises.

Peer Evaluation

Peer validation is very important to students and, if a teacher has a class that will respect ground rules, a wonderful sense of community and support can develop when the teacher asks peers to comment on what they liked about their classmates' performance. Student communicators benefit both from receiving the comments of their peers and from contributing their own comments. By focusing on the strengths and weaknesses of other peoples' speeches, students can improve their own speaking.

Two examples of peer evaluation are illustrated in Exhibits 5.11 and 5.12. Exhibit 5.11 is an analytic scoring method for a group discussion. Exhibit 5.12 is a holistic scoring method that may be used with a number of cooperative-learning activities.

Students take peer evaluation seriously if they understand that their feedback is valuable. Most students genuinely want to help their classmates. Another advantage of peer evaluation is that students who are weak in certain areas of speaking—for example, organization—improve their own speaking as they hear other group members discuss strategies for improvement (Grice & Skinner 1995).

In the peer evaluation shown in Exhibit 5.12, a peer completes the top half of the evaluation form. The teacher then writes comments on the bottom half or on the back, and may reinforce or disagree with comments made by the speaker's peers.

Exhibit 5.11 Peer-Group Discussion Evaluation

Group Member: _____ Topic: _____

Circle the number that best fits your evaluation of this group on each of the criteria listed below. A score of 7 means that you very strongly agree with the statement; a score of 1 means that you very strongly disagree with the statement.

1. I am very happy with how my group decided the issues we discussed.
    7   6   5   4   3   2   1

2. This discussion raised a lot of new and interesting issues.
    7   6   5   4   3   2   1

3. Everyone tried hard to support their opinions with facts and logic.
    7   6   5   4   3   2   1

4. Our group was organized in its approach to the topic.
    7   6   5   4   3   2   1

5. Everyone in our group contributed to the discussion and felt okay about participating.
    7   6   5   4   3   2   1

6. People took turns leading our group.
    7   6   5   4   3   2   1

7. We were interested in our group topic.
    7   6   5   4   3   2   1

Comments:

Exhibit 5.12 Sample Peer-Evaluation Form (Intermediate)

Your name: _____

Listener or speaker you are evaluating: _____

How did this person show that they were a good [speaker/listener] when we [engaged in activity]? Can you give an example?

What is one way that this person could try to improve for next time?

A FINAL WORD ABOUT EVALUATION: GUIDELINES FOR OFFERING CONSTRUCTIVE CRITICISM

Students need to know what was positive about their performance and what they can do to improve. Constructive criticism that meets these needs can be delivered orally to the student or as part of a written evaluation. We try to make sure that our numerical assessments also include personal comments to reinforce positive learning and to assist the student in setting goals for the next time.

Grice and Skinner (1995, p. 415) offer the following suggestions for constructive criticism:

1. Begin with a positive, sincere statement.
2. Be specific: "I was really impressed that you didn't read from your notecards, but referred to them instead," as opposed to, "You did a good job."
3. Be honest, but tactful.
4. Be careful to use "I" rather than "you" when phrasing criticism: "I had difficulty following your words because your rate seemed fast to me," as opposed to, "You lost my attention because you spoke too fast."
5. Reinforce the positive; it's very easy to focus too much (or even only) on the negative.
6. Problem-solve the negative; offer suggestions on how to improve.
7. Organize your comments: focus on delivery, content, and organization separately.

Other Key Principles of Effective Evaluations.   In addition to the Grice and Skinner factors cited above, we offer these additional suggestions.

1. As you develop content (or performance) standards, identify your own expectations for the level of behavior you are hoping to see before you make the assignment.
2. Create a criteria that can be applied consistently to each student and that respects diversity in gender, culture, and race. Criteria should be appropriate for the context.
3. Once you've determined the objectives and identified your own expectations, stick to them. Evaluate only the oral communication behaviors for which you explicitly gave instruction and adequate opportunity to practice before the graded exercise. If the assignment involves a specific set of cognitive skills, follow a similar procedure.
4. Learn to recognize your own biases toward style, dialect, or demeanor; adjust your grading and feedback to maintain objectivity.
5. Never give an evaluation without a thorough explanation of what a student has done well and without specifically suggesting areas for improvement and, if possible, strategies to help improve those areas (constructive criticism).

REFERENCES

Arneson, P. (1994). *Small group performance assessments*. Greeley, CO: University of Northern Colorado, Department of Speech Communication.

Backlund, P. (1983). Methods of assessing speaking and listening skills. In R. B. Rubin (Ed.), *Improving speaking and listening skills: New directions for college learning assistance, No. 12* (pp. 59–73). San Francisco: Jossey-Bass.

Barnes, D. (1992). *From communication to curriculum* (2nd ed.). Portsmouth, NH: Heinemann, Boynton/Cook Publishers.

Bergen, D. (1993, Winter). Authentic performance assessments. *Childhood Education*, pp. 99, 102.

Chaney, A. L., & Burk, T. L. (1997). *The Chaney-Burk direct performance oral communication instrument*. Williamsburg, VA: College of William and Mary.

Flores, N. L. (1995). *Assessment of oral communication and pronunciation competency*. Huntington Beach, CA: Golden West College.

Goulden, N. R. (1992). Theory and vocabulary for communication assessments. *Communication Education, 41,* 259–269.

Grace, C. (1992). The portfolio and its use: Developmentally appropriate assessment of young children. *ERIC Digest*. Urbana, IL: ERIC Clearinghouse on Elementary and Early Childhood Education.

Grice, G., & Skinner, J. (1995). *Mastering public speaking: Instructor's manual* (2nd ed.). Boston: Allyn and Bacon.

Guskey, T. R. (1994, March). What you assess may not be what you get. *Educational Leadership*, pp. 52–54.

Lucas, S. E. (1995). *The art of public speaking: Instructor's manual* (5th ed.). New York: McGraw-Hill.

National Forensics League. (1995). Original oratory judge's ballot. Ripon, WI: Author.

O'Keefe, V. (1995). *Speaking to think, thinking to speak*. Portsmouth, NH: Heinemann, Boynton/Cook Publishers.

Rochester City School District, Department of Curriculum Development and Support. (1995). *Portrait of a learner: Portfolio guidelines at a glance, Pre-K–8*. Rochester, NY: Author.

Van Tassel-Baska, J., Johnson, D., & Boyce, L. (Eds.) (1993). *A curriculum framework in the language arts*. Williamsburg, VA: College of William and Mary, Center for Gifted Education.

_____. (1996). *Developing verbal talent*. Boston: Allyn and Bacon.

Viechnicki, K. J., Barbour, N., Shaklee, B., Rohrer, J., & Ambrose, R. (1993). The impact of portfolio assessment on teacher classroom activities. *Journal of Teacher Education, 44(5),* 371–377.

6

Making the Most of Your Language Arts Textbook

OVERVIEW

As the debate continues over the efficacy of language arts instructional practices, so too does the debate over which (if any) commercial text to adopt. It is likely that the basal text will gain in popularity as authors strive to find the balance between whole language and traditional drill-and-skill approaches to language learning. In addition, many school districts suffer from a lack of funding and are unable to update their textbook series on a regular basis. Since a stronger emphasis on speaking and listening is a relatively recent phenomenon, this chapter suggests three strategies for enhancing traditional language arts textbooks that might not otherwise offer a balanced treatment of oral communication.

PRACTICALLY SPEAKING

What are some guidelines for ranking language arts texts according to their emphasis on oral communication?

How can traditional language arts texts be adapted to emphasize oral communiction?

What are some guidelines for creating supplemental oral communication activities?

THE BASAL APPROACH AND ORAL COMMUNICATION INSTRUCTION

Traditional *basal* texts allow teachers to group students according to literacy level and to track them in graduated reading and writing tasks designed to meet the learner where he or she is. Basals are often characterized by focused instruction in spelling, vocabulary, grammar, syntax, and phonics. Students learn to read and write language by adding up its parts to make the whole.

The tendency of such traditional texts to compartmentalize language into consonants, suffixes, and homophones eventually led to the revolution in teaching philosophy known as *whole language*. In a whole language approach, students are immersed in authentic, interesting literature that motivates them to learn language by using their higher-order thinking skills. For instance, students might use clues from the text to draw inferences about the meaning of a new vocabulary word. In reading authentic literature, students learn to recognize features such as spelling, parts of speech, and sentence structure. Students create meaning by comparing what they read and write to what they previously knew or experienced.

With respect to oral communication, neither the whole language approach nor the traditional *drill-and-skill* approach has completely satisfied the need to teach oral communication as a process occurring in a wide variety of contexts with its own unique set of behavioral, cognitive, and affective attributes. Some adaptation of texts has always been necessary for teachers who desired a stronger emphasis on oral communication.

The Basal Advantage: Oral Language Used to Develop Literacy

The advantage of basal texts, particularly for K through 2 and 3 through 5, is their efficacy in teaching young learners to recognize aural symbols and to distinguish among them. Certain other skills fundamental to the discriminative listening function (see Chapter 4), such as listening for main ideas, following organizational patterns, and listening for detail, have also always been present in basals. The use of oral language to sound out phonemes, words, and sentences is consistent with leading theories about how young children learn to think about language and construct meaning.

The Basal Disadvantage: Scope and Sequence of Oral Communication Skills May Be Narrow

Beyond using oral language as a tool to develop literacy, however, basal texts may struggle to engage learners in progress toward oral communication competence. The compartmentalized approach to topics does not adequately portray oral communication as a transactional process involving speaking, thinking, and listening. It does not challenge students to think on their feet and to use and recognize nonverbal language. The scope of speaking and listening contexts may also be limited.

THREE STRATEGIES FOR STRENGTHENING ORAL COMMUNICATION SKILLS

Devoting more attention to phonics and drill-and-skill teaching practices, however, need not compromise efforts to teach oral communication as process and to build oral communication competency. The strategies that follow—ranking textbooks for strong oral communication emphasis, adapting reading and writing lessons to include oral communication components, and developing supplemental oral communication lessons—can help strengthen oral communication skills in any language arts curriculum.

Strategy #1: Ranking Textbooks for Strong Oral Communication Emphasis

An oral communication ranking criteria may be helpful if your school is in the process of ranking language arts textbooks for adoption into the language arts curriculum. If your school has already adopted a language arts textbook, taking stock of its approach to oral communication may suggest content areas and instructional practices that can be improved through adaptation or with supplemental curricula.

In evaluating reading and writing texts, Aldrich and McKim (1992) developed an extensive integrated language arts curriculum criteria that measured the achievement of three primary curricular goals: (1) appropriateness of literacy content, (2) engagement of the learner, and (3) development of a literacy community. Their holistic approach included reading, writing, speaking, and listening. In applying the criteria to basal texts, state language arts curricula, and supplemental curricula issued by nonprofits and other educational organizations, Aldrich (1996) found that while many publishers claimed to address certain key aspects of that criteria within the introductory statements of philosophy, in actuality such texts often failed to truly embody those philosophies.

Similarly, we also surveyed seven popular basal language arts series published over a ten-year period (1984–1994) for oral communication content and found that although several texts marketed themselves as promoting speaking and listening, upon closer inspection *speaking* was limited to instances of reading aloud and whole-class discussion, while *listening* was limited to following directions or listening to a story in order to create a written response (not necessarily a bad practice in itself, but it is frequently overused).

One strategy for teachers and administrators is to develop a ranking system similar to this one from Aldrich (1996, pp. 232–234) and apply it to the criteria on the next page.

6 = extensively	5 = adequately	4 = moderately
3 = infrequently	2 = rarely	1 = not at all

In theory and practice, does the text consistently portray oral communication:

- as a way that learners build meaning?
- as a way that learners share meaning?
- as a process involving speaking, listening, and critical thinking?
- as a process that takes place in a number of situations and contexts?

In practice, does the text provide regular opportunities for:

- listening to learn and distinguish aural symbols?
- listening (observing) to distinguish nonverbal symbols (body language)?
- listening for comprehension of main ideas and organization?
- listening to draw inferences, critique reasoning and perspective, and predict?
- listening to recognize vocal expression of feelings?
- listening for enrichment?
- formal informative speaking (group and individual)?
- formal persuasive speaking (group and individual)?
- enrichment speaking (storytelling, mass media programming, oral history)
- discussion in small groups?
- conversation and interpersonal activity?
- whole-class discussion?
- dramatic performance (plays, skits, reader's theatre, oral interpretation)?

Very few texts will meet these criteria. Those that come closest will probably be those with a strong collection of dramatic material. For many years, speaking and listening have been categorized as expressive and receptive arts, which, in combination with the imaginative appeal of dramatic literature, has led to the popular use of plays, skits, and puppetry as typical oral language activities. To help develop natural turn-taking behaviors, critical thinking skills, and meaning-making skills, dramatic performance should be part of a curriculum that includes contexts such as conversation, small-group discussion, and persuasive speaking/evaluative listening. Most language arts texts would benefit greatly from some form of adaptation or supplementary curricula.

Strategy #2: Adapting Reading and Writing Lessons

This section on adapting reading and writing lessons reminds us of how cookbooks often suggest ways to disguise leftovers or stretch a pound of hamburger so that it lasts though the week. Essentially, we are doing the same thing: suggesting innovative ways to present, invigorate, or reuse material that was originally prepared for a different purpose.

Alternate Writing and Speaking Responses.   When the text calls for listening to a passage and then writing a response, consider substituting oral response for written response, especially when the task calls for critical thinking. Students will learn to think critically in response to an oral message. Remember that writers have the luxury of re-reading a written text if they did not understand it the first time; oral communicators must be adept at grasping symbols and comprehending them without that same luxury; knowing what questions to ask and having the willingness to ask them are also attributes that an oral communicator can develop only with practice. Students will learn to take healthy risks in asking questions, and will get practice in expressing their opinions.

Analyze Stories for a Variety of Purposes.   Read stories from a text out loud for different purposes than the authors intended. For instance, read a story to the class (or ask a student to read the story) two or three times and ask students to listen carefully and to write down every word they hear that fits a certain part of speech, such as adjective, verb, conjunction, and so on. Use characters in the stories to perception-check and challenge stereotypical thinking with whole-class discussion and journal assignments. Students develop discriminative and evaluative listening skills and increase their ability to identify aural symbols quickly and efficiently.

Challenge Students to Think About Communication Context.   Include stock oral communication questions in your literature discussions, such as the following:

If this person had said [such and such] to someone else, how do you think that person would have felt?

What would you have said if you had been listening?

What are other ways that this person could have expressed their feelings?

Was that statement a fact or opinion?

What do you think are the most important goals for this speaker?

What would you think about if you were the listener?

Use Games to Expand on Concepts in the Text.   Students can be challenged to listen for detail and for deeper understanding. For instance, create bingo cards that display words instead of numbers (Exhibit 6.1); call out words with target phonemes and ask students to cross off the corresponding words on their card.

Another version of bingo is vocabulary bingo (Exhibit 6.2). Using words featured as vocabulary in that week's spelling or vocabulary lessons, create cards with the definitions and call out the words (or vice-versa). Students can review their answers in small groups or as a class. Games like this foster recognition of phonemes and aural symbols, thus building discriminative listening and critical thinking skills.

Another type of game involves "meaning making." Students learn to make meaning with oral communication when they listen to a sentence with a missing word and volunteer a vocabulary or phonics-related word that completes the sentence. With young children, the sentences can be rhymes, such as "Roy, Roy, where's the _____?" (Hunsacker 1994).

Older children can tell group stories using vocabulary from the text, homonyms, synonyms, and so forth. One child starts the story with a sentence using a

Exhibit 6.1   Phonics Bingo

pick	boil	curl	girl
bring	arm	going	check
taking	toys	trouble	saw
clock	pearl	grass	noise

Possible Questions:

Do you have a word or words rhyming with "twirl," as in "Can you twirl a baton?"
Do you have any words beginning with the "cl" sound?
Do you have any words with the vowel sound similar to the "o" in "oven?"
Do you have any words ending with the "ck" sound?
Do you have any words with the vowel sound of "a" in "ball?"

Exhibit 6.2   Vocabulary Bingo

choose one over the other; select and remove	to become so hot as to evaporate; to seethe in rage	a young female child
to take something with you where you are going	one of the human limbs; attached at the shoulder and ends in a hand	a mark shaped like a V, often used to keep track of items on a list
a valuable gem created when an oyster secretes a film around a grain of sand to stop its irritation	objects that children use in playtime to help stretch their imaginations	the past tense of the verb "to see"

Possible Questions:

Do you have a definition for the word "pick?"
How about the word "boil?"
How about the word "pearl?"
Do you have a definition for a word that rhymes with "king?"

word from the lesson. Another student adds to the story with a second sentence using a homonym or synonym; the rest of the class identifies the word used by the speaker and its relationship to the previous target word.

Another technique is to read a paragraph of a story to the class. Insert in the paragraph a sentence that does not belong. Ask the class to find the inserted sentence.

Highlight Differences Between Oral and Written Communication.   Particularly as students begin to understand the distinction between expository and persuasive writing, discussion questions or small-group projects can focus on a writing assignment from the text and instead challenge students to uncover ways in which the finished oral communication product might be different from the finished written product. Allow for discussion about different kinds of oral communication contexts—not just oral reports or formal speeches.

Match pictures to sound. Make a tape of corresponding sounds and ask students to match the sounds to the pictures. Other variations:

1. Identify sounds made from behind a screen or on a tape, such as the sound of a vacuum cleaner, hair dryer, running water, dishwasher, and so on.
2. Develop awareness of pitch by playing notes on a piano or other instrument. Discuss with the class what a person would be feeling if someone made that sound to send a message. How might a story character have used pitch or music to express their feelings?

Pantomime Stories.   These activities focus on nonverbal aspects of expression.

Utilize Peer Reading and Writing Conferences.   Used successfully within the whole language approach, peer conferences can be used to enhance a basal approach in which students complete worksheets or write stories and response papers that are read out loud to a "buddy" or group of peers who assist in editing and revising the work. Students learn discriminative, evaluative, and sometimes empathic listening skills, as well as interpersonal and group-discussion skills.

Tell Stories in Conjunction with Other Activities.   Develop mental images by having the class listen to, and then draw a picture of, something in the story. Ask students to listen for details, plot development, or clues to solve a problem or mystery in the text. To develop speaking and oral composition skills, ask students to retell stories, either to you, to the class, or to an older student or peer (Sweet 1994).

Strategy #3: Developing Supplemental Oral Communication Lessons

A third strategy for enhancing textbooks is, of course, to supplement them with additional curricula. Using a set of grade-appropriate competencies, you may wish to supplement your textbook with oral-intensive lessons such as those featured throughout this book. If you are interested in creating your own lessons using themes and materials from your textbook or teaching resource kits, consider the guidelines in Exhibit 6.3.

The main benefit of supplementing traditional texts with independent oral communication lessons is that students are exposed to more "authentic" oral

---

Exhibit 6.3   Oral Communication Lesson Checklist

Learning Objectives:

1. _____ What is the main purpose of this lesson? How will it be introduced to students?
2. _____ What specific competencies will be targeted in the lesson?
3. _____ How many students will participate?
4. _____ How difficult or complex is this assignment in relation to previously introduced concepts?
5. _____ Does the exercise provide adequate opportunity for both learning and application?
6. _____ Has enough time been allocated for accomplishment of the lesson?

Teacher Preparation:

1. _____ How much classroom time will you devote to the lesson?
2. _____ What kind of feedback will you use in evaluating learning outcomes? Have you developed a specific criteria that correlates closely with the principles and skills you will emphasize the most?
3. _____ Have you anticipated how you might handle different types of emotional behavior from your students? How will you respond if they are unusually frightened? Competitive? Giggly? Indifferent?
4 _____ How much time have you allocated to provide detailed, thoughtful, positive feedback?
5. _____ What adjustments to your teaching style might this lesson require?

Student Participation:

1. _____ How mature are your students? Can they handle the complexity or sophistication of the lesson? Is the topic appropriate for this group of students?
2. _____ What ground rules would be helpful in managing classroom dynamics?
3. _____ Does the exercise include all students or is it likely to favor students with certain personality traits or backgrounds?
4. _____ Will students be able to place this lesson within a framework of their own experience both inside and outside of school? Is it relevant to their lives?
5. _____ Does the exercise foster active learning for everyone?

communication situations. Students learn about the many components of the oral communication process and about the relationship between speaking, listening, and thinking.

SUMMARY

Teaching a balance of phonics and whole language can present challenges and opportunities for competency-based oral communication instruction. Three strategies for working within a more traditional language arts framework are developing an oral communication criteria and using it to rank textbooks; adapting the rote exercises and methodologies often found in traditional texts to include more oral response and discriminative, evaluative, and empathic listening; and supplementing texts with stand-alone lessons that explore unique oral communication concepts and situations. The major challenge in teaching oral communication with traditional texts is the lack of opportunity to portray oral communication as a process involving many different roles and behaviors.

REFERENCES

Aldrich, P. (1996). Evaluating language arts materials. In J. Van Tassel-Baska, D. Johnson, & L. Boyce (Eds.), *Developing verbal talent* (pp. 218–239). Boston: Allyn and Bacon.

Aldrich, P., & McKim, G. (1992). *The consumer's guide to English-language arts curriculum.* New York: Saratoga–Warren Board of Cooperative Educational Services.

Hunsacker, R. (1994). In M. Snively (Ed.), *Listening activities for K–12.* Belleville, VA: East Forensics.

Sweet, A. (1994). *Transforming ideas for teaching and learning to read.* Washington, DC: U.S. Department of Education, Office of Educational Research and Improvement, Office of Research.

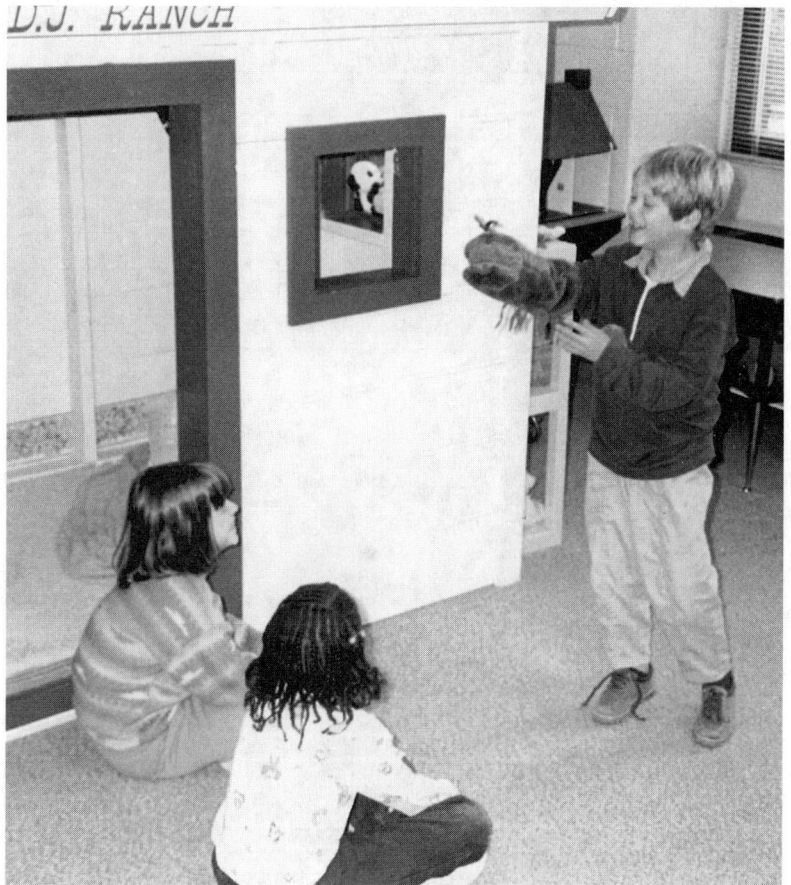

Telling stories with puppets

7

Exercises and Activities for Grades K Through 2

OVERVIEW

At the K through 2 stage, children are learning the most basic competencies in oral communication. The biggest challenge for oral communication instruction in K through 2 is probably in providing students with opportunities to practice listening in contexts other than following directions, although we've included at least one exercise involving directions.

LISTENING, THINKING, AND ORAL RESPONSE

Younger children should learn how to identify and distinguish sounds. Later on, they should be able to follow simple directions and attach meaning to different vocal tones and inflections.

EXERCISE 7.1   WHAT'S THAT SOUND?

Objectives:

1. To identify sources of sound
2. To describe differences in sound

Materials Needed: An audio tape of common household sounds, such as appliances, pets, running water, etc.; smaller objects that make sounds, such as musical instruments, papers rustling together, coins dropping into a piggy bank; a bed sheet or screen of some sort that can be used to conceal objects from view while allowing for clarity in sound

Procedures:

1. If using an audio tape, play sounds one at a time, several times each if necessary, and allow children to guess the source. Ask follow-up questions, such as:

   Can you think of something else that this sound might come from?

   Do you think this sound could come from a _____?
   Why/why not? (Repeat with other suggestion; encourage children to try and explain or imitate similarities and differences)

2. If using smaller objects that you manipulate to create a familiar noise, conceal the objects from sight with a light bed sheet or behind a screen of some sort; make the noise with the object and ask questions as above.

Simple Assessment (teacher checks off):

_____ I can identify some sounds in my world such as (teacher lists): _____

_____

_____ I can describe the difference between some sounds and say when sounds are similar. _____

_____

Adapted from Hunsacker (1994, p. 53). Reprinted with permission of Morris Snively/East Forensics.

EXERCISE 7.2   I CAN MAKE THAT SOUND!

Objectives:	1. To identify source of sounds
	2. To reproduce sounds
Materials Needed:	Toys that generate animal sounds, such as common pull-string toys; also, audio or video tapes (with audio) of animal sounds.
Procedures:	1. Use the toy to generate a common animal sound or play the tapes.
	2. Ask students to identify the animal, if it is not already obvious.
	3. Ask students to repeat the sound in unison ("When I say GO!" or "On the count of Three. One, Two, THREE.").
	4. Ask students to name the sound (for example, a lion's roar, a dog's bark).
Variations:	Make a list of other common sounds that children can imitate with their voices (sirens, cheering, wind, automobile engines, and so on) and repeat as above. A slightly more challenging version: when reading from storybooks with large pictures, point to a picture and ask, "What is this? What sound does it make?"

Simple Assessment:

_____ I can imitate sounds of animals/other things, such as (teacher lists): _____

_____

_____ I can recognize animals that make sounds and I can name or imitate that sound:

_____

_____

EXERCISE 7.3   THE HIGH–LOW SOUND GAME

Objective:	To identify differences in pitch
Materials Needed:	A musical instrument that has a range of pitch: a recorder, flute, or piano would work very well. You can supplement the musical instrument if you wish with a recording of sounds in nature that have a clearly identifiable pitch, such as a bird chirping, a dog barking (preferably a large dog so as to get the deeper pitch), a cow mooing, a person laughing, and so on.
Procedures:	1. Introduce the concept of pitch. "Pitch is the word we use to describe the highness or lowness of a sound. A sound with high pitch is like this: (play a very high pitch note on the instrument). A sound with low pitch is like this: (play a very low note on the instrument)."
	2. Ask students to tell you whether sounds have a high pitch or a low pitch. Use the musical instrument and/or other recorded sounds to do this. For the moment, stick with sounds that clearly fall into either extreme—high pitch or low pitch.
	3. Ask students to tell you whether one sound is higher than the other, or whether one sound is lower than the other. Start out with sounds from either extreme; then begin to use sounds that are closer in pitch to each other. This part of the exercise will be more challenging for students.

Simple Assessment:

_____ I can identify sounds with a high or low pitch.

_____ I can tell when one sound has a higher or lower pitch than another.

EXERCISE 7.4   WHAT IS IT?

Objectives:
1. To identify common objects by name
2. To identify pictures of that object

Materials Needed:
A collection of objects commonly found in a school, outside, or in the home; pictures of those objects (animated drawings or real photographs; magazines are good sources of photographs), a pillowcase or bag

Procedures:
1. Create a place in the classroom where objects can be seen by all students, a table for display, a pillowcase or bag that conceals the objects until you pull them out.
2. Pull an object out and ask students to name the object. If it is unknown to them, name it and explain how it is used.
3. Hold up pictures mounted on construction paper or in a scrapbook. Ask students to name the object as it appears in the picture. Sometimes objects look different in a photograph, or sometimes an object can have a different shape or style. You can ask students to identify and describe these differences and then to identify and describe similarities. "How do you know this is a _____?"

Variations:
1. This exercise can be designed around a theme or topic of study. Consider making a small museum exhibit. Students can collect and name artifacts that might be used in an exhibit about that topic, or they can make drawings or art objects that represent the object. Use labels to identify each object on display.
2. A discussion can probe different uses for objects identified in class. "What does this object do/what do people use this object for? How else is it used? Can animals use this object? Why/why not?"
3. If you will be taking a field trip with your students to a special place where there are unusual objects, try to find pictures of them in advance; identify them and discuss with students. On the field trip itself, ask students to tell you when they encounter the actual object itself.

EXERCISE 7.5   NAMING ACTIVITIES

Objectives: 1. To identify activities by name
                          2. To describe the activity

Materials Needed: Pictures (from books and magazines) of people participating in
                     different everyday activities, such as eating, playing, reading,
                     sleeping, cleaning, driving, walking, running, talking, watching
                     television, working, etc.

Procedures: 1. Explain to students that you are going to show them pictures
                             of people doing different things and you want them to tell you
                             what the people are doing.
                          2. Show the picture; ask what the person is doing. When the
                             students respond, follow up with, "How can you tell that's
                             what the person is doing? How do you know? What clues from
                             the picture help you know what the person is doing?"

Simple Assessment:

_____ I can identify activities that people do everyday, such as (teacher or student lists):

_____

_____ I can tell when people are _____ (doing the activity) because

_____ (describes signs of activity).

EXERCISE 7.6   REPEAT AFTER ME

Objectives:	1. To learn to repeat simple phrases and sentences
	2. To speak in unison
Materials Needed:	Select a fairy tale or nursery rhyme in which there is a refrain often said by a character. For instance, in the "Three Little Pigs" the pigs say, "Not by the hair on my chinny-chin chin!" and the Wolf says, "Then I'll huff and I'll puff and I'll blow your house in." Or one of our favorites, from Dr. Seuss: "Pale green pants with nobody inside them!"
Procedures:	1. Identify a phrase that students are to repeat when it is time in the story. Tell students they are to say it together when the time comes.
	2. Read the story slowly. When you get to the refrain, coach students through it as a group. "Let's all say it together now."

EXERCISE 7.7   EVALUATIVE LISTENING—PREDICTING OUTCOMES

Objective:	To draw inferences about actions and use them to predict outcomes
Materials Needed:	A large picture showing a person engaging in an activity; a short story or an action sequence from a story. The picture does not need to be related to the story.
Procedures:	1. Show the picture to the class.
	2. Ask the class to identify what the person is doing in the picture.
	3. Ask the class what is likely to happen next. How do they know what is likely to happen next?
	4. Read a short passage from the story. Stop before the story reveals an action about to be taken by the character.
	5. Ask the class what is likely to happen next. How do they know what is likely to happen next?

EXERCISE 7.8   FOLLOWING DIRECTIONS

Objective:	To build discriminative listening skills: attention to detail and concentration
Materials Needed:	Each student will need a sheet of paper and four crayons—one each in red, blue, green, and orange.
Procedures:	Explain to the class that they are going to practice listening and following directions. Tell them to use their eyes and ears and to do as you ask, so that each student follows the directions given by the teacher. Tell students you will not repeat directions. Give them a reasonable amount of time to complete the task, but do not repeat, even if some students appear frustrated. When the exercise is over, ask students what they might have done better when listening to make it easier to follow the directions. This exercise can be used more than once during the same week to help build confidence.
Instructions:	1. Put the paper in front of you on the desk. 2. Fold the paper so the top and bottom are together. 3. Open the paper. 4. Put the paper so that the long side goes up and down, from top to bottom (demonstrate). 5. Take a red crayon. Draw a red circle at the top of your paper. 6. Take a blue crayon. Draw a box on the bottom part of your paper. 7. Take a green crayon. Print your name in circle at the top of your paper. 8. Take an orange crayon. Put an X in the box at the bottom of your paper.

Adapted from Hunsacker (1994, p. 51). Reprinted with permission of Morris Snively/East Forensics.

EXERCISE 7.9   RHYMING WORDS

Objective:	To help students recognize and associate similar sounds of language
Procedures:	Read the following sentences or make up some of your own that have missing last words. Ask students to complete the missing words so the sentence is a rhyme.

Ann, Ann, get the _____ .   Pat, Pat, find your _____ .
Roy, Roy, where is the _____ ?   Fred, Fred, go to _____ .
Sue, Sue, where are _____ ?

Adapted from Hunsacker (1994, p. 51). Reprinted with permission of Morris Snively/East Forensics.

EXERCISE 7.10   DISCRIMINATIVE LISTENING— RECOGNIZING SEQUENCES

Objectives:
1. To identify the steps in a sequence
2. To organize the steps in a sequence into logical order

Materials Needed: Stories featuring action sequences

Procedures:
1. Read the story to the class, or have students read the story together or in pairs.
2. Ask: What happened first in this story? What happened next? Then what happened?
3. Ask: Would the story make sense if [name a step] happened before [name a step]? Why or why not?
4. Ask: When you talk to other people and you tell a story, are you careful to tell them in what order things happen? Why or why not?
5. Ask: When you listen to a story, do you want to know in what order things happened? Why or why not?

EXERCISE 7.11   LEARNING ABOUT CONSONANT SOUNDS

Objectives:
1. To identify consonant sounds
2. To identify when a consonant sound is used to describe an object
3. To identify the letter(s) responsible for the consonant sound

Procedures:
1. Show a picture and say the name of an object that begins with a consonant, deliberately exaggerating the initial consonant.

2. Show students two or three pictures of objects; ask them to identify the one(s) that begin with the same consonant sound.

3. Discuss:

   Can you think of other words that begin with this sound?
   Do you know what letters make that sound?
   Can someone draw that letter on the bulletin board/point to that letter on the alphabet chart/show us that letter on a poster in the classroom?

SPEAKING, THINKING, AND NONVERBAL COMMUNICATION

Drama

In K through 2, children learn to use their voices and bodies to express themselves creatively. They also begin to develop an awareness of different literary genres, such as poetry, prose, and dramatic works. Frequently, language arts textbooks will provide literary selections suitable for informal, impromptu dramatization, as well as other structured selections. The following are examples of some dramatic performances you can do with your class that are less likely to appear in a text:

Ideas for Other Forms of Drama

- Create and perform puppet shows
- Create and perform plays or skits
- Engage in choral reading
- Read or enact stories for younger children or parents
- Create a television or radio broadcast

Pantomime

Pantomime is a form of nonverbal drama that is particularly useful for helping children learn to recognize nonverbal behaviors common in everyday communication. Children learn to use their own bodies to communicate meaning and learn to recognize nonverbal behaviors or symbols used by others. Pantomimes can have a simple informal structure of introduction, body, and conclusion (see ideas in Exercise 7.12). You may wish to encourage your students to use structure in longer pantomimes and then discuss how the structure might have made the pantomime more effective.

Storytelling

Storytelling is a highly creative activity that encourages students to think on their feet, to listen for detail and listen appreciatively, and to use rich language and nonverbal expression. Our favorite book on storytelling is *Look What Happened to Frog: Storytelling in Education* by Pam Cooper and Rives Collins (1995).

More advanced students can be challenged to meet four basic criteria as they are building their stories: (1) using descriptive language and nonverbal expression; (2) making sure the plot of the story is clear; (3) creating a beginning, middle, and end to the story; and (4) working to keep the audience interested in the story. See Exercise 7.13 for some good ideas.

EXERCISE 7.12   PANTOMIME ACTIVITIES

1. Pantomime how you would look if you were feeling:

   angry   curious   sad
   bored   happy   scared
   cold   hot   sleepy

2. Pantomime a short scene about the following:

   You are eating spaghetti but it keeps slipping off your fork.

   You are caught in a very heavy snowstorm, and the wind is so strong that it keeps blowing you backwards.

   You are settling down to go to sleep, but you start to imagine there might be a monster under your bed.

   You are watching a baseball game and someone hits a home run into the stands near you.

   You are reading a book, when all of the sudden you see a really big spider drop down from the ceiling in front of your face.

   You are walking in the park and you find a hurt animal. You try to get near it to help it, but you don't want to scare it.

   You are on vacation with your family, camping outside. You discover that a skunk has crept into your tent in the middle of the night.

3. In small groups of three or four, pantomime the following:

   You are jumping rope.

   You are playing baseball or softball: an umpire, a batter, a pitcher, maybe a runner.

   One person is sick. The other people are doctors, nurses, emergency technicians at a hospital.

   You are delivering a very heavy piano to a customer's house. The house has two sets of stairs.

   You are fighting a large fire.

   You are news reporters interviewing a politician after an important speech.

   You are drivers caught in a traffic jam when the person in front gets a flat tire.

   You are astronauts in a space station working on an experiment together.

4. In small groups, pantomime scenes from stories, fairy tales, or nursery rhymes, and so on.

5. Discussion questions for use with pantomime:

   What was described by the pantomime?

   How did you know? What actions or expressions did your classmates use to show what they were feeling or thinking?

   Where have you seen similar actions or expressions used in everyday life?

   Which actions or expressions do you use when you are around other people?

   Which actions or expressions do you use when you are by yourself?

   Why do you think people use some actions or expressions when they are around people, but not when they are by themselves?

EXERCISE 7.13   FIVE IDEAS FOR STORYTELLING

1. Wake-Up Call. Assign a different student each morning to briefly retell a story that has been told previously in class, or to tell one that they have been reading at home, or to make up one if they wish. There should be no pressure here to "get it right." Make available large picture books, flannel or felt boards, and costume pieces or accessories.

2. Before a puppet-making activity, ask students to make a puppet that represents a character in a story. Again, the story could be one they have learned in class, one they have learned at home, or one they would like to make up. After the puppets are finished, students take turns telling their stories, using their puppets.

3. Draw a picture that represents . . .

   something you and your friends or family like to do for fun
   an event that would make you very happy
   what you think the world will be like in 100 years
   what you would like to do when you are a grown-up
   your favorite hobby
   your favorite story
   something that interests you very much

   When you have finished your picture, use it to tell a story to the class. The story can be about something that has already happened or something that you hope will happen.

4. If you could be a character from your favorite story, who would you be? Tell the story from that person's point of view.

5. Sit in a large circle on the floor. One person starts a story by saying the first sentence of the story. The person to his or her left tells the next phrase or sentence. The person to that person's left adds on, continuing until the story has gone around the circle at least twice. The teacher can use discretion in asking one student to begin wrapping up the story.

Storytelling Assessment
1. Did the storyteller use descriptive and imaginative language?
2. Did the storyteller make it clear what was happening in the story?
3. Did the story have a beginning, a middle, and an end?
4. Did the storyteller try to keep the audience interested in the story?

These next few exercises contain ideas for practicing fundamental speaking, thinking, and nonverbal competencies in both formal and informal contexts.

EXERCISE 7.14   GREETINGS

Objective: To introduce oneself to another

Procedures: Ask students to introduce themselves to another person in the class by
   1. saying a greeting, such as "Hi" or "Hello"
   2. finishing the sentence, "My name is _____."
   3. saying one interesting thing about themselves, such as "I have a pen pal."
   4. allowing everyone in the class a chance to practice greeting someone else from the class.

Simple Assessment *(check as appropriate)*:

_____ I can greet another person.

_____ I can tell another person what my name is.

_____ I can tell another person something interesting about myself.

EXERCISE 7.15   INTRODUCING ANOTHER PERSON

Objectives: 1. To learn introduction skills
                2. To practice recall of details from conversation

Procedures: 1. In pairs, students greet each other, say their names, and tell each other one thing that is interesting about themselves.
                2. Each pair takes a turn in front of the rest of the class. One person introduces the other person to the class, as in, "This is Li Chi. She is from the country of China and is going to become a citizen of the United States soon."

EXERCISE 7.16   STARTING A CONVERSATION

Objectives:	1. To initiate correct speech patterns
	2. To take turns in a conversation
Materials Needed:	Brightly colored paper featuring one age-appropriate word or a simple picture. Each child should get a sheet of paper with a different word or picture on it. Consider using words from current class topics or stories that might trigger student interest.
Procedures:	1. Explain to students that they are going to play a game. Each student will get a sheet of paper with a word on it, and they are to hold on to their word. The teacher will divide the students into pairs. One person will start the game by saying hello to the other person and asking a question that uses the word held by that student.
	For instance, if Natasha is holding the word "flower," her partner Rhonda might begin the conversation in this way: "Hello, Natasha. What is your favorite flower?" Meanwhile, Rhonda holds a picture of a set of musical notes.
	2. The student holding the word answers the question and then asks the other student a question using the word that they are holding. For instance, Natasha might say, "My favorite flower is the daisy. What kind of music do you listen to?"
	3. The student who initiated the conversation closes it by answering the question ("I listen to rock and roll.") and making a closure statement ("It was nice talking to you today." Partner answers, "It was nice talking to you, too. Goodbye. " Goodbye.")
Variations:	This exercise can be used to introduce different rules about conversation, such as how to greet people and how to maintain a conversation with follow-up questions or with additional statements of interest. The word on the card is merely a stimulus for students to say something related to in-class learning. The exchange between students can be lengthened at the teacher's discretion.

EXERCISE 7.17   THREE-POINT SPEECH

Objectives: 1. To practice a formal presentation
                2. To structure ideas

Procedures: 1. Ask each student to think of a favorite story, either read in class or at home. Ask them to write down on paper the names of two or three people or objects that appear in the story.
                2. Ask students to stand and explain to the class what their favorite story was and what the two or three things in the story were. Remind students to look at the audience when they are speaking.

Simple Assessment:

Student identified favorite story.
3 = definitely   2 = somewhat   1 = not at all

Student identified two or three concrete concepts in the story.
3 = definitely   2 = somewhat   1 = not at all

Student explained role of concepts in the story.
3 = definitely   2 = somewhat   1 = not at all

Student faced audience and maintained eye contact.
3 = definitely   2 = somewhat   1 = not at all

EXERCISE 7.18   USING EMOTIONAL TONE

Objectives: 1. To use emotional inflections in the voice to create meaning (speaking)
2. To recognize differences in meaning brought about by differences in emotional tone (listening)

Procedures: 1. Ask students to practice saying the phrase "You're kidding" as if they were:

   surprised at something very good that just happened
   laughing at a funny story told by a friend
   angry that another person accidentally broke a favorite toy
   disappointed that a favorite TV show has been canceled

2. Have some students perform their interpretations in front of the class.

3. Discuss:

   How is this person probably feeling?
   How can you tell?
   When do you use emotion in your voice when you are talking to someone.

Variations: You can substitute other phrases for "You're kidding," such as "Really?" "I'm not hungry anymore," "Let's go," "This is not what I expected," and so on. You can also ask students to brainstorm their own list of phrases and emotions to practice.

EXERCISE 7.19   NONVERBAL BEHAVIOR—AVOIDING DISTRACTIONS

Objective:	To identify positive and negative effects of nonverbal behavior when speaking and listening
Materials Needed:	A large flip chart or a chalkboard. You will need two pages or spaces on the board, one for *Listening* and one for *Speaking*
Procedures:	1. Ask the question: "When a person is listening to you, how do you know?" Follow up with probes:

> How does a person's face show that he or she is listening?
> How does a person's body show that he or she is listening?
> How does a person's voice show that he or she is listening?

For each answer, summarize the findings on one side of the page.

2. Ask the question: "When a person is not listening to you, how do you know?" Follow up with probes:

> How does a person's face show that she or he is not listening?
> How does a person's body show that he or she is not listening?
> How does a person's voice show that he or she is not listening?"

For each answer, summarize the findings on one side of the page.

3. Ask the question: "When a person is speaking, how does he or she use his or her face, body, and voice to keep the listener's attention?" Follow up with probes and summarize findings, as before.

4. Ask the question:

> When a person is speaking, what sort of things does she or he sometimes do with her or his face, body, or voice that makes the audience want to *stop* listening?

Follow up with probes and summarize findings, as before.

REFERENCES

Cooper, P., & Collins, R. (1995). *Look what happened to frog: Storytelling in education.* Scottsdale, AZ: Gorsuch Scarisbrick.

Hunsacker, R. (1994). In M. Snively (Ed.), *Listening activities for K–12.* Belleville, VA: East Forensics.

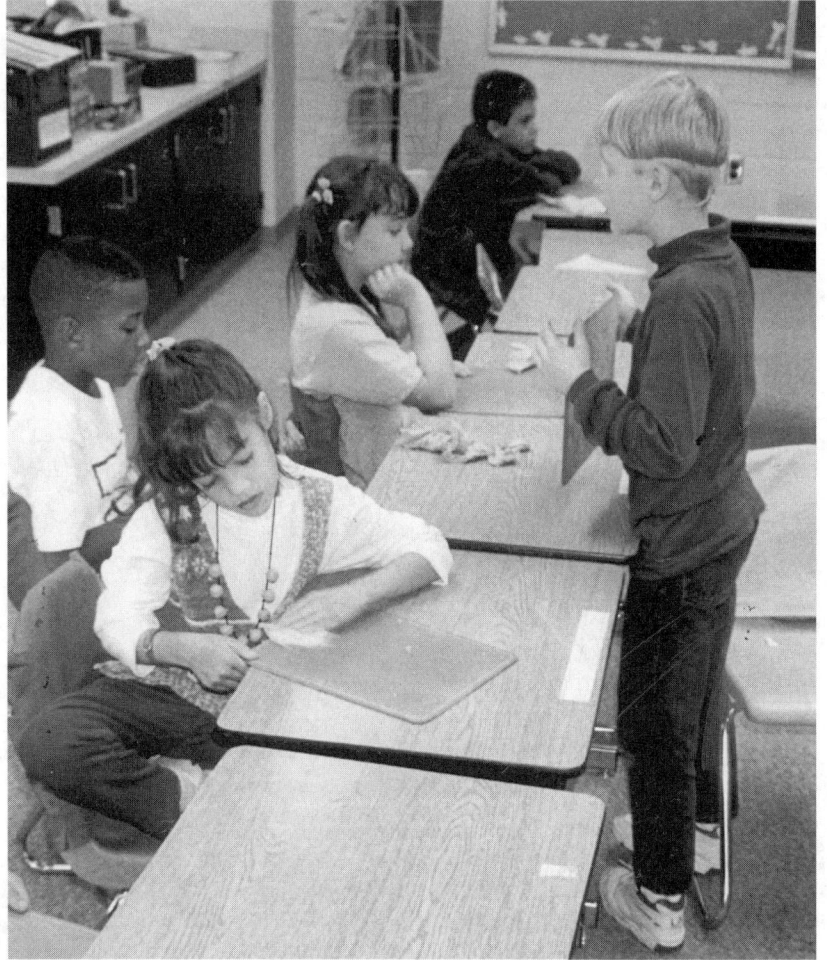

8

Exercises and Activities for Grades 3 Through 5

OVERVIEW

Grade 3 through 5 learners are capable of understanding some of the same concepts, and performing some of the same skills, as students in Grades 6 through 8. For instance, students are able to debate and deliver persuasive speeches. However, learners at the 3 through 5 level may be significantly limited in the range of skills that they can demonstrate simultaneously in one exercise. When this is the case, we have included useful activities from Chapter 9 (for Grades 6 through 8) but have modified the objectives, instructions, and evaluation forms so that they are more appropriate for Grades 3 through 5.

EXERCISE 8.1 DISCRIMINATIVE LISTENING: MARKET STREET MAP ACTIVITY

Objectives:	1. To practice discriminative listening 2. To highlight why good listeners must concentrate on details 3. To practice following directions
Description of Exercise:	Each student should be given a large piece of paper on which a large square or rectangle has been drawn and, next to it, a north–south–east–west compass so that students know the top of the page is north. The rectangle represents a town map about which the teacher will give instructions. Students should be told to follow all instructions carefully. The idea behind this lesson is to discuss why some maps are correctly drawn and some are not.
	Although students are cautioned to follow instructions accurately, some students will assume instructions to mark when there really were none. In particular, instructions 5, 6, and 8 do not ask students to mark anything on their maps. Discuss with students the difference between what is assumed and what is instructed.
	Read the following instructions, asking students to make the appropriate marks on their maps.
Student Instructions:	Pay very careful attention. In the next few minutes you will draw a map using the square on your sheet of paper. The square represents a town. When I tell you to draw a street on your map, use a straight line. When I tell you to draw a building on your map, use a small square. When I tell you to draw a railroad on your map, use a line with little cross-marks on it. Are you ready?

1. Market Street runs east–west through the center of town. Put it on your map and label it.
2. Center Street runs north–south through the center of town. Put it on your map and label it.
3. A railroad runs east–west along the northern edge of town. Put it on your map.
4. Liberty High School is on the southwest corner of town. Put it on your map.
5. Liberty Street runs parallel to Market Street and just north of the school from the edge of town to Center Street.
6. The town library is on the northwest corner of Market and Center.
7. School Street runs north–south along the east side of Liberty High School from the edge of town to Market Street. Put it on your map and label it.
8. The bus stop is on the northeast corner where Center Street crosses the tracks.

Adapted from Hunsacker, R. (1994). In M. Snively (Ed.), *Listening activities for K–12*. Belleville, VA: East Forensics. (p. 46). Reprinted with permission of Morris Snively/East Forensics.

EXERCISE 8.2 EVALUATIVE LISTENING: UNDERSTANDING THE DIFFERENCE BETWEEN REALITY AND FANTASY

Objective:
: To help students learn to distinguish between the concepts of reality and fantasy as expressed orally and visually

Description of Exercise:
: The concepts of reality and fantasy can be introduced by videotaping or audiotaping two commercials. One commerical should use real people and the other should use some cartoon characters or other nonhuman characters. Discuss with the class the difference between the two concepts, using analogy to real people and fantasy people.

Procedures:
: 1. Split the class into two teams. Each student will go to the board and write a response to a single statement. Students should not check the other team's answer before responding. Students list *R* for real and *F* for fantasy.

  2. Read the following sentences and start the game!
     - The boy was as small as your thumb.
     - The sun made the sidewalk very hot.
     - The horse dove off the springboard.
     - The kite followed the boy home.
     - The squirrel carried a nut in its cheek.
     - The room started to spin around.
     - The farmer plowed the fields for planting.
     - The creek overflowed and flooded the house.
     - Dirty clothes were hidden under the bed.
     - The chicken told the farmer she could lay hard-boiled eggs.
     - When the king cut open the pie, birds flew from it.
     - They lived in a two-story house.
     - The duck swam across the lake.
     - Her brother is older than she.
     - It rained all night the day I was born.
     - The water is very cold and dry.
     - The dish ran away with the spoon.
     - The teacher read the class a story.
     - The baseball team scored three runs.
     - The nuns had runs in their stockings.
     - The clothes washed themselves.
     - The sun was so hot she was freezing.

Adapted from Hunsacker, R. (1994, p. 52). Reprinted with permission of Morris Snively/East Forensics.

EXERCISE 8.3   LISTENING ESSAY

Objective:	To practice discriminative listening skills, including taking notes and identifying main ideas
Set-up:	A guest speaker in the classroom, at a schoolwide assembly, or on a field trip; or a fifteen- to thirty-minute videotaped presentation.
Procedures:	1. Students attend an interesting oral presentation of fifteen to thirty minutes or watch one on videotape.
	2. Students act as discriminative listeners as they observe the presentation. They should write down the main ideas of the speaker.
	3. Students write a one- to two-page essay focused on the following topics:
	a. What main ideas did this speaker talk about?
	b. In your opinion, was the speaker a good speaker? Why or why not?

EXERCISE 8.4   THINKING CRITICALLY ABOUT THE MEDIA I

Objective: To practice evaluative listening skills in identifying propaganda techniques and persuasive strategies, including:

- exaggeration
- "weasel words"
- misleading pictures
- leaving out important information
- emotional appeals
- false reasoning

Set-up: This exercise can work in one of two ways: (1) Select a series of full-page magazine advertisements that rely on many of the concepts listed above and mount them on construction paper for use in small groups; or (2) videotape television commercials with the same characteristics for use with the whole class.

Procedures: Students read (in small groups) or watch and listen to the ad (whole class). Ask students to collaborate in their groups, or discuss as a whole class, the reasons that a consumer might have for not trusting the advertiser's message. Ask the class to name as many reasons as they can about why the ad or commercial might be misleading.

Tip for Teacher Preparation: This exercise should follow a short unit on propaganda and persuasive strategies that introduces students to specific propaganda techniques (such as those listed above). Questions to ask students include:

Does the ad exaggerate the benefits of the product?

Does the ad use words that are confusing (that is, "weasel words," small fine print, or quickly spoken submessages, such as "X sold separately. Batteries not included.")?

Does the ad show pictures that are misleading?

Does the ad leave out important information about the product?

Does the ad try to make people feel a certain way? How? Why do you think this is the case?

EXERCISE 8.5   THINKING CRITICALLY ABOUT THE MEDIA II

Objective:	To practice evaluative listening skills
Description of Exercise:	Students will think critically about the persuasive appeals in their favorite television commercials.
Student Instructions:	1. Can you name your favorite television commercial? 2. Why do you like that commercial? How does it make you feel? 3. What are some reasons a person might decide not to buy that product, even though he or she liked the advertisement? this ever happened to you?

EXERCISE 8.6   APPRECIATIVE LISTENING: ORAL HISTORY PROJECT

Objectives:	1. To introduce students to appreciative listening 2. To build respect for others as communicators 3. To learn interesting information about the life of another person
Description of Exercise:	Contact a senior citizen or adult member of the community with a very interesting past. Invite them to come to your class and tell some stories about what it was like when they were growing up, going to school, coming to this country, and so on.
Procedures:	1. Contact senior citizens or adult relatives and community members who are informed of the exercise's purpose and are interested in participating. 2. Discuss with students the concept of oral history and why it is valuable. 3. Students listen to the oral history. 4. Students write an essay about what they learned from the person.

EXERCISE 8.7   SOME SHORT LISTENING ACTIVITIES

Clap, Snap, Stomp
Read a passage aloud to the class and have the students clap their hands every time they hear a certain word. Read the same passage again, only this time add another word for them to identify by snapping fingers. On the third reading, add still another word with the stomp as a response.

Giving Directions
Select several students to present what they would consider accurate directions (no demonstrations) for how to do some mundane, everyday things. Examples of assignments: tie a shoe, walk in swim fins, jump rope without falling, etc. Have someone physically do exactly what is being directed as the information is presented. Separate the giver of directions from the actor so no feedback is allowed or observed.

Summarize, Please
Select a student to summarize what the class has been talking about. Other students should listen for mistakes and add anything that is omitted.

Word of the Day
At the start of the school day, give the day's word to the class. Sometime during the day, that word should be used in a class discussion or presentation. The student who identifies the word should be awarded a special prize.

Picture, Picture
Describe a picture to the class. Do not allow them to see the picture until later. During the description the teacher should insert incorrect bits of information. When the students see the actual picture, they are to discover what was false in the description.

May I Take Your Order?
The class will role-play parts as if they were in a restaurant. Some will be customers and others servers. The customers give the orders to the waiters who must then remember the requests and repeat them to the cook (teacher). Some teachers have even gone so far as to use menus for this project and to decorate the room as if it were a restaurant.

Trail of Sounds
Students should make a map of how to get from their house to the school. On the map, the students should identify as many different sounds they could hear if that route were taken to school on any given day.

Adapted from Hunsacker, R. (1994, p. 54). Reprinted with permission of Morris Snively/East Forensics.

EXERCISE 8.8   WRITING A PURPOSE STATEMENT FOR A SPEECH

Objective:

To practice writing specific purpose statements for a variety of topics

Student Instructions:

A purpose statement is the goal you hope to accomplish with your speech. Today you are going to practice thinking about purpose statements. Write the following topics down on your paper and see if you can think of two or three different purpose statements for each topic (both informative and persuasive).

Topic: Exercise and Health
Topic: The Environment
Topic: Writing
Topic: Music
Topic: Vacationing

Example:

Topic: Sports

1. I want my audience to understand that many sports played in America, such as football, soccer, and baseball, actually came from other countries.
2. I want my audience to know about an athlete I admire very much.
3. I want my audience to learn how to play my favorite sport.

EXERCISE 8.9   VOCAL DELIVERY: ARTICULATION

Tongue Twister Exercise

1. A big baby buggy with rubber buggy bumpers
2. She sells sea shells down by the sea shore
3. Six slim slick slender saplings
4. Eat fresh fried fish free at the fish fry
5. The sixth sheik's sixth sheep's sick
6. Truly rural
7. Strange strategic statistics
8. Lemon liniment
9. Double bubble gum bubbles double

EXERCISE 8.10 CONVERSATION: THE GOLDEN GLOBE OF TRUTH

Objectives:

1. To seek another person's opinion in a communication-friendly manner.
2. To express an opinion in an organized, concise, and straightforward manner
3. To facilitate a conversation both as a listener and as a speaker by making statements that promote the exchange of interpersonal communication

Description of Exercise: The Golden Globe of Truth is useful in several different contexts—as a prelude to formal speaking assignments, improving interpersonal communication, and organizing thoughts on the spot, as is necessary in argumentation and debate. Here, it is used to teach students a variety of basic speaking, critical thinking, and listening skills.

Set-up: Arrange chairs or desks in a large semicircle, if possible. Obtain a large foam rubber (very soft) ball (the size of a volleyball or soccer ball) to use as the "Golden Globe of Truth."

Procedures:

1. Students prepare questions suitable to ask a classmate about that person's opinion of a character's actions in a story, about a favorite game or hobby, or, for older or high-ability learners, about a current events issue. Questions should be phrased in an open-ended, nonjudgmental manner, such as:

   "What is your favorite hobby?" or "Do you think that the city should require pet owners to keep their dogs on leashes at all times?"

   as opposed to:

   "Are you one of these people who plays chess all the time?" or "Don't you think it's unfair that the city requires pet owners to keep their dogs on leashes at all times?"

   It may be helpful to model the right and wrong ways to ask questions (for purposes of this exercise). Students will need adequate time to write down one or two questions. In the alternative, teachers can generate a set of appropriate topics on strips of paper and let students draw topics from a hat. Each student in the class should have a different topic, if possible. A good source of topics might be activities or stories that students have been working on/reading in class that week.

(continued)

EXERCISE 8.10 *Continued*

Procedures:
(Cont.)

2. After students have chosen their questions, the teacher introduces the Golden Globe of Truth and explains that each person who touches the ball will take a turn answering a question posed by a classmate. The teacher explains that the purpose of the exercise is not only to learn how to seek the opinion of another person, but that it is also important to be able to express an opinion using organization and reasoning.

   The teacher explains that in this exercise, when a student is asked to give an opinion, he or she should answer the question and support the answer with one or two reasons. It may be helpful to model the form of an answer, for example:

   Question: "What do you think about violence on television?"

   Answer: "I think there is too much violence on TV because sometimes people get confused about what they see on TV and they might think that violence is the way to solve their problems. I also think that young children who don't have an adult or older brothers and sisters to help explain TV to them might be frightened by what they see on TV."

   Explain that in this exercise there are no right or wrong answers, and encourage students to feel comfortable expressing what they think.

3. A volunteer stands in front of the class so that he or she is able to make eye contact with everyone. Holding the globe, the student asks the audience if anyone has a question to ask. Audience members raise their hands, and the student calls on someone to ask a question. That person asks his or her question, which the teacher may rephrase if necessary. The person holding the globe answers the question with an opinion, using the format modeled earlier. Since the point of the exercise is to learn how to express an opinion and how to seek and respect the opinions of others, there should be no attempt to evaluate the strength or weaknesses of the reasons given in this exercise; it is enough that the student is able to identify and offer them.

4. When a student has finished answering a question, he or she tosses the ball to another classmate (similar to hot potato games) who has not yet taken a turn in front of the class.

EXERCISE 8.10   *Continued*

Tips for Teacher Preparation:	Teachers can adjust this exercise to the maturity and knowledge level of their students. Younger students who know very little about current events can still benefit from the experience of expressing opinions about a story they have read, a favorite game or hobby, or some other relevant topic.

With older students, however, it may be especially important to set ground rules. In particular, students should be instructed not to ask anything that might be embarrassing, and students who are holding the ball may be told that they can pass on a question if they feel uncomfortable answering it.

It is important to carefully monitor this exercise since it involves interpersonal risk-taking and self-disclosure. Allow extra time and be generous with encouragement for shy or apprehensive students, who may benefit greatly from this exercise. Do not pressure a student who appears to be in great distress about participating to do so. There is certainly a balance to be struck. The classroom climate may improve remarkably as the exercise progresses, and it is always possible that a student who is reluctant in the beginning may choose to participate toward the end; but in any event, it is always best not to force participation or to afterwards scold a shy student who did not participate.

Feedback:

This exercise is best left ungraded because of the risks that students are taking in engaging in this kind of self-disclosure. Teachers may, however, reward students when they show respect and tolerance for others and when they demonstrate that they value what others have to say. Listeners can be rewarded with "Good Listener stars" or awards; teachers can make comments to individual speakers that reward their courage in standing up in front of the class; students may be reminded that their comments and questions indicate that they are becoming good communicators and the kind of people that others will be interested in having a conversation with.

Positive feedback in teaching constructive interpersonal communication and any kind of public speaking is at a premium, since peer pressure and common fears about speaking in front of an audience can be very powerful in hindering students' development as confident communicators. Students should never be criticized in front of the class for their answers or questions (with the exception of appropriate discipline for disruptive behavior); instead, the teacher should coach the student through an alternate phrasing of the question or answer in as positive a manner as possible while explaining why a different phrasing might be more appropriate.

EXERCISE 8.11   EXTEMPORANEOUS SPEECH ASSIGNMENT: INFORMATIVE OR PERSUASIVE

Objectives:

1. To practice quick organization of thoughts and supporting materials
2. To develop confidence in expressing ideas before an audience without a prepared manuscript
3. To practice basic delivery skills

Set-up:

Students will need an appropriate place to deliver the speech—one that will allow eye contact with the audience. A podium is not necessary; in fact, we often prohibit our students from using a podium so that they learn to be more conscious of their posture, gestures, and other nonverbal movements.

Procedures:

1. Give students a topic from class discussion or a class unit that is appropriate for a short informative or persuasive speech.
2. Ask them to prepare a list of three ideas related to that topiic.
3. Make available to students a number of interesting reference sources, such as almanacs and encyclopedias (computer-based encyclopedias would work well, too). Ask students to find some interesting information about each of the three ideas.
4. Students stand at their desks or at the front of the room and tell the rest of the class about the three ideas they have—one at a time.

EXERCISE 8.12   PERSUASIVE SPEAKING

Objectives:	1. To introduce students to persuasive speaking 2. To practice impromptu delivery 3. To practice basic delivery
Description of Exercise:	Bring a large number of interesting objects to school, or collect them from your colleagues. Objects should be fun and it helps if they are unrecognizable. Place the objects in a pillowcase. Ask students to reach into the bag and pull out an object. The object they select will become the topic of their speech.
Procedures:	1. Make sure all students have paper. 2. After each student has selected an object, tell them that they are to give a speech to their classmates trying to persuade them to buy the object they picked. Students can make up a name and purpose for their object if they want. Encourage them to have fun and be creative in their planning. 3. Tell students to write two or three reasons why their classmates should buy the object. Use only one sentence for each reason. 4. When everyone has written two or three reasons, students take turns giving short persuasive presentations based on those reasons.

PERSUASIVE SPEAKING EVALUATION

Name: _____   Object/Product: _____

Put a check-plus, a check, or a check-minus mark by the characteristics of this speech and speaker.

Content:

1. _____ This speaker tried to be creative and thoughtful.
2. _____ This speaker thought of two or three reasons classmates should buy the object/product.
3. _____ This speaker explained each of the reasons to the class.
4. _____ This speaker was organized when he or she spoke.

Delivery:

1. _____ This speaker looked directly at the audience.
2. _____ This speaker stood up straight and tall.
3. _____ This speaker used hands, facial expressions, and other kinds of body language to help express himself/herself.
4. _____ This speaker spoke loudly and clearly.

Listening:

1. _____ This listener was courteous and polite when his or her classmates were speaking.
2. _____ This listener used body language and facial expressions to let classmates who were speaking know that the listeners cared.
3. _____ This listener was very patient and paid attention to other peoples' speeches.

EXERCISE 8.13   IMPROMPTU SPEECH ASSIGNMENT

Objectives:	1. To develop organizational skills 2. To practice using a standard speech introduction, body, and conclusion format 3. To develop poise and confidence 4. To practice critical thinking skills under time pressure
Materials Needed:	Small- to medium-sized index cards; enough so that every student has three
Description of Exercise:	Impromptu speeches are especially useful as ungraded exercises that reinforce basic speech structure and delivery concepts. It is important to limit criticism and feedback to these basic concepts, because even the most experienced high school and college students lack control under such limited preparation and delivery circumstances. Instead, consider stressing the basics and encouraging students to be creative with their topics. Making the impromptu speech an exercise in fun will help relieve student expectations that the speech will be a failure if it is not perfect.

Procedures:	1. Distribute no more than three index cards to each student.
	
	2. Tell students that they will have ten minutes to develop a one- or two-point speech on any aspect of the topic they choose. The speech will be less than three minutes in length. Encourage students to be creative and to use examples or facts that they know from personal experience to support their main points. Index cards should state the following:
	  • The specific purpose of the speech (goal for this speech and audience)
	  • The main points
	  • Any ideas they have for supporting each point
	
	3. Students draw their topics from a hat or bag.
	
	4. Students have fifteen minutes to think about their topics and to write down the basic concepts of specific purpose, main points, and supporting materials.
	
	5. Students deliver the speech in front of the class as they are called on by the teacher. It is probably best not to use a podium. Encourage students to use gestures and maintain direct eye contact.

(continued)

EXERCISE 8.13   *Continued*

Ideas for Topics:

1. Make a list of interesting nouns and cut them up into strips of paper. Make sure there are enough words so that each student selects a different word. The words do not have to be light or humorous in nature. Sometimes serious words lend themselves easily to impromptu speeches. Some examples of good words for impromptu topics include:

pollution	computer	respect	youth
sports	health	humor	culture
popcorn	music	frozen food	concrete
grandparents	insects	history	space
rain	friends	candy	theater
best vacation	comics	pets	technology

2. Make a list of interesting quotations, using a popular quotation book. Each student selects and interprets a different quotation.

3. Make a list of interesting self-disclosure questions. It is not necessary to use a different question for each student, but there should be enough different questions to keep things interesting. Examples:

   What is your favorite movie and why?
   If you had a million dollars, how would you spend it, and why?
   Who is the person you admire the most, and why?
   When I grow up, I want to be . . .
   If I could put three things in a time capsule to represent me, they would be . . .

It's important to add the "and why" in order to foster the use of main points and supporting materials.

IMPROMPTU SPEECH EVALUATION

Name: _____

Speech Topic: _____

Length of Speech: _____

Criteria	Comments
EFFORT: Makes a good effort even though topic might be difficult, preparation is limited, or notes are not allowed	
INTRODUCTION: Identifies topic of speech; previews main points	
ORGANIZATION: Main points are clear and distinct; organized	
CONTENT: Adapts to audience; explains main points	
VERBAL DELIVERY: Uses effective rate, pitch, volume; articulates clearly; does not say "uh" "um" very often	
NONVERBAL DELIVERY: Eye contact; gestures; posture	
CONCLUSION: Summary of points; thoughtful ending	

Additional Comments:

EXERCISE 8.14   INTERVIEWING

Objectives:

1. To practice discriminative listening skills
2. To learn more about nonverbal communication skills

Description of Exercise:

Students will interview a classmate about that classmate's use of nonverbal communication skills. Students write a short report using questions generated by the teacher.

Student Instructions:

1. Prepare a set of three or four questions before interviewing your classmate.
   - Describe a time when you used nonverbal skills to express yourself. What happened in that situation?
   - Describe what I would see you doing and saying if I had been there to watch you in that situation.
   - Have you ever experienced a time when you thought you were expressing yourself well with nonverbal skills, but it turned out that the other person misunderstood you? What happened in that situation? What did you do to try and make the person understand?

2. When you interview your classmate, take notes. You will later write a short report about what you learned.

EXERCISE 8.15 SPIRO MOUNDS: OKLAHOMA'S NATIVE AMERICAN HISTORY

Objectives:

1. To acquaint students in Grades 3 through 6 with a part of Oklahoma's heritage

2. To build oral communication competencies in the following contexts:
   a. informing others about an historical event
   b. discussing and interpreting characteristics of another culture
   c. listening as part of an audience to a formal presentation

3. To build the following oral communication competencies:
   a. writing and delivering a formal presentation using a spatial or chronological organizational pattern
   b. discussion skills: description, questioning for clarification, and turn-taking
   c. listening for information and understanding

Resources/Materials:

Student handout, "Spiro Mounds: Prehistoric Gateway . . . Present-Day Enigma," on the two pages following this exercise.

Procedures:

1. Read the adaptation of Don G. Wyckoff and Dennis Peterson's "Spiro Mounds: Prehistoric Gateway... Present-Day Enigma." Either read the story out loud to students, or let them read it for themselves. Discuss unfamiliar vocabulary terms or provide each student with a vocabulary handout like the one that follows the story here.

2. Engage students in a discussion of the material.

3. Divide the class into small groups and assign one or more of the following activities:
   a. Make a model of a Spiro village—include grass roofs and evidence of farming, hunting, and pottery making.
   b. Make a three-dimensional map or chart of the Spiro trade network. Use real materials to illustrate your work.
   c. Pretend you are an archaeologist. Use the classroom as a site. Write an exact description of all you find and then describe how you think these things were used.
   d. Write a story describing your life as a member of the Spiro village. Illustrate your story.
   e. Compare and contrast other mound builders in other parts of the United States and elsewhere.
   f. Corn grinding—use a matate and dried corn.

(continued)

EXERCISE 8.15 *Continued*

4. Have the small groups give presentations to the rest of the class about their projects. The rest of the class asks questions. Stimulate discussion about the small-group projects. Ask students:

How is this similar to your home/life/clothing/food today?

How is this different from your home/life/clothing/food today?

What do you think it would have been like to be a person of your age in this culture?

Adapted and reprinted with permission of Ernestine Hightower (1995), a fourth-grade teacher at Whittier Elementary School, Lawton, Oklahoma.

SPIRO MOUNDS

Prehistoric Gateway . . . Present-Day Enigma

Don G. Wyckoff and Dennis Peterson
Oklahoma Archaeological Survey

The mounds at Spiro, Oklahoma, are some of the most important archaeological remains in the United States. The people of Spiro once had a large trading network, a highly developed religious center, and a political system which controlled the region. Today, the Spiro site and its artifacts are among Oklahoma's richest cultural resources, and the site is Oklahoma's only National Historic Landmark.

The archaeological site at Spiro includes the remains of a village and eleven earthen mounds. Although several different groups of people camped on or near the Spiro area during early prehistoric times, Spiro did not become a permanent settlement until approximately A.D. 600. The permanent settlement was led by a series of priest-chiefs, and its inhabitants constructed mounds and grew corn, beans, and squash.

In 1933, a group of treasure hunters began excavating the largest mound. They discovered many spectacular artifacts, including objects of wood, cloth, copper, shell, basketry and stone. Unfortunately, the diggers were only concerned with finding and selling the relics. They were not interested in preserving the relics or recording information about them. These treasure hunters looted the mounds and sold many important artifacts to people who took them out of Oklahoma. Like pages ripped from a rare book, valuable information about Oklahoma's past was lost forever.

After 1933, another group of archaeologists excavated what was left of the Spiro mounds. They carefully recorded the layers of earth and artifacts, burials, and other features which remained in the Craig Mound. The Craig Mound was the largest and most severely damaged mound. It was 33 feet high and 400 feet long, and was actually four smaller mounds joined together. The Craig Mound was built to cover the graves of the Spiro society's most important leaders.

The Spiro site was one of the most important trading and religious centers of prehistoric America. From its location in a narrow valley of the Arkansas River, the Spiro people were able to control traffic, trade and communications along the river, especially between small villages that were scattered to the south and to the north. Later on, the Spiro people even played a role in controlling trade and information between bison-hunting farmers to the west and farmers in the Southeast.

Some Spiro political and religious leaders also became successful traders. These leaders collected and saved exotic goods which they wore to show their status, and sometimes used in special ceremonies. The Spiro leaders favored exotic goods such as conch shells from western coastal Florida, copper from the Southeast and other regions, lead from Iowa and Missouri, pottery from northeast Arkansas and Tennessee, quartz from central Arkansas and flint from Kansas, Texas, Tennessee and Illinois. Spiro artisans fashioned many of these materials into elaborately decorated ornaments, ceremonial cups, batons and other symbols of status and authority. Among the prehistoric societies, such objects were a sign of wealth, and Spiro's priestly leaders were very wealthy.

Spiro's artisans influenced the ideas and works of many southeastern people. The artisans used conch shells and copper to engrave and emboss pictures of dancing, hunting, warriors, and mythological creatures such as winged serpents, antlered serpents, spiders, and catlike monsters.

(continued)

SPIRO MOUNDS *Continued*

Around A.D. 1250, the Spiro inhabitants began to change their way of life. Some of them abandoned their frontier settlements. Some people completely left northeast Oklahoma. Others began settling along the Grand and Arkansas rivers. Few people continued to live at Spiro, although they lived nearby and visited the mounds for special religious ceremonies. The people who lived near the Spiro site continued to build mounds and to bury more people in Craig Mound. In fact, more than 700 burials have been discovered at Craig Mound.

By A.D. 1450, the priest-chiefs were no longer the centers of political power in Spiro society. Trade and influence among Southeastern chiefdoms had ended; and ritual mound construction at the Spiro site had also ceased. About a hundred years later, Spiro's descendants lived in settlements of small houses scattered along the Arkansas River. The houses had many nearby storage and trash pits. For the first time in their history, the Spiro people hunted bison extensively. They had become part-time hunters and farmers.

Vocabulary

archaeology:	the study of ancient cultures by looking for evidence of their daily activities and settlements
artifacts:	objects made or modified by people, such as arrowheads, pottery, and jewelry, that show how they once lived and what their culture was like
conch:	a type of large seashell, used for ornaments, cups, and other decorative purposes
excavate:	to carefully dig through layers of soil at an ancient site and record information that describes the site and the artifacts that are found there
priest-chief:	the spiritual and political leader of the people
trade network:	a system in which people from different villages and regions of a country exchanged goods for money or other valuables

Adapted from Wyckoff, D. G., & D. Peterson (1995), "Spiro Mounds: Prehistoric Gateway, Present-Day Enigma." Norman, OK: Oklahoma Museum of Natural History. Used with permission.

EXERCISE 8.16   PROPOSING AND DEFENDING A POLICY

Objectives:
1. To think critically to develop a plan of action
2. To think critically about how to defend a plan of action

Procedures:
1. Divide the class into small groups. Assign each group a different hypothetical problem to solve. The problem can be based on a current issue, a topic studied in a thematic unit, or any other area of interest on which the class has been focused.

2. Students must work together cooperatively to develop a plan to solve the problem. As a group, they will decide:
   - how the plan will solve the problem they were asked to solve;
   - why the "pros" of their plan outweigh the "cons";
   - why other possible approaches might not work as well.
   A member of the group should record these agreed-upon statements on a worksheet.

3. The group makes a presentation focused on the three questions listed in #2.

4. After the group has had a chance to present and explain their policy, classmates can ask questions—like a press conference. Members of the policy-making group can use their worksheet as a guide to answering the questions; each member of the policy-making group should try to answer a question.

Tips for Teacher Preparation:
This exercise needs monitoring to make sure that each member of the group has a chance to make significant input into the policy-making process and in responding to questions during the press conference.
   It might be necessary to advise students that when they are in front of the class, the group is responsible for making sure that any member who is speaking can be heard and seen by the rest of the class.

Feedback:
1. *Small-Group Assessment:*   Consider videotaping this exercise and developing a self-assessment exercise for each small group.

2. *Individual Self-Assessment:*   Have students complete a self-assessment exercise, answering questions such as:
   How did you feel when you were in front of the class, presenting and defending your policy?
   What did you like about the answers you gave?
   What advice would you give someone who is about to present a policy to an audience and answer questions about the plan?

EXERCISE 8.17   MASS MEDIA: TEN IDEAS FOR MANUSCRIPT DELIVERY

1. Create a public service announcement about what to do in case of a natural disaster, such as a fire, hurricane, tornado, or thunderstorm.
2. Design an invention and make a model or drawing of it. Create a radio or television advertisement to sell the invention, complete with a persuasive strategy and a jingle.
3. Create a program celebrating a particular culture, describing important symbols, holidays, customs, and clothing; use music, language, and stories from the culture.
4. In teams of four to six, create news broadcasts. Assign each team member a different responsibility, and give each member a total of three or four minutes on the air. It may help to assign two members as news anchors, who take turns reporting on different stories; a sports anchor; a weather anchor; and a series of one or two feature reporters.
5. Develop a "rockumentary"—in small groups, select a popular song and create a video that lasts the length of the song. The video should focus on a theme that is present in the song. Each member of the group should appear in the video.*
6. Hold a competition for the best thirty-second public service video on issues such as drug awareness, staying in school, dangers of cigarette smoking, and nutrition.
7. Create a television tribute to an inspiring person from the community.
8. Create a version of a reader's theater for the radio, complete with sound effects.
9. Create a slide show for the beginning or end of the school year about the school or some of its events, such as spirit week, a winter carnival, or a special guest speaker.
10. Write and deliver a political campaign speech.

* *Note:* This idea was suggested by David A. Wendt, Keokuk High School, Keokuk, IA, during a presentation at the Speech Communication Association Annual Convention, New Orleans, October, 1994.

EXERCISE 8.18   DISCUSSION: THE GOLDBERG TECHNIQUE

The Goldberg technique is a simple and effective way of sparking discussion on any topic. The teacher prepares a list of statements and asks students to rank their level of agreement with the statement. Students then discuss their rankings and the reasons behind them.

For example, in reading a story about animals, a teacher could create a Goldberg scale centered around various issues related to animals.

Cats make better pets than dogs.

Strongly disagree   1   2   3   4   5   6   7   Strongly agree

EXERCISE 8.19　CLASSROOM CONTINUUM

The continuum exercise is reminiscent of the Goldberg discussion technique, although used here it has a narrower purpose in defining points of view rather than exploring and challenging those perspectives. It is particularly helpful in motivating students to take a position on an issue and then explain their reasons for that position.

Objectives:	1. To articulate a point of view on a topic
	2. To evaluate how that point of view might be similar to or dissimilar to another person's point of view on the topic
	3. To appreciate how many different points of view can emerge on one topic
Description of Exercise:	Students will physically form a continuum against a wall in the classroom or hallway that depicts the range of class opinions on a given topic.
Set-up:	An unobstructed wall of a classroom or hallway is required for this exercise. The wall should be long enough so that all students can fit against it if necessary (although this is rarely an outcome).
Procedures:	1. Provide students with a statement or question about a problem or controversy that has been the subject of class-room study. A question should be close-ended. For example, "Should our country spend more money on exploring outer space?"
	2. The teacher marks three places on the wall with pieces of masking tape: an end of the continuum to symbolize strong agreement with the proposition; a middle of the continuum to symbolize neutrality toward the proposition; and an end of the continuum to symbolize strong disagreement with the proposition.
	3. Students are asked to decide whether they agree or disagree with the proposition, and then how strongly they agree or disagree. They should be prepared to explain their rationale to the class.
	4. The teacher calls on students one by one to go up to the wall and stand at the point on the continuum that they feel best expresses their level of agreement or disagreement with the proposition.
	5. After the student has picked a spot on the continuum, he or she explains the reasons for that spot. If the student has picked a spot slightly higher or lower on the continuum than another student, he or she must explain the differences in opinion that resulted in different places on the continuum.
	6. After each student has had a chance to take a place on the continuum, students take their seats. The teacher wraps up the exercise with whole-class discussion.

(continued)

EXERCISE 8.19   *Continued*

Feedback: If you are using a communication journal in your classroom,
                             this exercise would be a good topic for a journal entry. Students
                             can write about how they felt expressing their opinions in front
                             of the class, their reactions to the range of opinions (or lack of
                             range of opinions), and the value of discussing and respecting
                             differences in opinions.

EXERCISE 8.20   GROUP STORYTELLING

Objectives:	1. To encourage group members to accept and build on the ideas of others 2. To build self-esteem 3. To practice active listening skills—in particular, concentration
Description of Exercise:	A brainstorming game that can be used with large or small groups
Set-up:	Students will need enough room to form a circle.
Procedures:	Students stand or sit in a circle. The instructor helps the group choose a theme for a story and begins the game by creating an introductory phrase, which is then passed on to the next person. Going clockwise or counterclockwise, each player adds one word to the story. When someone wants to end a sentence, he or she says "period" and begins a new sentence with a word. The group should work together to keep the story line moving forward.
Tips for Teacher Preparation:	Sentences should be short, and the story told in the third person. After group members become comfortable in their roles, they should be encouraged not to use *and* and *because*. Encourage students to listen carefully to everything!
Variations:	1. A group member points at another person when saying a word, and that person then speaks and points. 2. Group members stand in a line, facing out. Each player steps forward and gives a phrase or sentence; stops (and can stop in mid-phrase or sentence) and steps back; another player must take the initiative to step forward and continue the story exactly where the previous player stopped, even if in mid-word. Players need to constantly move the story line forward. 3. Teacher directs the story by choosing a style of story, such as a fairy tale, murder mystery, or adventure; pointing to individual group members to indicate that it is their turn to speak; and cutting off speakers to point to a new speaker.

Adapted from a similar exercise by Spolin, V. (1986). In A. Morey & M. A. Brandt (Eds.), *Theatre games for the classroom: A teacher's handbook.* Evanston, IL: Northwestern University Press. Reprinted with permission.

EXERCISE 8.21 STORYTELLING: FAMILY COAT OF ARMS

Objectives:

1. To use pictures to symbolize meaning
2. To tell a story to an audience
3. To practice basic delivery

Description of Exercise: Students will create a family coat of arms using symbols to represent four topics about their families. Students will give a short oral presentation to the class explaining their coats of arms.

Student Instructions:

1. Using a large piece of posterboard and markers, draw a family coat of arms. Your coat of arms should have four symbols on it:
   a. a symbol that represents what your family means to you
   b. a symbol that represents where you and your closest family members live
   c. a symbol that represents a funny event in your family history
   d. a symbol that represents you

2. In front of the class, explain each of the symbols in your coat of arms, one at a time.

3. Write a short report about your coat of arms for your portfolio.

EXERCISE 8.22   STORYTELLING: SIGNS

Objectives:
1. To understand signs
2. To explain how signs are used to convey meaning
3. To explain how human nonverbal behavior conveys meaning

Description of Exercise:
Students will work cooperatively to create a group collage that is focused on an assigned topic. The pictures in the collage can come from a collection of old magazines or other photo resources. Students will need art supplies for making a simple collage on posterboard.

Procedure:
1. Discuss with students the concept of a sign: a sign is a picture or something else that represents a thought or message. Ask students to think about signs in their community. Talk about what those signs mean.

2. Divide students into groups of three or four. Give each group a topic, such as:

Expressing happiness	Expressing friendship
Taking care of other people	Reminding people about safety
Expressing authority	Celebrating holidays

3. Instruct students to look through the magazine or photo collection for pictures (words would be okay if they are part of a larger picture) that relate to their group's topic.

4. Students make a collage using the pictures.

5. Students deliver a short presentation about their collage.

6. Ask each group some of the following questions:

When you were looking for pictures about your topic, did you think of some ways that people express their thoughts on this topic that don't involve speaking or writing?

Do you use signs to express yourself sometimes? What are they?

EXERCISE 8.23   INFORMATIVE CULTURAL HERITAGE SPEECH

Length: Three to four minutes

Objectives: 1. To provide a low-key atmosphere for an introductory
                                     speech
                                  2. To demonstrate the usefulness of an interview for collect-
                                     ing supporting material
                                  3. To bring about a greater understanding of our cultural
                                     backgrounds

Student Instructions: 1. Choose an aspect of your cultural heritage to research,
                                     such as a cultural tradition your family keeps, the origins
                                     of your family name, or an experience that you had living
                                     in your native country that tells the class something about
                                     your country.
                                  2. Interview a family member or other person familiar with
                                     your cultural heritage. Tape-record the interview or take
                                     very good notes about the person's answers.
                                  3. Use the information from your interview to write a short
                                     speech. Describe your cultural heritage; tell about any
                                     new facts or interesting information you learned; talk about
                                     a goal you might set for yourself to learn even more about
                                     your cultural heritage.

EXERCISE 8.24   ORAL INTERPRETATION: MULTICULTURAL STORIES

Objectives:

1. To learn something new and valuable about another culture
2. To creatively interpret a story for an audience
3. To enhance verbal and nonverbal delivery skills
4. To practice appreciative listening skills

Description of Exercise: Students will research short stories, narrative poems, or other short forms of literature produced by a particular culture and present an oral interpretation of that literature to the class or another audience.

Procedures:

1. Students locate an authentic short work of literature from a country or culture of their choice (alternatively, teachers can assign different cultures or can allow students to choose their assignment from a hat).

2. Teacher makes a photocopy of the story so that it can be marked on and eventually cut up and pasted onto separate sheets of paper.

3. Students should prepare a *cutting* of the story or poem that is suitable for an oral interpretation presentation. A cutting begins by marking up the story: placing brackets around the most interesting material, crossing out passages or sentences that are too long or too pastoral and thus unsuited for an interesting reading-aloud. Transitions between main ideas should be preserved or modified. Give students these tips for making effective cuts:

   • The entire story does not have to be told in the oral interpretation—only a sequence that is long enough to convey a main idea or two while preserving the authenticity of the story.

   • Oral interpretation tends to be more interesting if it is made up of characters' voices, rather than told by a third-person narrator. Dialogue is thus always a good choice for a cutting, although it may be difficult to interpret more than two or three characters.

   • Try to end the story in a way that resolves any tension or conflict that arose in an earlier part of the cutting.

   • Separately, prepare a short introduction (maybe two or three sentences) that describes the general theme of the story, the major characters involved, and orients the audience to the place and time at which the cutting begins. Similarly, a conclusion may be prepared if necessary to bring closure to the piece.

(continued)

EXERCISE 8.24   *Continued*

4. Students physically cut and paste the script pieces together onto new sheets of paper or write out the new version of the story. Put these sheets into a notebook of some sort that is easy to hold open in one hand while turning the pages with the other hand.

5. Now the student is ready to begin practicing the oral interpretation. The student should stand up straight on both feet, face the audience squarely, and begin the presentation with the notebook closed and held neatly, parallel to the floor (not hugged close to the body), in both hands. The student should recite the introduction from memory, then open the notebook, turn to the front page, and begin the oral interpretation. The student should be as dramatic and creative as possible with voice, facial expressions, shoulder movements, and gestures from the free arm. Some students may even want to develop distinct character voices and accents native to the culture.

6. After practicing for several days, hold a classroom performance. Consider inviting parents, other classes and grades of students.

Feedback: Consider awarding prizes; have the class vote on the top three presentations. Consider videotaping the performances; consider including tapes of the performances and the cuttings in a student portfolio.

MULTICULTURAL ORAL INTERPRETATION EVALUATION

Name: _____

Oral Interpretation of: _____

Criteria	Comments	Points
ATTITUDE: Student shows interest and effort in researching the story. Prepares the cutting thoughtfully; practices to achieve excellence; willing to be creative.		/10
SELECTION: The selection is an authentic example of literature from a unique perspective. The story is challenging and interesting. The story imparts new information about the culture to the audience.		/15
CUTTING: The cutting meets time and content requirements; is interesting and effective as a script. The introduction and conclusion are concise and helpful overall.		/20
PRACTICE: The student diligently practiced the script to develop a polished presentation.		/15
DELIVERY: Delivery was polished and showed use of a variety of vocal skills. Gestures and facial expression enhanced the dramatic content of the presentation.		/25
AUDIENCE ADAPTATION: The oral interpretation is creatively and thoughtfully designed for the enrichment of the audience.		/15

Additional Comments:

9

Exercises and Activities for Grades 6 Through 8

OVERVIEW

Middle or junior high school is an exciting time to challenge students with exercises that explore group and interpersonal communication, intercultural communication, debate, and impromptu speaking. Empathic and evaluative listening skills can dramatically improve at this level. The exercises in this chapter can be used in multiple learning situations: across the curriculum, as supplements to language arts units, or as stand-alone communication skills lessons. Many of the exercises integrate reading, writing, speaking, and listening.

EXERCISE 9.1   EXPERIENCING THE IMPACT OF LISTENING BEHAVIOR

1. Create a selection of large name tags, perhaps with construction paper or index cards, and use a dark marker to write the following instructions on the tags:

   Tell me I'm wrong.
   Ignore me.
   Interrupt me.
   Agree with me.
   Ask me a follow-up question.
   Ask me to tell you more.
   Laugh at everything I say.
   Look away from me.
   Give me advice.
   Make a lot of nonverbal noise when I talk.
   Summarize what I say.
   Act very interested in what I am saying.
   Smile at me and nod your head.
   Applaud when I finish speaking.

2. Divide students into manageable groups. Have the groups sit in circles, so that everyone in a group can see and hear the others in the group. Give each student in a group a different tag. Tell students not to look at their own tags. A small piece of tape is usually sufficient to attach the tag to clothing.

3. Explain that the purpose of the exercise is to understand how different listening behaviors can have a positive or negative effect on communication. It is important to mention that some students may experience some uncomfortable or surprising feelings. This is normal and they will be asked to tell the rest of the class about it shortly.

4. Give students an interesting question to talk about, such as "What is your favorite movie, and why?" Tell students that there will be a group discussion on this question for about ten minutes and that every person in the group should take a turn answering the question. While that group member is talking, the other group members should respond to them according to the instructions on the speaker's name tag.

5. Start the discussion and allow it to continue for at least ten minutes, long enough to ensure that all students have had a chance to talk. Walk around and monitor the groups.

6. End the small-group discussion. Students may take their tags off and look at them now. Begin a whole-class discussion on the following topics:

   How did you feel when listeners responded to you?
   Have you ever noticed people using this behavior in real life when they listen?
   Would you say that particular listening behavior has a positive or negative effect on communication? Why or why not?
   What changes do you think you might make in your own listening behavior because of this exercise?
   What listening behaviors do you like that people use in real life?
   What do you like about your own listening behavior?
   How do you think it is best to handle unpleasant feelings when people behave negatively in real life?

EXERCISE 9.2   A (WRITTEN) DISCRIMINATIVE LISTENING ASSESSMENT

Objectives:

1. To assess knowledge of active listening concepts, including
   a. distinguishing between discriminative, evaluative, empathic, and evaluative listening
   b. identifying the specific purpose of the speaker
2. To practice discriminative listening skills, including
   a. identifying the main point(s) previewed by the speaker
   b. identifying specific information used to explain at least one main point
   c. formulating some questions to ask the speaker about the topic

Set-up:

Videotape a short, interesting news segment (needs to be strictly informative) that focuses on one topic only. The segment should preview the topic of the segment and should list one or two points or subpoints that are supported by additional information. A clip from a documentary or how-to feature might also work well, but it is important to make sure that the clip previews the topic and any main points that will come later in the program. It is also important to show at least one of the main points as it is being developed in the presentation (see Tips for Teacher Preparation for helpful hints).

Use a television and VCR to play it back for the class. Rearrange desks, if necessary, to make sure that all students can see the video segment.

Procedures:

Give students the handout that follows. Ask them to read the instructions at the top of the handout along with you. After everyone understands the instructions, play the video segment two or three times so that students have a chance to absorb it. Encourage the class to remain quiet while you are rewinding and replaying the video.

Tips for Teacher Preparation:

Omit or add other questions depending on the concepts you have discussed in your listening instruction. It may help to determine the questions you would like to ask first and then look for a video segment that provides material for each question.

Often, "how-to" videos that you can check out from the school or public library work well for this assessment. Most commercially produced how-to videos have short introductions that preview the topic and the main points, and most feature transitions between main points. You can fast forward as you need or edit the clip to get the information you need for the assessment.

DISCRIMINATIVE LISTENING ASSESSMENT—PRACTICING ACTIVE LISTENING

In the next few minutes you will watch and listen to a video. I will play it several times for you so that everyone has a chance to hear and understand it fully. While you are watching and listening to the video, you may take notes on the piece of scratch paper. After you have had a chance to hear the video several times, I will turn off the television and you will have time to write answers to the following questions. Let's read the questions together now, so that you will know what to listen for when I play the commercial.

Question 1:   Which of the types of active listening that we have discussed in class should a listener use during this video?

Question 2:   What are two or three main points described in this presentation?

Question 3:   Can you give an example of something the speaker said that was used to help explain a main point?

Question 4:   If one of your friends wanted to learn about [this topic] would you recommend watching this video? Why or why not?

Answer to Question 1:   Discriminative (or a combination of discriminative and appreciative). The student's response should indicate recognition that the main purpose of the presentation is to inform the audience about the topic/steps in the process, and so on; but the student may also point out that sometimes people listen to these sorts of presentations because they want to expand their knowledge or increase their enjoyment of life—hence, appreciative listening.

EXERCISE 9.3   A (WRITTEN) EVALUATIVE LISTENING AUTHENTIC ASSESSMENT

Objectives:
1. To assess knowledge of active listening concepts:
   a. distinguishing between discriminative, evaluative, and empathic listening
   b. identifying common persuasive strategies
   c. identifying specific reasoning patterns
2. To assess application of evaluative listening skills:
   a. determining the purpose of the speaker's message
   b. analyzing an argument made by the speaker using the Toulmin model of argument (see Chapter 3)
   c. evaluating the strength of the logic in the persuasive message
   d. determining appropriate decision-making response to a persuasive message

Set-up:
Video tape an interesting thirty- or sixty-second television advertisement. Use a television and VCR to play it back for the class. Rearrange desks, if necessary, to make sure that all students can see the commercial.

Procedures:
Give students the student handout. Ask them to read the instructions at the top of the handout along with you. After everyone understands the instructions, play the commercial two or three times so that students have a chance to absorb it. Encourage the class to remain quiet while you are rewinding and replaying the commercial.

Tips for Teacher Preparation:
Omit or add other questions depending on the concepts you have discussed in your listening instruction. It may help to determine the questions you would like to ask first and then look for an advertisement that provides material for each question. We've found that political campaign advertisements are especially effective for this assessment.

EVALUATIVE LISTENING ASSESSMENT—PRACTICING ACTIVE LISTENING

In the next few minutes you will watch and listen to a videotape of a television commercial. I will play the commercial several times for you so that everyone has a chance to hear and understand it fully. While you are watching and listening to the commercial, you may take notes on the piece of scratch paper. After you have had a chance to hear the commercial several times, I will turn off the television and you will have time to write answers to the following questions. Let's read the questions together now, so that you will know what to listen for when I play the commercial.

Question 1: Which of the types of active listening that we have discussed in class should a listener use when watching this commercial?

Question 2: Using the Toulmin model, identify an argument in the advertisement that includes a claim, evidence, and warrant.

> HINT: Remember that in the Toulmin model of argument, a *claim* is a statement or depiction of reality, that the speaker (or advertiser) wants the audience to believe. *Evidence* can take the form of facts or images that the speaker uses as support for the claim. A *warrant* is the reasoning or logical assumptions stated or implied by the advertiser.
>
> Claim:
>
> Evidence:
>
> Warrant:

Question 3: Can you name some propaganda techniques used by the ad that we discussed in class?

Question 4: Does the advertiser use images in the ad to try and persuade you? If so, can you explain why those images might be persuasive?

Question 5: What advice would you give to a younger brother or sister about whether or not to do what the ad says?

Answer to Question 1:   Evaluative; although students are also correct if they suggest a combination of evaluative and discriminative. In general, the answer should suggest that the student recognizes the persuasive purpose of the advertisement and recognizes that the claims made by the advertisement must be evaluated before taking action.

EXERCISE 9.4   LISTENING ESSAY

Objectives:	1. To practice evaluative listening skills, such as identifying persuasive strategies and propaganda techniques 2. To practice organizing thoughts and supporting an opinion
Set-up:	A guest speaker in the classroom, at a schoolwide assembly, or on a field trip; or a fifteen- to thirty-minute videotaped presentation or television broadcast (presidential campaign speeches are great for this exercise, as are infomercials), using a TV and VCR in the classroom.
Procedures:	1. Students attend a persuasive oral presentation of fifteen to thirty minutes or watch one on videotape. 2. Students act as evaluative listeners as they observe the presentation. They may take notes if they wish. 3. Students write a three- to five-page essay focused on the following topics: a. What was the persuasive message delivered by the speaker? b. What were the main points of the presentation? c. In your opinion, was the speaker effective? Why or why not? d. Explain how the speaker's use of (or failure to use) reasoning, evidence, emotional appeals, good physical and vocal delivery, or other communication characteristics influenced your opinion.
Tips for Teacher Preparation:	When choosing a speaker and topic for this exercise, select a topic that: a. students can easily understand; b. will interest students; and c. is open to a critical analysis with respect to both content and delivery.
Feedback:	Grade this essay as you would any other, based on the essay requirements of the assessment.

EXERCISE 9.5   THINKING CRITICALLY ABOUT THE MEDIA

Objective:	To practice evaluative listening skills
Description of Exercise:	Students will think critically about the persuasive appeals in their favorite television commercials.
Student Instructions:	1. On an index card, write down your favorite television commercial. 2. Think and write down your response: Does the commercial persuade you? Inspire you? Make you feel good about yourself? 3. Apply one principle of persuasion that makes this commercial effective.

EXERCISE 9.6   APPRECIATIVE LISTENING: ORAL HISTORY PROJECT

Objectives:	1. To introduce students to appreciative listening 2. To build respect for others as communicators 3. To learn interesting information about the life of another person
Description of Exercise:	Students will interview an adult (preferably, a senior citizen) using interview questions that they have constructed. This exercise can be a wonderful way to increase pride in one's culture or heritage.
Procedures:	1. Locate senior citizens or adult relatives and community members who are informed of the exercise purpose and are interested in participating. 2. Discuss with students the concept of oral history and why it is valuable. 3. Assign a different adult to each student. Assist students in developing two or three appropriate, open-ended questions that invite the adult to tell a story about their past or to recount a sequence of events from their memory and perception of history. 4. Introduce students to efficient note-taking techniques. 5. Students interview the adult outside of class. 6. Students write an essay about what they learned from the person.

EXERCISE 9.7   WRITING A PURPOSE STATEMENT FOR A SPEECH

Objective: To practice writing specific purpose statements for a variety of topics

Student Instructions: Topics for speeches are listed below. Think of three different specific purpose statements that you could use to develop each topic into a speech.

    Topic: Exercise and Health
    Topic: The Environment
    Topic: Writing
    Topic: Music
    Topic: Vacationing

Example:

Topic: Sports

1. I want my audience to understand that many sports played in the United States, such as football, soccer, and baseball, actually were adapted from sports played in other countries.
2. I want my audience to know how to treat some common sports injuries, such as a twisted ankle, shin splints, and cramps.
3. I want my audience to support drug testing for all Olympic athletes.

EXERCISE 9.8   PERSUASIVE OR INFORMATIVE SPEECH: FULL-SENTENCE OUTLINE ASSIGNMENT

Good speakers begin their preparation with a full-sentence outline. When you are writing your outline, use the following format:

Purpose Statement: A *purpose statement* describes the specific goal you wish to achieve in your speech. An example of a purpose statement is:

> "The purpose of my speech is to inform my audience about basic first aid techniques."

Introduction: Do you remember these key principles of a strong speech *introduction?* Check them off one by one as you finish putting them into your outline:

_____ *Attention-getting question, anecdote, quotation, or statistic.* For instance:
> "What would you do if someone nearby was choking and couldn't breathe?"

_____ *Central idea.* An example of a central idea is:
> "You can learn three basic first aid tips that can save a person's life in an emergency."

_____ *Preview statement* listing your main points. An example of a preview statement is:

> "In the next few minutes, I will demonstrate three basic first-aid tips: first, what to do if someone is choking; choking; second, what to do if you suspect a baby has swallowed something poisonous; and third, how to to temporarily stop a wound from bleeding until help arrives."

Body: The *body* of the speech includes the *main points* as well as *supporting materials.* Your speech should have between two and five main points and should have at least one or two pieces of supporting material for each point. Example:

    I. Main point
       A. Supporting material
       B. Supporting material

Conclusion: Do you remember these key elements of a *conclusion?* Check them off as you include them in your outline:

_____ *Summary* of main ideas

_____ A memorable *ending* thought

EXERCISE 9.9   SPEECH CONTENT CHECKLIST

For all speeches in this class, including the impromptu speeches you will be giving throughout the session, use this checklist.

1. Does your speech introduction:

    _____ clearly state the topic of the speech?

    _____ catch the audience's attention?

    _____ establish credibility (if necessary)?

    _____ preview the main points in the order in which they will appear?

2. Does the body of your speech have:

    _____ clear, distinct main points?

    _____ transitions into the main points?

    _____ an organizational pattern, such as one of the following, that fits the purpose of your speech?

       spatial
       topical
       chronological
       problem–solution
       cause–effect

    _____ properly cited, credible supporting materials, FOR EACH MAIN POINT?

       For example, "According to the June 3, 1996, issue of *Digest Magazine*, more than 300 whales are killed annually by illegal whaling ships."

    _____ use language that includes everyone in your audience and is respectful toward them?

3. Does your speech conclusion:

    _____ clearly end the speech?

    _____ summarize the main points (in the same order in which they were presented)?

    _____ end in a thoughtful and memorable way?

EXERCISE 9.10   VOCAL DELIVERY: ARTICULATION

Tongue Twister Exercise

1. A big baby buggy with rubber buggy bumpers
2. She sells sea shells down by the sea shore
3. Six slim slick slender saplings
4. Eat fresh fried fish free at the fish fry
5. The sixth sheik's sixth sheep's sick
6. Truly rural
7. Strange strategic statistics
8. Lemon liniment
9. Double bubble gum bubbles double

EXERCISE 9.11   STAGE FRIGHT

On three-by-five-inch cards, students write their biggest fears about speaking in front of the class. Collect the cards and redistribute them. One student goes up to the front of the class, shares what is on his or her card, gives a response with problem-solving advice for that fear, then leads the group in any further suggestions. This exercise helps students see that others have the same feelings and anxieties that they do about speaking in public. Most will feel reassured.

EXERCISE 9.12   AN EXTEMPORANEOUS SPEECH ASSIGNMENT: INFORMATIVE OR PERSUASIVE

Objectives:
1. To practice quick organization of thoughts and supporting materials
2. To develop confidence in expressing ideas before an audience without a prepared manuscript
3. To practice basic delivery skills

Set-up:
Students will need an appropriate place to deliver the speech—one that will allow eye contact with the audience. A podium is not necessary; in fact, we often prohibit our students from using a podium so that they learn to be more conscious of their posture, gestures, and other nonverbal movements.

Student: Instructions:
1. Select a current event topic that is appropriate for an informative or persuasive speech.
2. Take a position on the topic and prepare a rough three-point analysis explaining and advocating the position (persuasive speech). Determine three points to share with the audience about the topic (informative speech).
3. Collect two or three newspaper or magazine articles and use facts, testimony, or illustrative examples from them to help support points. Any and all sources must be cited in the speech, whether quoted directly or paraphrased.
4. Prepare a speaker's outline of the speech on index cards. Encourage students to use four-by-six-inch cards—they will hold more handwritten information and are easier to reference during the presentation.
5. Practice the speech at least three times from the outline. Time the speech to make sure that it is between three and five minutes.
6. If it is longer, look for areas to pare down—perhaps the introduction—or take out an entire point, if necessary.
7. Deliver the speech to the class from the outline.

Tips for Teacher Preparation:
In spite of the fact that most speakers in real life use an extemporaneous method, the stereotype of a well-delivered public speech is one that is delivered completely from memory or read from behind a podium from a manuscript. For this reason, it may be necessary to manage both your own and student expectations by exploring the differences between manuscript or memorized delivery and extemporaneous delivery (see Chapter 3).

Feedback:
This exercise can be graded or ungraded. For ungraded speeches, consider using a holistic evaluation form combined with a peer or self-evaluation form. For an informative extemporaneous speech, use an atomistic evaluation form; for a persuasive extemporaneous speech, use an atomistic evaluation form or perhaps a holistic form (see examples in Chapter 5).

EXERCISE 9.13   INFORMATIVE SPEECH ASSIGNMENT

The purpose of the informative speech is to provide the audience with new information. The goal is to create awareness of your subject matter and to increase audience knowledge concerning your topic. Be certain that your speech is *not* persuasive.

1. Select an appropriate topic for your audience. Selecting a topic with which you have some personal connection or interest is often helpful in establishing credibility. You may want to choose a topic because you find it intriguing and believe your audience will also. Avoid trivial topics such as building sandcastles or distinguishing between brands of toothpaste.

2. This speech will require you to do research. If you select a topic about which you have personal knowledge, such as how to play a violin, you must still supplement your personal knowledge with outside information. This may include statistics on the number of people who attend orchestra concerts every year, testimonial evidence about which companies or individuals make the best quality violins, and so on. You must incorporate the sources for information you cite within the text of the speech as you present it. For example, "According to the May 23, 1992, issue of *Orchestra World* magazine . . ."

3. Clear your topic and any visual aids with me prior to the speech.

4. The presentation must be four to five minutes in length. Grades will be lowered for speeches which do not meet the time requirements or that extend beyond five-and-a-half minutes in length.

5. Use a speaker's outline, rather than writing the speech word-for-word, on index cards. It is often helpful to write directions to yourself on your speaker's outline, such as "smile," "eye contact," "gesture," or "slow down."

EXERCISE 9.14   EDITORIAL SPEECH ASSIGNMENT

Objectives:
1. To learn about persuasive appeals
2. To practice offering persuasive appeals
3. To practice refuting persuasive appeals

Student Instructions:
1. Locate a recent editorial in a newspaper or magazine, or tape one from a radio or television station, with which you disagree.

    Make sure that the author is clearly making a persuasive appeal. A persuasive appeal asks the reader to take a particular course of action, or adopt or maintain a belief about a controversial issue.

    Sometimes, editorials are entertaining or informative, but they may not include a persuasive appeal to the reader. If you have a question about whether your editorial has a persuasive appeal, ask me and we will figure it out together.

2. Read or analyze the editorial. See if you can identify the persuasive appeal, the reasons offered by the author to support his or her appeal, and the evidence used by the author to support his or her reasons.

    Remember that evidence can include quotations, statistics, examples, and short anecdotes or stories.

3. After you have read the editorial, prepare a two-point speech that meets the following requirements:
    a. Length
       Your speech must be three to five minutes in length. Practice in front of someone who will time you so that you meet this criteria.
    b. Introduction
       1. Catch the audience's attention.
       2. Introduce the thesis statement—that you disagree with the persuasive appeal of the editorial.
       3. Preview the two main points (see below, Body).
    c. Body
       1. *Point one:* Describe the persuasive appeal of the editorial. Use subpoints to show how the author supported the appeal with reasoning and evidence.
       2. *Point two:* Explain why you disagree with the persuasive appeal made by the author.
    d. Conclusion
       1. Summarize.
       2. End thoughtfully.
    e. Delivery
       Deliver the speech from notecards, using an outline.

EDITORIAL SPEECH EVALUATION

Name: _____

Topic: _____

Length of Speech: _____

Criteria	Comments	Points
TOPIC: Interesting editorial topic, appropriate for audience; persuasive purpose		/ 5
INTRODUCTION: Catches audience's attention, identifies topic of speech, previews main points		/ 15
ORGANIZATION: Main points are clear, subpoints are clear, uses transitions		/ 15
CONTENT: Identifies and explains reasons for disagreement with appeal, cites sources (if used), refers to the text of the editorial, adapts to audience		/ 20
VERBAL DELIVERY: Uses effective rate, pitch, volume; articulates clearly; does not say "uh" or "um" very often		/ 15
NONVERBAL DELIVERY: Uses outline on notecards; eye contact; gestures; posture		/ 15
CONCLUSION: Summary of points; thoughtful ending		/ 15

Additional Comments:

EXERCISE 9.15   IMPROMPTU SPEECH ASSIGNMENT

Objectives:
1. To develop organizational skills
2. To practice using a standard speech introduction, body, and conclusion format
3. To develop poise and confidence
4. To practice critical thinking skills under time pressure

Materials Needed: Small- to medium-sized index cards (enough that every student can have three)

Description of Exercise: Impromptu speeches are especially useful as ungraded exercises that reinforce basic speech structure and delivery concepts. It is important to limit criticism and feedback to these basic concepts since even the most experienced high school and college students lack control under such limited preparation and delivery circumstances. Instead, consider stressing the basics and encouraging students to be creative with their topics. Making the impromptu speech an exercise in fun will help relieve student expectations that the speech will be a failure if it is not perfect.

Procedures:
1. Distribute no more than three index cards to each student.

2. Tell students that they will have ten minutes to develop a two- or three-point speech on any aspect of the topic they choose. The speech will be less than three minutes in length. Encourage students to be creative and to use examples or facts that they know from personal experience to support their main points. Index cards should state the following:
   - The specific purpose of the speech
   - The preview statement
   - Each main point and an idea or two for supporting the point

3. Students draw their topics from a hat or bag. (See ideas for topics under Tips for Teacher Preparation.)

4. Students have ten minutes to think about their topics and to write down the basic concepts of specific purpose, central idea, preview statement, main points, and supporting materials.

5. Students deliver the speech in front of the class as they are called on by the teacher. It is probably best not to use a podium. Encourage students to use gestures and maintain direct eye contact.

(continued)

EXERCISE 9.15   *Continued*

Tips for Teacher
Preparation:

There are several interesting ways to assign impromptu
speeches:

1. Bring a pillowcase full of interesting objects to school. These
   can be objects that may or may not be recognizable to students. Ask students to pick an object out of the bag that will
   serve as their topic. They should try to persuade the audience to buy the object. They can name it, make up uses for
   it, or tell stories about it. Of course, every student's specific
   purpose will be phrased as, "My specific purpose is to persuade the audience to buy this [thingamabob]."

2. Make a list of interesting nouns and cut them up into strips
   of paper. Make sure there are enough words so that each
   student selects a different word. The words do not have to
   be light or humorous in nature. Sometimes serious words
   lend themselves easily to impromptu speeches.

   Some examples of good words for impromptu topics
   include:

pollution	computers	respect	youth
sports	health	humor	culture
popcorn	music	frozen food	concrete
grandparents	insects	history	space
rain	friends	candy	theater
best vacation	comics	pets	technology

3. Make a list of interesting quotations, using a popular quotation book. Each student selects and interprets a different
   quotation.

4. Make a list of interesting self-disclosure questions. It is not
   necessary to use a different question for each student, but
   there should be enough different questions to keep things
   interesting.

   Examples:

   What is your favorite movie, and why?

   In your opinion, what is the greatest problem facing
   America today, and why?

   If you had a million dollars, how would you spend it,
   and why?

   Who is the person you admire the most, and why?

   It's important to add the "and why" in order to foster the
   use of main points and supporting materials.

EXERCISE 9.15 *Continued*

5. Make a list of statements and ask students to agree or disagree with the statement.

   Examples:

   People should be allowed to burn the American flag if they are engaging in nonviolent protest.

   There should be tougher penalties for people convicted of drunk driving.

   Our city should have a mandatory recycling program for its offices

   Endangered species should be protected, even if it means that land can't be used for buildings and other investment purposes.

   There are forms of extraterrestrial life.

Feedback:

1. Consider using an ungraded, holistic speech evaluation (see example in Chapter 5).
2. After each student has spoken, ask them to remain standing in front of the class for a moment. Then, ask for class volunteers to identify two or three things the speaker did really well. Do not ask the class for negative comments on this assignment. Save those for the evaluation form.
3. Consider holding a round of impromptu speeches without an evaluation form, limiting feedback to positive comments from the class. Then hold a final round of impromptu speeches, after which you address some of the skills and concepts that you feel the class, as a whole, could improve on.

IMPROMPTU SPEECH EVALUATION—UNGRADED

Name: _____

Speech Topic: _____

Length of Speech: _____

Criteria	Comments
EFFORT: Makes a good effort even though topic might be difficult, preparation is limited, or notes are not allowed	
INTRODUCTION: Catches audience's attention, identifies topic of speech, previews main points	
ORGANIZATION: Main points are clear and distinct, organized with an appropriate pattern, preceded by transitions	
CONTENT: Adapts to audience, supports main points with examples; cites sources as appropriate	
VERBAL DELIVERY: Uses effective rate, pitch, volume; articulates clearly; does not say "uh" or "um" very often	
NONVERBAL DELIVERY: Eye contact; gestures; posture; stayed within time limits	
CONCLUSION: Summary of points; thoughtful ending	

Additional Comments:

EXERCISE 9.16   INTERVIEWING

In this exercise, students will role-play the interview process. Everyone in the class will play one of two roles: (1) a representative of a not-for-profit organization that needs to hire people for the positions listed below, or (2) an applicant for one of the positions. Use the four student handouts that follow as guidelines for the class.

About the Organization

Youth for a Better America is a not-for-profit organization whose purpose is to enrich the lives of young people by providing free recreational activities, art and music lessons, and classes about such topics as pet care, fashion, and woodworking.

Youth for a Better America was founded five years ago by a generous millionaire who left enough funds for the organization to continue its activities and expand its facilities well into the twenty-first century.

Unfortunately, Youth for a Better America has had trouble attracting young people to its services, largely because of ineffective publicity. It also needs to add to its physical equipment and expand its facilities, but no one on the current board of directors seems to have any ideas on how to do this. A final concern is the need to increase the number of activities.

In order to help achieve these goals, Youth for a Better America is hiring people to fill the following positions:

Public Relations Manager: The public relations manager will write press releases and help generate new marketing strategies to increase the public's familiarity with Youth for a Better America. Must possess strong written and oral communication skills. Work or volunteer experience in community organizations a plus. Must be able to get along well with other people. Must be creative and energetic.

Physical Plant Manager: The physical plant manager will be responsible for purchasing and maintaining equipment used by Youth for a Better America. He or she will also make recommendations to the board of directors about how to expand the facilities to meet the needs of more people. Experience in working with recreational and/or landscaping equipment preferred. Creative, efficient, technically talented person needed.

Activities Coordinator: The activities coordinator will plan and coordinate all the activities that take place at Youth for a Better America. Academic, work, or volunteer experience involving community service, planning for entertainment, or counseling preferred. Person must be very organized and must have some ideas for new recreational activities for young people. Will supervise staff of volunteers.

INSTRUCTIONS FOR INTERVIEWERS

In real life, interviewers have a tough job. They must evaluate whether a person is suited for a job on the basis of that person's resume and an interview. Unfortunately, most interviews are only about twenty-minutes long, and interviewers must choose between many qualified candidates.

Interviewers with strong communication skills are more likely to pick the right person for the job because they are more likely to ask insightful questions, listen carefully to the responses, and ask follow-up questions. These good communication skills help interviewers form an accurate picture of an applicants' potential.

Your Responsibilities:

Before the interview, prepare a list of at least five initial questions to ask the applicant. You will have the benefit of reviewing the applicant's resume before the interview.

During the interview, greet the applicant and give them a compliment about their resume to help make them feel comfortable. Then you may begin to ask questions. Take notes during the interview and ask follow-up questions every now and then. The applicant may also have some questions for you about the job or about the company. If you do not know the answers to these questions, just improvise. At the close of the interview, thank the applicant for coming in. Let the applicant know when you expect to make a decision and shake the applicant's hand.

After the interview, evaluate the applicant's interview performance using the form provided for you.

Tips: 1. Use open-ended questions that allow the applicant to give a quality answer. Try not to ask questions that can be answered with a simple yes-or-no response.
2. Try to ask questions that allow the applicant to talk about his or her strengths and why he or she might be right for the job.
3. Try to ask at least one challenging question that the applicant might not be expecting, like, "What would you do if, while you were in this job, . . ."
4. Remember to use active listening skills!

INSTRUCTIONS FOR JOB APPLICANTS

Interviewing is a very challenging process. Job applicants are evaluated on their skills, education, work experience, and other positive attributes. They may be competing with many other qualified applicants, but only one may be hired for the position. In addition, most interviews are actually only twenty- to thirty-minutes long, which is not very much time to get to know an applicant.

However, good communication skills can help a job applicant move successfully through the interviewing process. Successful interviewees use good active listening skills, give thoughtful answers, and ask questions that show their interest in the position or the company itself.

You will be trying to convince the interviewer that you are the best person for the job.

Your Responsibilities:

Before the interview, decide to apply for one of the three positions. Think about your strengths and positive attributes. Fill out the resume using as many facts about your life as possible. If you would like to add some hypothetical experiences or activities in order to fit the job description better, feel free to do that as long as you are prepared to talk about those experiences or activities in the interview. Your resume will be collected and given to your assigned interviewer. You will be allowed to keep a copy of it.

During the interview, greet the interviewer with a handshake. When answering the interviewer's questions, try to respond in a way that tells the interviewer about the kind of person you are by referring to your strengths and positive attributes and to the experiences and activities you wrote about on your resume. Ask a few questions about the job and/or the organization to show that you are truly interested in the position. At the close of the interview, shake hands with the interviewer and thank him or her for meeting with you.

After the interview, evaluate the interviewer using the form provided for you.

HOW TO PREPARE APPLICANT'S RESUME

_____
Name

_____
Street Address

_____
City, State, Zip Code

Education

_____
Date   Favorite School Subjects   School Name

_____
Date   Favorite School Subjects   School Name

Work or Volunteer Experience

_____
Dates   Position Held   Company Name   Location

Description
_____
_____

_____
Dates   Position Held   Company Name   Location

Description
_____
_____

_____
Dates   Position Held   Company Name   Location

Description
_____
_____

Hobbies and Activities

_____
_____

Special Skills

_____
_____

EVALUATING THE INTERVIEWEE

Applicant: _____   Interviewer: _____

Write about your interviewing experience by answering the following questions.

1. Circle the topics that you think the applicant discussed with the most confidence during the interview:

   academic interests or achievements

   volunteer or work experience

   hobbies and activities

   leadership abilities

2. What verbal or nonverbal characteristics impressed you the most about the applicant?

   _____ Personality: friendly, easy to have a conversation with

   _____ Verbal expression: good at answering and asking questions

   _____ Poise: seemed relaxed, calm, confident

   _____ Listening: good at listening while you were speaking and asking follow-up questions

   _____ Turn-taking: helped maintain the flow of the interview; did not interrupt, but asked questions or elaborated on answers without your prompting

3. Describe at least two of the strengths of this applicant as an interviewee. If you can, use examples from the interview itself.

4. What is one way that the applicant could become an even stronger interviewee? If you can, use examples from the interview itself.

EVALUATING THE INTERVIEWER

Applicant: _____   Interviewer: _____

Write about your interviewing experience by answering the following questions:

1. Circle the topic areas that the interviewer asked you about:

   academic interests or achievements

   volunteer or work experience

   hobbies and activities

   leadership abilities

2. What verbal or nonverbal characteristics impressed you most about the interviewer?

   _____ Personality: friendly, easy to have a conversation with

   _____ Verbal expression: good at answering and asking questions

   _____ Poise: seemed relaxed, calm, confident

   _____ Listening: good at listening while you were speaking and asking follow-up questions

   _____ Turn-taking: helped maintain the flow of the interview; did not interrupt, but asked questions or elaborated on answers without your prompting.

3. Describe at least two strengths of the interviewer. If you can, use examples from the interview itself.

4. What is one question that you wished the interviewer had asked, but didn't? Why do you think this question would have been helpful?

EXERCISE 9.17   PROPOSING AND DEFENDING A POLICY

Objectives:

1. To think critically to develop a plan of action
2. To think critically about how to defend a plan of action

Procedures:

1. Divide the class into small groups. Assign each group a different hypothetical problem to solve. The problem can be based on a current issue, a topic studied in a thematic unit, or any other area of interest on which the class has been focused.

2. Students must work together cooperatively to develop a plan to solve the problem. As a group, they will decide on statements that address the following issues:

   • The nature and extent of the problem they were asked to solve
   • How the policy will solve the problem they were asked to solve
   • The advantages and disadvantages of the policy, and why the advantages outweigh the disadvantages
   • Why they decided on this policy as opposed to other possible approaches

   A member of the group should record these agreed-on statements on a worksheet.

3. The group next issues a press release about the policy that briefly summarizes the problem they were asked to address and further explains the policy. The press release does not have to address the other issues listed in #2 above.

4. Distribute the press release to one of the other small groups. That group will use the press release to formulate questions about the policy. Every small group thus serves as a policy maker/defender and as journalists/questioners. Questions should focus on the advantages and disadvantages of the policy, why it should prevail over other alternatives, and other strengths and weaknesses of the policy.

5. The groups hold press conferences.

   Presentation of the policy.   Each small group takes a turn presenting its policy to the class. One or two people in the group make a brief presentation, explaining <u>only</u>:
   a. the problem they were asked to solve, and
   b. how the policy they designed will solve the problem.

   Defense of the policy.   After the group has presented and explained their policy, the journalists ask questions. Members of the policy-making group can use their worksheet as a guide when answering the questions; each member of the policy-making group should try to answer a question.

   (continued)

EXERCISE 9.17   *Continued*

Tips for Teacher Preparation:

This exercise needs monitoring to make sure that each member of the group has a chance to make significant input into the policy-making process and in responding to questions during the press conference. It might be necessary to advise students that when they are in front of the class, the group is responsible for making sure that any member who is speaking can be heard and seen by the rest of the class.

Feedback:

1. Consider videotaping this exercise and developing a self-assessment exercise for each small group.

2. Questions to use for individual self-assessment include:

How did you feel when you were in front of the class presenting and defending your policy?

What did you like about the answers you gave?

What new insights emerged as a result of your group's discussion?

Based on your group's experience in policy-making, have your perceptions of politicians and community leaders changed or remained the same? Why?

What advice would you give someone who is about to participate in a press conference?

EXERCISE 9.18   MASS MEDIA I

TEN IDEAS FOR MANUSCRIPT DELIVERY

1. Create a public service announcement about what to do in case of a natural disaster, such as a fire, hurricane, tornado, or thunderstorm.

2. Design an invention and make a model or drawing of it. Create a radio or television advertisement to sell the invention, complete with a persuasive strategy and a jingle.

3. Create a program celebrating a particular culture, describing important symbols, holidays, customs, and clothing, and using music, language, and stories from the culture.

4. In teams of four to six, create news broadcasts. Assign each team member a different responsibility, and give each member a total of three or four minutes on the air. It may help to assign two members as news anchors, who take turns reporting on different stories; a sports anchor; a weather anchor; and a series of one or two feature reporters.

5. Develop a "rockumentary"—in small groups, select a popular song and create a video that lasts the length of the song. The video should focus on a theme that is present in the song. Each member of the group should appear in the video.*

6. Hold a competition for the best thirty-second public service video on issues such as drug awareness, staying in school, dangers of cigarette smoking, and nutrition.

7. Create a television tribute to an inspiring person from the community.

8. Create a version of a reader's theater for the radio, complete with sound effects.

9. Create a slide show for the beginning or end of the school year about the school or some of its events, such as spirit week, a winter carnival, or a special guest speaker.

10. Write and deliver a political campaign speech.

Note: This idea was suggested by David A. Wendt, Keokuk High School, Keokuk, IA, during a presentation at the Speech Communication Association Annual Convention, New Orleans, October, 1994.

EXERCISE 9.19   MASS MEDIA II

TEN IDEAS FOR EXTEMPORANEOUS
OR IMPROMPTU DELIVERY

1. Design a talk show about an important community, school, or national issue, complete with a talk show host, commercials, and guests who improvise their roles.

2. Create and record a panel discussion on an important topic that allows more than one point of view. Each member of the panel must develop and discuss the issue from a distinct point of view. This exercise may require research. One or two students should serve as moderators.

3. A variation on the above panel discussion is a debate among several presidential candidates, with several journalists serving as moderators.

4. Interview a member of the school administration or a community activist about an important issue. Develop a series of questions in advance; but during the interview, ask follow-up questions. After the interview, record introductory and closing comments to create a complete program.

5. Record an oral history of a time in your family history or a favorite family story.

6. Create a fifteen-minute radio program featuring music, public service announcements, and news.

7. Interview a member of the class about an essay or story that he or she wrote.

8. Videotape and call a school sports event.

9. Hold a press conference about a topic discussed in a thematic unit. Some students represent a hypothetical organization reporting on the topic, and others represent journalists asking questions. Still other students create feature stories based on what they heard at the press conference.

10. Create an awards show, complete with emcees and presenters, for class awards at the end of the year.

EXERCISE 9.20   EXPRESSING AND JUSTIFYING OPINIONS: THE GOLDEN GLOBE OF TRUTH

Objectives:

1. To seek seek another person's opinion in a communication-friendly manner
2. To express an opinion in an organized, concise, and straightforward manner
3. To facilitate a conversation both as a listener and as a speaker by making statements that promote the exchange of interpersonal communication

Description of Exercise:

Students prepare short, impromptu opinion statements for presentation to the class. A large foam rubber ball serves as a "hot potato" that determines turn-taking. This exercise is useful in several different contexts—as a prelude to formal speaking assignments, improving interpersonal communication, and organizing thoughts on the spot as is necessary in argumentation and debate. Here, it is used to teach students a variety of basic speaking, critical thinking, and listening skills.

Set-up:

Arrange chairs or desks in a large semicircle, if possible. Obtain a large foam rubber (very soft) ball (the size of a volleyball or soccer ball) to use as the "Golden Globe of Truth."

Procedures:

1. Students prepare questions suitable to ask a classmate about that person's opinion of a current event issue. Questions should be phrased in an open-ended, nonjudgmental manner, such as:

    "What do you think about violence on television?"
    or "Do you think our president is doing a good job?"

    as opposed to:

    "Don't you think kids our age should be allowed to watch whatever they want on television, even if it's violent?"

    or

    "You don't think our mayor is doing a good job, do you?"

    HINT: It may be helpful to model the right and wrong ways to ask questions. In the alternative, generate a set of current event topics on strips of paper and let students draw them from a hat. Each student in the class should have a different topic, if possible. Some suggested topics are:

    What is the most important social issue in America right now?

(continued)

EXERCISE 9.20 *Continued*

Would you rather live in the country or city, and why?
What would you say if you could talk to the President of the United States?
What do you think is the most important environmental issue right now?

2. After students have chosen their questions, introduce the Golden Globe of Truth and explain that each person who touches the ball will take a turn answering a question posed by a classmate. Explain that the purpose of the exercise is to learn how to seek the opinion of another person and to express an opinion using organization and reasoning.

Further explain that students should phrase the opinion as a direct response to the question and support it with one or two reasons. It may be helpful to model an answer:

Question: "What do you think about violence on television?"

Answer: "I think there is too much violence on TV, because sometimes people get confused about what they see on TV and they think that violence is the way to solve their problems. I also think that young children who don't have an adult or older brothers and sisters to help explain TV to them might be frightened by what they see on TV."

In this exercise, there are no right or wrong answers. Encourage students to feel comfortable expressing what they think.

3. A volunteer stands in front of the class so that he or she is able to make eye contact with everyone. Holding the globe, the student asks the audience if anyone has a question. Audience members raise their hands, and the student calls on someone to ask a question. That person asks their question, which the teacher may rephrase if necessary. The person holding the globe answers the question with an opinion, using the special format.

4. When a student has finished answering a question, he or she tosses the ball (similar to hot potato games) to another classmate who has not yet taken a turn in front of the class.

Tips for Teacher Preparation:

Teachers can adjust this exercise to the maturity and knowledge level of their students. Younger students who know very little about current events can still benefit from the

EXERCISE 9.20   *Continued*

experience of expressing opinions about a story they have read, a favorite game or hobby, or some other relevant topic.

With older students, however, it may be especially important to set ground rules. In particular, students should be instructed not to ask anything that might be embarrassing, and students who are holding the ball may be told that they can pass on a question if they feel uncomfortable answering it.

It is important to carefully monitor this exercise since it involves interpersonal risk-taking and self-disclosure. Allow extra time and be generous with encouragement for shy or apprehensive students, who may benefit greatly from this exercise. Do not pressure a student, who appears to be in great distress about participating, to do so. There is certainly a balance to be struck. The classroom climate may improve remarkably as the exercise progresses, and it is always possible that a student who is reluctant in the beginning may choose to participate toward the end; but in any event, it is always best not to force participation, or to afterwards scold a shy student who did not participate.

Feedback:

This exercise is best left ungraded because of the risks that students are taking with this kind of self-disclosure. Teachers may, however, reward students when they show respect and tolerance for others and when they demonstrate that they value what others have to say. Teachers can make comments to individual speakers that reward their courage in standing up in front of class; students may be reminded that their comments and questions indicate that they are becoming good communicators and the kind of people that others will be interested in having a conversation with.

Since the point of the exercise is to learn how to express an opinion and how to seek and respect the opinions of others, there should be no attempt to evaluate the strength or weaknesses of the reasons given in this exercise; it is enough that the student is able to form an opinion and share it with the class.

It is important to give positive feedback when teaching interpersonal communication and public speaking because peer pressure and common fears about speaking in front of an audience can be very powerful in hindering students' development as confident communicators.

EXERCISE 9.21   GROUP DISCUSSION AND PROBLEM-SOLVING EXERCISE: THE FOUR D'S

An effective discussion tool is the creation of a hypothetical scenario that deliberately evokes the critical issues necessary for discussion. A carefully crafted "case study" can stimulate a focused discussion if the *Four D's* are employed in creating the hypothetical scenario.

Define the issue—Isolate a critical issue or two that needs to be discussed.

Dramatize—Imagine you are writing a short story when creating the case study. Use details to intrigue the audience. What happened? When did the event take place? Who was involved? Where did the event happen? There must be a plot that builds to the discussion point.

Dialogue—Consider creating dialogue between the characters, or sharing a character's internal thoughts.

Discuss—Students play roles in order to create interesting insights in the discussion. Some suggested roles are characters in the scenario, friends of the characters, expert witnesses, and so on.

EXERCISE 9.22   DISCUSSION: THE GOLDBERG TECHNIQUE

The Goldberg technique is a simple and effective way of sparking discussion on any topic. The teacher prepares a list of statements and asks students to rank their level of agreement with the statement. Students then discuss their rankings and the reasons behind them.

For example, in beginning a unit on drug abuse and drug awareness, a teacher could create a Goldberg scale centered around the various misconceptions about drugs and addictive personalities.

Initial exploration into drugs is usually encouraged by low self-esteem.

Strongly disagree   1   2   3   4   5   6   7   Strongly agree

EXERCISE 9.23   CLASSROOM CONTINUUM

The continuum exercise is reminiscent of the Goldberg discussion technique, although used here it has a narrower purpose in defining points of view rather than exploring and challenging those perspectives. It is particularly helpful in motivating students to take a position on an issue and then explain their reasons for that position.

Objectives:	1. To articulate a point of view on a topic
	2. To evaluate how that point of view might be similar to or dissimilar to another person's point of view on the topic
	3. To appreciate how many different points of view can emerge on one topic
Description of Exercise:	Students will physically form a continuum against a wall in the classroom or hallway that depicts the range of class opinions on a given topic
Set-up:	An unobstructed wall of a classroom or hallway is required for this exercise. The wall should be long enough so that all students can fit against it if necessary (although this is rarely an outcome).
Procedures:	1. Provide students with a statement or question about a problem or controversy that has been the subject of classroom study. A question should be close-ended. For example, "Should our neighborhood have a mandatory 10 P.M. curfew for teens?" An analogous statement would be phrased so that students can agree or disagree with it: "Our neighborhood should have a mandatory 10 P.M. curfew for teens."
	2. The teacher marks three places on the wall with pieces of masking tape: an end of the continuum to symbolize strong agreement with the proposition; a middle of the continuum to symbolize neutrality toward the proposition; and an end of the continuum to symbolize strong disagreement with the proposition.
	3. Students are asked to determine whether they agree or disagree with the proposition, and then to decide how strongly they agree or disagree. They should be prepared to explain their rationale to the class.
	4. The teacher calls on students one by one to go up to the wall and stand at the point on the continuum that they feel best expresses their level of agreement or disagreement with the proposition.
	5. After the student has picked a spot on the continuum, he or she explains the reasons for that spot. If the student has picked a spot slightly higher or lower on the con-

(continued)

EXERCISE 9.23   *Continued*

tinuum than another student, he or she must explain the differences in opinion that resulted in different places on the continuum.

6. After each student has had a chance to take a place on the continuum, students take their seats. The teacher wraps up the exercise with a whole-class discussion.

Feedback: If you are using a communication journal in your classroom, this exercise would be a good topic for a journal entry. Students can write about how they felt expressing their opinions in front of the class, their reactions to the range of opinions (or lack of range of opinions), and the value of discussing and respecting differences in opinions.

EXERCISE 9.24   NOMINAL-GROUP TECHNIQUE

The strength of the nominal-group technique is that it encourages students to think "laterally" as opposed to "vertically" about a problem and solution. This technique can be very effective at eliciting participation from quieter students.

1. The teacher (for whole class) or a student group leader (for small groups) offers a discussion question.
2. Students generate written lists of ideas, silently and independently.
3. The facilitator asks each participant to offer one idea from his or her list. Each idea is recorded on a chalkboard or flip chart. The process continues until all participants have shared all ideas or agree that a sufficient number of ideas have been introduced.
4. Students rank the ideas. Once a vote is tallied, then the teacher or group leader decides how to direct the discussion around the highest-ranking ideas.

Nominal-group technique can be used for both whole-class and small-group discussion. If initiated with the whole class, the teacher can form groups to deal more specifically with the top ten ideas. For example, a class of fifty might come up with some form of a top ten list and then break into groups of five assigned to one of the topics listed.

Adapted with permission from a similar exercise by Richard K. Olsen (1995), Regent University, Virginia Beach, VA.

EXERCISE 9.25   SELF-MODERATING DISCUSSION

In this exercise, students are responsible for holding a discussion and generating ideas about a text. The teacher plays a very minimal role as facilitator in guiding students to stay focused on the topic.

Objectives:

1. To build meaning from a text through the exchange of ideas
2. To practice turn-taking
3. To foster attitudes of respect for the opinions and ideas of others

Description of Exercise: This exercise is constructed around a text of some sort that students are currently studying. The group maintains a self-moderating discussion, using a set of guidelines.

Set-up: Seat students and teacher in a circle. A small- to medium-sized class can interact as a whole class; if not, divide the class into two or three groups, and assign a student facilitator for each group.

Procedures:

1. Select a thought-provoking text or portion of a text that students are currently studying. The text can be a document, a photograph or piece of artwork, a short story, a poem, or an essay. Be creative.

2. Formulate an open-ended question that is not too broad or too narrow. The question might be about a conclusion, purpose, intended meaning of the author/artist, or about something that is described in the text itself.

3. Give each student a copy of the following guidelines:
   - Everyone in the group is responsible for maintaining the discussion.
   - When you want to make a comment or raise a question for further thought, take initiative to do so.
   - Listen carefully and thoughtfully to what others are saying in the group.
   - Expand on or disagree with an idea, but do not address the person who stated the idea, and keep the idea open for discussion by others. Try not to start your sentences with the pronoun "I." Instead, try to refer to the idea you are working with first. For instance, "This idea sounds like something else I saw in the text . . ." or "That point of view reminds me of . . ."
   - Whenever possible, use material from the text to support your points.
   - If there are people in your group who have not contributed, ask them what they think about a particular

EXERCISE 9.25 *Continued*

idea. Remember, everyone is responsible for the discussion, and that means making sure that everyone feels comfortable participating. It is not a discussion if only a few people do all the talking.

- Be courteous and do not interrupt each other. It is okay if there are a few seconds of silence between ideas. Use it to think.
- Compare the ideas in your discussion with what you have learned or already know from other experiences or studies.

4. Begin the discussion by asking the question. As the discussion progresses, the only role played by the facilitator (teacher or student) should be to ask the group to take a moment to review the guidelines, if the discussion seems to become personal or a few group members dominate the discussion or remain silent.

5. After everyone in the group appears to have contributed meaningfully to the discussion, close and evaluate the exercise, using the following form as a model.

A GENERAL EVALUATION FOR THE GROUP PARTICIPANT

Name: _____ Discussion Topic: _____

Rate the participant using one of the following:
   5 = superior   4 = excellent   3 = average   2 = below average   1 = poor

Criteria	Rating
1. *Attitude.* Objective, open-minded, willing to modify views when presented with new evidence	_____
2. *Knowledge.* Understood the issue under discussion, showed skill in introducing information about the topic	_____
3. *Thinking.* Analyzed the issue for discussion well, able to develop relationships between ideas	_____
4. *Listening.* Kept track of the discussion and comments made by others, avoided obviously irrelevant or repetitive contributions	_____
5. *Speaking.* Expressed ideas clearly, clarified confusing or vague comments	_____
6. *Spontaneity.* Reacted to what was happening at the time, did not merely recite pre-prepared remarks	_____
7. *Consideration.* Was courteous of others, disagreed without being disagreeable, avoided dominating the discussion, interested in helping the group achieve its goal	_____

Additional Comments:

EXERCISE 9.26   PANEL DISCUSSION

Objectives:

1. To learn how to phrase a question for group discussion
2. To research and prepare an effective panel presentation
3. To practice turn-taking skills in the context of a panel discussion
4. To practice using research to support a point of view

Description of Exercise:

Student groups will conduct an investigation of topics related to their school, community, or state. Each group will write a discussion question that is broad enough to elicit as many points of view on the topic as possible and will research and prepare a panel discussion to explore those points of view. One student from each group will serve as a moderator.

Procedures:

1. Each group must pick a problem in their school, community, or state that is specific, controversial, and timely. The problem area must be one that can be fully researched to uncover several different points of view.

2. Groups write a discussion question that will be the focus of the group's investigation. The question should follow these guidelines:
   - Phrased so that it clearly identifies the problem
   - Phrased so that it provides the widest possible variety of answers
   - Phrased as succinctly as possible in clear, neutral language

   Present the question in writing to the teacher, with a list of preliminary resources and a short statement explaining why the group thinks the question is worth discussing.

3. Panel presentation, twenty to thirty minutes

   Responsibilities of the group: Develop an outline of the presentation. A successful group:
   - Researches the topic thoroughly and shares information
   - Encourages each other and works well together to create a successful presentation
   - Carefully describes the nature, extent, effects, and so on, of the problem
   - Discusses several possible solutions
   - Describes and justifies a criteria for evaluating the solutions
   - Explains the group's opinion as to which solutions might be the best
   - Develops audio/visual aids

(continued)

EXERCISE 9.26 *Continued*

Responsibilities of individual panel participants:
- Know and stick to the outline of the presentation
- Contribute frequently
- Keep contributions focused and brief
- Take turns by asserting yourself, but also be sensitive to others on the panel
- Listen carefully and critically
- Be fully prepared to discuss information relevant to your topic

Responsibilities of moderator:
- Begins presentation of panel by giving an introduction that captures audience attention, states the question for discussion, introduces the panelists, gives a brief overview of the main points to be discussed, and makes a transition into the discussion
- During the presentation, asks questions to facilitate the flow of the discussion, clarify comments made, and probe for additional details; balances communication among group members; keeps the group on its agenda
- Closes the presentation by summarizing and bringing the presentation to an end

Adapted and reprinted with permission from an exercise by John T. Morello (1995), Mary Washington College, Fredericksburg, VA.

PEER EVALUATION OF PANEL PRESENTATION

Group: _____

Topic: _____

Put a *check mark* by the features of this group presentation that you thought were effective. Put a *question mark* by the features of this group presentation that you thought needed more work.

_____ Approached the topic in a thought-provoking way

_____ Began the presentation with an introduction that made me interested in the topic

_____ Clearly stated and explored the discussion question

_____ Clearly indicated each main point of the presentation

_____ Presented material in a clear and interesting way

_____ Supported each panelist's points with interesting and useful supporting material

_____ Organized and easy to follow

_____ Ended with a good summary

_____ Tried to relate the presentation to the audience

- -

THIS PART OF THE FORM WILL BE DETACHED BEFORE IT IS GIVEN TO THE PANEL

Evaluator's name:

Adapted and reprinted with permission from an exercise by John T. Morello (1995), Mary Washington College, Fredericksburg, VA.

TEACHER EVALUATION OF PANEL PRESENTATION

Group: _____

Topic: _____

   5 = excellent   4 = good   3 = average   2 = below average   1 = poor

Criteria	Rating
1. The group's central topic was clearly stated; group stuck to it.	_____
2. Panelists explained their ideas clearly.	_____
3. Comments by panelists were relevant to the point under discussion at the time.	_____
4. Panelists spoke enthusiastically.	_____
5. There was a suitable balance of participation among panelists.	_____
6. Panelists' points were developed with interesting and relevant supporting materials.	_____
7. Panelists evaluated information, rather than merely presenting a series of facts or opinions.	_____
8. Visual and other presentational aids were well designed and enhanced the presentation; used when appropriate.	_____
9. Panel presentation was organized and easy to follow.	_____
10. The panel reached some kind of a conclusion about what to do, and the conclusion reached was clearly communicated during the presentation.	_____

Comments:

Adapted and reprinted with permission from an exercise by John T. Morello (1995), Mary Washington College, Fredericksburg, VA.

EXERCISE 9.27   GROUP STORYTELLING

Objectives:	1. To encourage group members to accept and build on the ideas of others 2. To build self-esteem 3. To practice active listening skills—in particular, concentration
Description of Exercise:	A brainstorming game that can be used with large or small groups
Set-up:	Students will need enough room to form a circle.
Procedures:	Students stand or sit in a circle. The instructor helps the group choose a theme for a story and begins the game by creating an introductory phrase, which he or she then passes on to the next person. Going clockwise or counterclockwise, each player adds one word to the story. When someone wants to end a sentence, he or she says "period" and begins a new sentence with a word. The group should work together to keep the story line moving forward.
Tips for Teacher Preparation:	Sentences should be short, and the story told in the third person. After group members become comfortable in their roles, they should be encouraged not to use *and* and *because*. Encourage students to listen carefully to everything!
Variations:	1. A group member points at another person when saying a word, and that person then speaks and points. 2. Group members stand in a line, facing out. Each player steps forward and gives a phrase or sentence; stops (and can stop in mid-phrase or sentence) and steps back; another player must take initiative to step forward and continue the story exactly where the previous player stopped, even if in mid-word. Players need to constantly move the story line forward. 3. Teacher directs the story by choosing a style of story, such as a fairy tale, murder mystery, or adventure; pointing to individual group members to indicate that it is their turn to speak; and cutting off speakers to point to a new speaker.

Adapted from a similar exercise by Spolin, V. (1986). In A. Morey and M. Brandt (Eds.), *Theatre games for the classroom: A teacher's handbook*. Evanston, IL: Northwestern University Press. Reprinted with permission of Northwestern University Press.

EXERCISE 9.28   GROUP BRAINSTORMING

Objectives:	1. To foster appreciation for new ideas
	2. To practice brainstorming ideas in a group by building on each other's ideas
Description of Exercise:	Student "marketing" groups will invent a product, its packaging, and its sales strategy.
Procedures:	1. In a class of more than twenty students, divide the class into two groups (the groups will take turns brainstorming while the other group listens and observes). This exercise will work equally well with one group, however, for smaller classes.

2. One group stands in a semicircle in front of the second group, which sits (or stands) and observes.

3. The teacher gives the brainstorming group a problem to solve—creating a consumer good or service. The group is to brainstorm what this good or service might be, how it will be packaged, and how it will be marketed to the public.

4. Brainstorming begins with one group member, who volunteers a *general* idea for a good or service, such as "We could sell food." The student that is clockwise or counterclockwise builds on that idea by starting with "Yes, and . . . ." For example:

   "Yes, and it could be a hot dog."

   Next student: "Yes, and it could be an extra long hot dog."

   Next student: "Yes, and we could sell all kinds of odd ingredients for it."

   Next student: "Yes, and they could be hot peppers and whipped cream."

   It matters little that the ideas may be nonsensical or not feasible—the purpose is to encourage creativity and to purposefully delay the evaluation process until after the brainstorming has been completed. Teachers should keep the brainstorming going at a fast pace.

5. When the first group has completed its brainstorming (allow about five or ten minutes), it changes places with the observing group. That group begins the brainstorming process.

EXERCISE 9.28   *Continued*

6. When both groups have had a chance to brainstorm, discuss the experience as a class. Some questions for discussion include:

What did you learn about the brainstorming process?

If this had been a brainstorming session for a real product or service, what do think would be a good next step?

Why do you think it might be important to suspend judgment of ideas until after the brainstorming process is over?

How did you feel at the beginning of the exercise?

How did you feel at the end?

Adapted from a similar exercise by Spolin, V. (1986). In A. Morey and M. Brandt (Eds.), *Theatre games for the classroom: A teacher's handbook.* Evanston, IL: Northwestern University Press. Reprinted with permission of Northwestern University Press.

EXERCISE 9.29   INFORMATIVE CULTURAL HERITAGE SPEECH

Length:

Three to four minutes

Objectives:

1. To provide a low-key atmosphere for an introductory speech
2. To demonstrate the usefulness of an interview for collecting supporting material
3. To bring about greater understanding of our cultural backgrounds

Student Instructions:

1. Choose an aspect of your cultural heritage to research by focusing on your membership in a particular ethnic or cultural group. You might want to examine different cultural traditions that you maintain, the origins of your family name, or why you have lost the connection with your specific cultural heritage. These are only suggestions for focus.
2. Interview a family member or other person familiar with your cultural heritage, asking them prepared questions about your topic. Tape-record the interview or take very good notes about the person's answers.
3. Use the information you uncover in the interview, along with other research, to write your speech. In your presentation, you should describe your cultural heritage, explain the insights you have gained, and relate your information back to the audience.

Minimum Requirements:

1. The speech must be between three and four minutes in length, give or take some seconds. Practice and time your speech beforehand.
2. The speech must contain specific references to your interview, explaining who you interviewed and why.
3. The speech must contain at least one additional non-interview source, properly cited.
4. Turn in your speech outline and any notes, or the tape you made of the interview, following your presentation.

EXERCISE 9.30   UNDERSTANDING DISCRIMINATION

Objectives:

1. To help students understand the emotional impact of discrimination
2. To initiate a discussion about the role of stereotypes and misperception in discrimination

Description of Exercise:

This exercise must be handled with the utmost sensitivity and careful planning. Students will momentarily experience a surprise feeling of discrimination. They are not told this in advance. This exercise should occur a day after a unit on perception when the term *discrimination* or *stereotype* has previously been introduced and discussed.

Procedures:

1. Teacher divides the class into two categories—tall and short, or people wearing blue jeans and everyone else. Seat one of the two groups in front and seat the other group in back.

2. Conduct class as usual, but give the students in front or back more attention. Praise them constantly when they make a comment; call on others but do not give any feedback at all to their responses. It is important to continue this long enough until students start to figure out what is going on and begin to get restless.

3. When students seem to have noticed and perhaps even become irritated with the preferential treatment, stop the activity and bring everyone together into a semicircle. Initiate a discussion along the following lines:

   - Based on what we have talked about (in a unit on perception/discrimination), what words would you use to describe my treatment of the group in front/back?
   - Group in front/back, how did that treatment make you feel? Why?
   - When did you start to notice the difference in treatment?
   - When did you start to have feelings about it?
   - Group in front/back, how did you feel when you noticed that the others were being excluded? Why?
   - What do you think people can do to avoid discriminating against other people?
   - What communication skills might be especially useful in helping to prevent discrimination?

EXERCISE 9.31   ORAL INTERPRETATION: MULTICULTURAL STORIES

Objectives:

1. To learn something new and valuable about another culture
2. To creatively interpret a story for an audience
3. To enhance verbal and nonverbal delivery skills
4. To practice appreciative listening skills

Description of Exercise:

Students will research short stories, narrative poems, or other short forms of literature produced by a particular culture and present an oral interpretation of that literature to the class or another audience.

Procedures:

1. Students locate an authentic short work of literature from a country or culture of their choice (alternatively, teachers can assign different cultures or can allow students to choose their assignment from a hat).

2. Teacher makes a photocopy of the story so that it can be marked on and eventually cut up and pasted onto separate sheets of paper.

3. Students should prepare a *cutting* of the story or poem that is suitable for an oral interpretation presentation. A cutting begins by marking up the story: placing brackets around the most interesting material, crossing out passages or sentences that are too long or too pastoral, and thus unsuited for an interesting reading-aloud. Transitions between main ideas should be preserved or modified. Give students these tips for making effective cuts:

   - The entire story does not have to be told in the oral interpretation—only a sequence that is long enough to convey a main idea or two while preserving the authenticity of the story.
   - Oral interpretation tends to be more interesting if it is made up of characters' voices, rather than told by a third-person narrator. Dialogue is thus always a good choice for a cutting, although it may be difficult to interpret more than two or three characters.
   - Try to end the story in a way that resolves any tension or conflict that arose in an earlier part of the cutting.
   - Separately, prepare a short introduction (maybe two or three sentences) that describes the general theme of the story, the major characters involved, and orients the audience to the place and time at which the cutting begins. Similarly, a conclusion may be prepared if necessary to bring closure to the piece.

EXERCISE 9.31 *Continued*

4. After the students have completed an initial marking on the photocopies, have them time a reading of the cutting in a slow, leisurely pace. Students should continue to make choices about what to exclude until the length of the cutting falls between five and seven minutes, including the introduction and conclusion.

5. Students next physically cut and paste the script pieces together onto new sheets of paper. Put these sheets into a notebook of some sort that is easy to hold open in one hand while the student turns the pages with the other hand.

6. Now the student is ready to begin practicing the oral interpretation. The student should stand up straight on both feet, face the audience squarely, and begin the presentation with the notebook closed and held neatly, parallel to the floor (not hugged close to the body), in both hands. The student should recite the introduction from memory, then open the notebook, turn to the front page, and begin the oral interpretation. The student should be as dramatic and creative as possible with voice, facial expressions, shoulder movements, and gestures from the free arm. Some students may even want to develop distinct character voices and accents native to the culture.

7. After practicing for several days, hold a classroom performance. Consider inviting parents and other classes and grades of students.

Feedback:

Consider awarding prizes; have the class vote on the top three presentations. Consider videotaping the performances; consider including tapes of the performances and the cuttings in a student portfolio.

MULTICULTURAL ORAL INTERPRETATION EVALUATION

Name: _____

Oral Interpretation of: _____

Criteria	Comments	Points
ATTITUDE: Student shows interest and effort in researching the story. Prepares the cutting thoughtfully; practices to achieve excellence; willing to be creative.		/10
SELECTION: The selection is an authentic example of literature from a unique perspective. The story is challenging and interesting. The story imparts new information about the culture to the audience.		/15
CUTTING: The cutting meets time and content requirements; is interesting and effective as a script. The introduction and conclusion are concise and helpful overall.		/20
PRACTICE: The student diligently practiced the script to develop a polished presentation.		/15
DELIVERY: Delivery was polished and showed use of a variety of vocal skills. Gestures and facial expression enhanced the dramatic content of the presentation.		/25
AUDIENCE ADAPTATION: The oral interpretation is creatively and thoughtfully designed for the enrichment of the audience.		/15

Additional Comments:

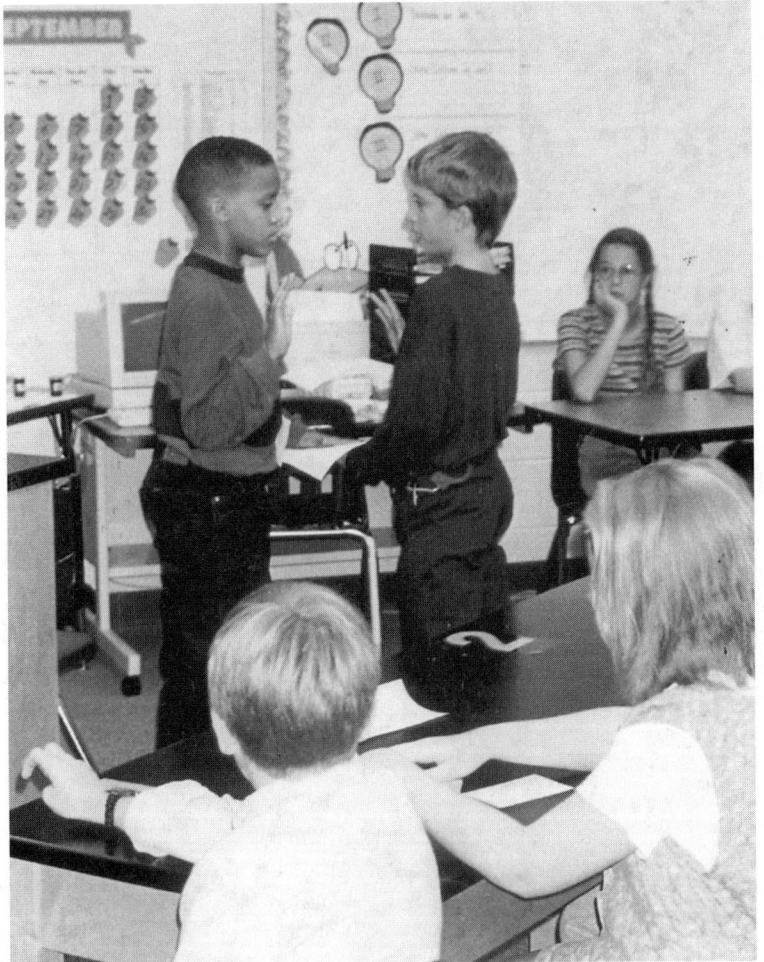

Swearing in a witness during a mock trial

10

Competitive Speech and Debate, Moot Courts, and Activities with Community Involvement

OVERVIEW

One of the exciting features of teaching oral communication in grades K through 8 is that new opportunities for oral-intensive co-curricular and extracurricular activities exist that formerly were available only at the secondary level. A particular example is the formation of a middle school debate and competitive speaking division by the National Forensics League, the primary sponsor of most high school competitive debate and speech activities. In addition, moot court and mock trial events have become popular at the middle school level; and for K through 5, increased parental involvement has resulted in activities such as cultural storytelling, authors' teas, and student-led tours of school facilities. This chapter suggests a number of oral-intensive co-curricular and extracurricular activities and provides specific information about how to implement competitive speech and debate activities. A sample moot court simulation is also provided.

ACTIVITIES WITH PARENTAL AND COMMUNITY INVOLVEMENT: GRADES K THROUGH 5

Parental and community involvement in the schools has been shown to improve chances for success in the area of literacy, especially for at-risk students. Some successful literacy programs have included oral-intensive activities such as the following:

- Senior citizens reading to young students
- Students reading or telling their own stories to younger students

- Authors' teas—young authors share their stories with parents after school
- Cultural folklore classes—parents and children learn folklore together after school or on weekends. Folklore may be learned and shared in the learner's native language.
- Drama and puppetry at assemblies and on special parent days
- Oral history or storytelling by a guest member of the community
- Students interview members of the community and report back to their classmates

Activities such as these introduce students to the many ways in which language is used around them. Communicating with adults in creative roles such as author, performer, and journalist, children build their self-esteem and learn to value language, literacy, and oral communication skills. See, for instance, the interview with Mary Helen Benitez, principal of Balderas Elementary School, Fresno, California, in Chapter 2.

SIMULATIONS: GRADES 5 THROUGH 8

Simulations of real world events can be used across the curriculum to integrate the language arts with other content areas. At the secondary level, popular simulations include a Model United Nations (teams of students represent individual countries in a mock General Assembly and Security Council); the Close-Up Foundation mock legislative session (students travel to their state capitol and debate whether to adopt a draft bill); and similarly, Student Congress, a legislative simulation sponsored by the National Forensics League.

Moot Courts and Mock Trials

At the middle school level, moot courts and mock trials are popular simulations of the American judicial process.

A moot court is an exercise in appellate advocacy that closely approximates oral argument before the U.S. Supreme Court. Attorneys for the petitioner (person who is raising the appeal) and the respondent (person who is opposing the appeal) present oral arguments to a panel of nine justices. The justices question each of the attorneys during their oral arguments and then confer to reach a decision. Throughout the simulation, teams of journalists interview the attorneys and create newspaper articles and broadcasts about the proceedings and the decision.

A mock trial is an exercise in advocacy before a mock judge and jury. Attorneys for the state present a case, complete with witnesses (who may be cross-examined) and evidence. Attorneys for the accused defend with their own witnesses and evidence. A judge, jury, and bailiff complete the mock trial team.

Because it simulates the appellate court process rather than the initial jury trial, a moot court is easier to coordinate than a mock trial. The appellate process does not require witness testimony, presentation of evidence, or a jury. Instead, appellate lawyers argue that a trial verdict should be overturned or upheld because of errors that may have occurred in the lower court's rendering of the case. As advocates, appellate attorneys rely on their persuasive writing and speaking skills. A moot court presents unique opportunities for critical thinking because, just as in real life, attorneys rarely have a chance to complete their arguments before they are interrupted by the justices with questions.

Although oral arguments and judicial decision making are the highlight of a moot court simulation, the preparatory work leading up to that day is rich in cooperative learning and integrated language arts activities. Throughout the simulation, students integrate reading, writing, listening, thinking, and speaking in the contexts of small groups, whole-class discussion, interviews, journalistic and persuasive writing, and formal argument.

The steps in a moot court simulation, allocated at the teacher's discretion over a one-, two-, or three-week period, are:

1. *Grounding*—Introduce students to basic facts about the U.S. legal system and civil appeals process (optional if students have learned this already in social studies or civics).
2. *Explanation*—Explain the moot court exercise to students.
3. *Facts of the case*—Introduce the case and its underlying facts.
4. *Brainstorming*—Generate arguments on each side of the case.
5. *Preparation*—Assign roles, prepare oral arguments and first news accounts.
6. *Simulation*—Argue the case and reach a decision.
7. *Wrap-up*—Optional, with writing assignments.
8. *Assessment*—Peer and/or self-assessment.

The moot court simulation that we will walk through, *Vernonia School District v. Acton*, demonstrates each of the eight steps listed. It is based on a recent Supreme Court case, in which a seventh grader, James Acton, and his parents challenged the Vernonia School District's mandatory drug-testing policy. The Actons claimed that the drug-testing policy was a violation of students' constitutional rights against unreasonable searches and seizures.

Step 1: Grounding

The first step in conducting a moot court simulation is to ground students in basic facts about the United States judicial system. Even fifth graders can master a basic knowledge of the appeals process, as long as the major concepts are emphasized and legal terminology is kept to a minimum. If you have already introduced this topic in a social studies class, you will not need to devote as much time to the grounding step. If this information has not already been introduced to students in the social studies curriculum, you may wish to create a handout for the moot court or adapt the one in Exercise 10.1 to the literacy level of your students.

EXERCISE 10.1   APPEALING A CASE TO THE U.S. SUPREME COURT

Do you know what these terms mean?

affirm	injunction
appeals process	opinion
circuit court of appeals	reverse
district court	U.S. Supreme Court

In the United States judicial branch of the government, there are three levels of courts. The first level (Level I), is the district court. The second level (Level II) is the court of appeals. The third and final level (Level III) is the U.S. Supreme Court.

LEVEL I

Most cases are heard at the first level of the judicial system, the *district court*. When a person believes that a government agency (such as a school district) has taken away a constitutional right, that person can ask the district court for an *injunction*. An injunction is a written court order that tells the government agency to stop the unconstitutional conduct.

The district court listens to the attorneys and witnesses for both sides as they present their cases. The judge issues a decision in a written document called an *opinion*. The opinion states the judge's decision and, in some cases, explains the reasoning behind the decision.

LEVEL II

After the district court issues a decision, the losing side can appeal to the *court of appeals*. The United States has eleven Courts of Appeals and one for the District of Columbia. Each court hears appeals from district courts for a different *circuit*, or group of states. For instance, in the case you are about to study, the losing side appealed from a district court in Oregon. The court of appeals handling appeals from the state of Oregon is the Court of Appeals for the Ninth Circuit.

If the court of appeals agrees with the district court's decision, it will *affirm* the decision. If the court of appeals disagrees with the district court's decision, it will *reverse* the decision.

LEVEL III

After the court of appeals issues its opinion, the losing side may appeal to the *U.S. Supreme Court*. The Supreme Court is the highest, or most authoritative, court in the land. When the Supreme Court makes a decision, it cannot be appealed or re-versed by another court, although on very rare occasions, the Supreme Court reverses one of its own decisions.

Step 2: Explanation

Explain the moot court simulation process so that students will understand the objectives. It may be helpful to explain the process in terms of the roles that students will be asked to play.

- *Attorneys.* Some students will serve as attorneys. Attorneys who are asking the Supreme Court to reverse the decision of the Ninth Circuit are called the *petitioners.* Their responsibility is to make arguments in favor of James Acton and his parents. Attorneys who are asking the Supreme Court to affirm the decision of the Ninth Circuit are called the *respondents.* Their responsibility is to make arguments in favor of the Vernonia school district.

- *Justices.* Some students will serve as justices. Their responsibility is to consider the arguments on both sides of the case, question the attorneys during their oral arguments, and reach a decision. The justices will later explain their individual reasoning to the rest of the class when they announce the verdict.

- *Journalists.* Some students will serve as journalists. Their responsibility is to study the issues on both sides of the case, interview attorneys about their plans for oral argument, and write news reports or create radio and video broadcasts about the upcoming appeal. During oral argument and the announcement of the decision, the journalists take notes; and at the close of the case, they prepare final news reports and broadcasts about the proceedings.

Step 3: Facts of the Case

Next, introduce the facts and legal issues in the case. This is an excellent opportunity for cooperative learning. One approach is to divide students into small groups and assign to each group the task of uncovering research on one of the two background topics listed below. Schedule a class visit to the library to conduct limited research into the controversy surrounding the case—perhaps your school librarian could have materials already selected and available.

Alternatively, provide students with materials for in-class use. Two or three newspaper and magazine articles should be sufficient. Newspaper and magazine articles are easy to read and tend to give a fairly balanced view of the issues suitable for background information. It's important to give students at least one fairly objective source about each of the following topics:

1. Why drug abuse among teenagers might be a problem for students, parents, and teachers
2. Why drug testing is favored by some and opposed by others as a solution to drug abuse at school and at work

After students have conducted this preliminary research on the factual issues in the case, students read about the facts of the *Vernonia v. Acton* case (Exercise 10.2) and why it was appealed to the Supreme Court.

EXERCISE 10.2   *VERNONIA V. ACTON*—BACKGROUND AND FACTS BEHIND THE CASE

Do you know what these words and phrases mean?

Fourth Amendment	reasonable suspicion
mandatory	warrant
probable cause	unreasonable search and seizure

In the case you are about to study, seventh grader James Acton refused to take a *mandatory* drug test administered by his school district. A drug test is mandatory when a person must either take it or face punishment of some sort. In the Vernonia school district, students who did not take a drug test were not allowed to participate in school sports, including football and basketball.

James Acton was interested in playing football, but the Vernonia school district believed that forcing athletes to take a drug test was the only way to stop drug use and discipline problems at school. James and his parents disagreed with the school district. They believed that forcing a student who did not show signs of drug use to take a drug test was an *unreasonable search and seizure* that violated the *Fourth Amendment* of the U.S. Constitution.The Fourth Amendment says that the government can not search its citizens without a *warrant* or *probable cause* to believe that the person has done something illegal.

A *warrant* is a piece of paper issued by a court giving the police permission to search a person or their house and belongings. Courts issue warrants when a police officer can show a strong possibility, or *probable cause*, that a person was involved in a crime. Sometimes courts will allow searches and seizures without probable cause, if there is a *reasonable suspicion* that a person has committed a crime. A reasonable suspicion is a lower standard than probable cause. School districts are sometimes allowed to search lockers and personal belongings of students if they have *reasonable suspicion* because of the special role that schools play in supervising and protecting students while they are away from their parents.

THE FACTS BEHIND *VERNONIA V. ACTON*

Vernonia is a small logging town in Oregon with a population of about 3,000. James Acton was a seventh grader attending school there when the Vernonia school district established a mandatory drug-testing program for student athletes. Students who refused to take the drug test were not allowed to participate in school sports.

The drug-testing program was a response to reports of increasing student drug use and disciplinary problems in the schools. According to the school district, students began to boast that they were using drugs. In 1989, teachers reported double the number of disciplinary problems with students than they had reported in 1988. Several students were suspended. A teacher observed small groups of students smoking marijuana at a nearby restaurant before school and during school hours. One student was so noticeably drunk in school that he was sent home by his teacher. Another student was singing and dancing in the back of a classroom. When the teacher asked him what was going on, he replied, "Well, I'm high on life." School officials stated that the disciplinary problems had reached epidemic proportions.

EXERCISE 10.2   *Continued*

Vernonia teachers and school administrators attributed these and other disciplinary problems to drug and alcohol use among athletes. The school district was also concerned that student athletes who used illegal drugs might suffer more injuries during sports because of their drug use. As a result, the Vernonia school district offered anti-drug–education programs. It received assistance from the local police department in patrolling the school grounds to help deter drug use and even brought a drug-sniffing dog onto the school grounds. After these options did not appear to help, school district officials called a special meeting of parents. At that meeting, parents, teachers, and administrators agreed to develop a drug-testing policy that would be used to deter drug use among student athletes.

The Vernonia drug-testing policy required a urinalysis test of all students desiring to participate in athletics for any season. It required weekly, random testing of 10 percent of the athletes. When taking the drug test, students were monitored in the school bathrooms by adults of the same gender. Results were analyzed for marijuana, cocaine, and amphetamines. Additional tests of certain drugs, such as LSD, could be ordered if necessary. The test had an accuracy rate of 99.94 percent, but if a student tested positive, the sample was retested. A second positive result led to a hearing for the student and parents at which the student had the choice of either suspension from athletics or participation in a six-week drug-assistance program. After the drug-testing policy was implemented, teachers reported a 50 percent decrease in disciplinary problems and an apparent decrease in student drug use and favorable attitudes toward drug use.

Although James Acton wanted to play on the district football team, he refused to take the drug test. He and his parents challenged the drug-testing policy in court because they believed that it violated James's right to be free from an unreasonable search under the Fourth Amendment to the U.S. Constitution. Since James had not shown any signs of drug use, the school lacked reasonable suspicion or probable cause; and without those factors, the Actons argued, the drug test was an unreasonable search and seizure.

Step 4: Brainstorming

The next step in a moot court simulation is to identify arguments on both sides of the case. Divide all students into small groups once again. Each group should discuss the arguments in Exercise 10.3 and decide which ones support the school district's drug-testing policy and which ones oppose the policy.

Step 5: Preparation

Assign a team of four or five students to be attorneys on each side of the case. Each attorney will have between four and five minutes to make their part of the argument. Alternatively, the attorney teams can pick one person to deliver the entire oral argument to the judge. The disadvantage of this strategy is that only one student from each team reaps the benefit of experience in delivering the argument and in answering the questions posed by the justices. Assign a group of nine students to serve as justices in the case. Assign the remaining students to teams of print, radio, and/or television broadcasters. Provide students with instructions on their responsibilities (Exercise 10.4).

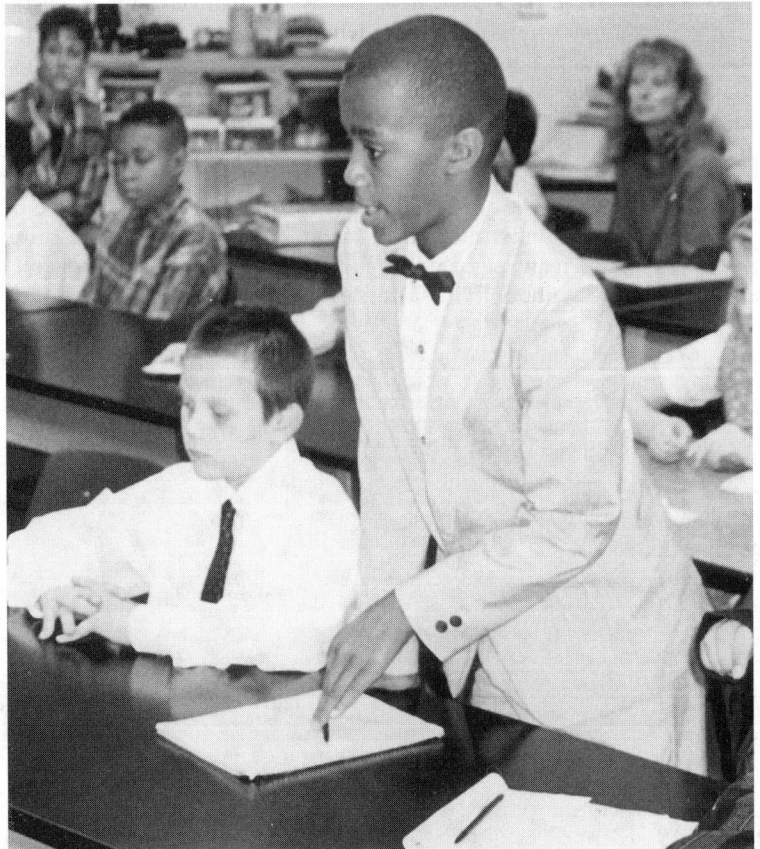

A young advocate makes an argument

EXERCISE 10.3   ARGUMENTS IN *VERNONIA V. ACTON*

In your group, read the following arguments and discuss whether each one supports or opposes the mandatory drug-testing policy of the Vernonia School District. Put the letter *Y* (for Yes) beside each argument that supports the policy and a letter *N* (for No) beside each argument that opposes the policy. If you think that an argument could be used both to support and to oppose the policy, put the letter *B* (for Both) beside the argument.

ARGUMENTS

_____ 1. The district's drug-testing program is a constitutionally reasonable search. Other Supreme Court cases have upheld mandatory, suspicionless drug-testing as constitutionally reasonable under the Fourth Amendment.

_____ 2. The evidence of drug use and disciplinary problems at Vernonia schools was not strong enough to justify suspicionless searches of students.

_____ 3. Because students are not yet adults, they have fewer constitutional rights at school than adults would have.

_____ 4. Another previous Supreme Court case requires reasonable suspicion that a student has violated the law or school rules, although it says that schools do not have to have a warrant and probable cause.

_____ 5. School searches are okay even without warrants, probable cause, or reasonable suspicion. Schools have a responsibility to protect students.

_____ 6. Another previous Supreme Court case says that "students do not leave their constitutional rights at the schoolhouse door."

_____ 7. Two previous Supreme Court cases allow suspicionless testing only of employees in sensitive positions affecting public safety and law enforcement. No similar compelling need to allow suspicionless drug-testing e exists in a public school.

_____ 8. The search in this case has many safeguards to make sure an innocent person isn't punished.

EXERCISE 10.4   INSTRUCTIONS TO ATTORNEYS, JUSTICES, AND JOURNALISTS

ATTORNEYS

Using the facts of the case, the arguments you discussed earlier in your small groups, and any supporting information you may have obtained, develop thorough arguments for your side's presentation to the Court. Remember that you will have to answer some unexpected questions from the justices. If you are a *petitioner*, you represent James Acton and his parents and are responsible for developing arguments that oppose the drug-testing policy. If you are a *respondent*, you represent the Vernonia School District and are responsible for developing arguments that support the drug-testing policy.

When you present your oral argument, you will begin by saying, "May it please the Court, my name is _____ and I am counselor for the petitioner/respondent. I will address the issue of _____." When a justice interrupts you, immediately stop speaking—even if you are in mid-sentence—and listen to the question. Begin your answer to the question with, "Your Honor . . ." When you have finished answering the question, return to your planned argument, but don't be surprised if you are interrupted again! Many attorneys never even finish presenting their entire argument to the Court. The Court is usually much more interested in asking questions and hearing the answers. For this reason, many attorneys try to use parts of their planned argument to answer the Court's questions.

Don't be surprised if you don't get to finish presenting your entire argument before your time is up. Sometimes that happens because the justices ask so many questions. The most important thing is to try to answer their questions as persuasively as possible.

JUSTICES

Carefully re-read the facts of the case and the arguments you discussed in your small groups. Become familiar with the arguments on both sides. Develop a series of questions and follow-up questions about each side to ask the attorneys when they are presenting their arguments to you. When the attorneys begin to speak, you may interrupt them with a question by addressing each attorney as "Counselor," as in, "Counselor, are you saying that. . . ."

After all the attorneys have spoken and answered at least two questions from the panel, meet quietly with your colleagues to reach a decision. When you meet, briefly explain your individual decisions and the reasons behind them to the rest of the panel. Then allow the chief justice to take a final tally. After about ten minutes, the chief justice announces the decision to the class. Each one of you will then once again briefly tell the class how you voted and what you found to be the most persuasive arguments in making your personal decision.

JOURNALISTS

While the attorneys and justices are working in small groups to prepare for the oral argument, you prepare news accounts, radio, or television broadcasts about the upcom-

EXERCISE 10.4 *Continued*

ing appeal. Review the research your class conducted about drug use in schools. Review the arguments you discussed in your small groups, then listen in on the attorney teams as they prepare for the oral argument to find out more about what they plan to argue. You may need to interview one or two attorneys from each team after they finish conferring to get more information. Use a combination of sources to prepare your first news accounts.

During the oral argument itself, take notes on what is said by the attorneys and on which justices asked what questions. After the justices announce their decision, take notes on the decision and the reasoning of the individual judges. See if you can identify a majority opinion and a dissenting opinion. Write or create a second and final news account of the oral argument and the decision.

Step 6: Simulation

Students are now ready to argue the case and reach a decision. On the day of the oral argument, set up the room to resemble a courtroom so that there is a long table or set of desks at the front of the room, facing the rest of the class, at which the justices will sit. Place a podium, facing the table, at a distance that will allow both the justices and attorneys to speak without straining to be heard. The attorney teams sit facing the panel, but behind the podium, at two adjacent tables.

Appoint a bailiff to call the court to order. When the justices begin to take their seats, the bailiff announces, "All rise," and everyone in the classroom stands until the justices have been seated. The bailiff then states, "Hear ye, hear ye, the Supreme Court is now in session, the Honorable Chief Justice _____ presiding. Remain silent while the court is in session." After these words from the bailiff, the chief justice announces, "Counsel for the petitioner, you may begin." The first attorney for the petitioner approaches the podium and begins his or her argument, as do all the attorneys who argue, with "May it please the Court, I am _____ , counsel for the petitioner/respondent in the case and I will be addressing the issue of _____ . "

The justices may interrupt whenever they choose but with the opening word of "Counselor. . . ." In most moot court simulations, as in real life, the attorneys will not be able to present their arguments as completely as they have planned on paper. However, this is very normal and it may help to caution attorneys to expect that they will not be able to finish their prepared argument, but rather that they should concentrate on being prepared to answer questions from the justices while they are speaking.

Each student speaks long enough (perhaps four or five minutes) to present some of their argument and to answer at least one or two questions from the panel. When all attorneys for the petitioner have spoken, the attorneys for the respondent begin their arguments in the same fashion. After about forty to forty-five minutes of oral argument, the justices confer with each other for about ten to fifteen minutes to reach a decision. While they are conferring, they should briefly explain to each other how they voted and why. At the end of the judicial conference, the justices return to their places and the chief justice announces the decision. Each justice briefly explains his or her reasoning to the class.

Step 7: Wrap-up

The exercise can be wrapped up, if time permits, with the following optional writing assignments.

Attorneys: Compose written versions of their oral arguments and compile them into a single "mini-brief," which can be displayed in a binder underneath a bulletin board featuring news accounts, photographs, or illustrations prepared by the journalists as part of their chronicling of the case.

Justices: The justices decide among themselves if majority, concurring, and dissenting opinions exist. Then each justice decides which category his or her opinion falls into, and the justices write individual opinions that can be compiled into a longer "mini-opinion" with majority, concurring (if applicable), and dissenting (if applicable) sections. The opinion can be put on display in a binder.

Journalists: Organize their final news accounts into a "mini-paper" for distribution to the class. If they have printed news accounts, photos, or illustrations, consider creating a bulletin board or other area of the room that tells the story of the trial.

Step 8: Assessment
Assessment of a moot court can be very simple. Ask students to respond to questions such as:

> What did you think was the strongest argument made in favor of [topic]? Why?
>
> What did you think was the strongest argument against [topic]? Why?
>
> What did you like best about your work in this moot court?
>
> What do you think you could do next time to improve?
>
> What are the most important two or three things you have learned about the U.S. judicial system?

Teachers can use assessment tools, such as those featured in Chapter 5, tailored to each role in the moot court. Videos of a student's performance are suitable for inclusion in a portfolio.

COMPETITIVE SPEECH AND DEBATE: GRADES 5 THROUGH 8

The National Forensics League, the national organization that sponsors high school debate and speech competitions, has organized a National Junior Forensics League, an honor society that will reward students and schools, using a system of points, for their participation in oral-intensive performance activities. Unlike the National Forensics League activities at the high school level, however, points can be awarded for classroom and intramural activities such as public speaking, radio and television "programs," impromptu speaking, oral interpretation, and different forms of debate. At the middle school level, the emphasis is less on competition and more on participation, especially in-class participation. The National Forensics League, suggests classroom or school festivals as an alternative to the high school speech and debate tournaments.

We have summarized here, with the permission of the National Forensics League, the judging criteria used in different types of competitive speaking events at the high school level. Middle school teachers can model their own activities after these or develop their own versions.

Possible Middle School Speech Events

Dramatic Interpretation

Dramatic interpretation is a form of oral interpretation of literature. At the high school level, it is usually distinguished from humorous interpretation, which as its name suggests, focuses on literature that is humorous.

- Five to ten minutes in length
- Selections are cut from novels, short stories, plays, or poetry; monologues are acceptable; a short introduction written by the student identifies the author and the title of the work from which the selection was cut.
- The selection and its cutting must be appropriate and suitable to the purpose and audience; adaptation of the author's words is allowed only if necessary to maintain continuity; literary merit of the selection is a factor.
- Delivery is from memory; concentrate on poise, quality and use of voice, inflections, emphasis, pronunciation, enunciation, and ability to interpret characters correctly and consistently.
- Gestures are discouraged—the emphasis is on vocal and facial expressiveness.
- Performed without costumes, props, and visual aids
- Any narrative portions in the cutting must be animated so as to be an interesting and integral part of the story.
- The overall impression should be that the hearer is carried away to the time and place of the story being unfolded.

Expository Speaking

Expository speaking is also known as informative speaking. In this event, the speech is usually prepared in advance on a topic of the student's choosing. At the high school level, expository speaking is usually distinguished from persuasive speaking (a speech to influence the audience's beliefs or choice of action) and from extemporaneous and impromptu speaking (both of which are shorter speeches and involve limited preparation on a topic that is randomly drawn by the student).

- Five to ten minutes in length
- Original composition
- Considered a speech to inform (describe, clarify, illustrate, or define an object, idea, concept, or process)
- Student chooses a "real-world" topic.
- Content should be well developed, explain concepts clearly, and well organized.
- Language should reflect high standards of usage, style, and vocabulary.
- Delivery is quite often from memory but may be from unobtrusive notes (index cards); concentrate on poise, quality and use of voice, gestures, audience contact, sincerity, and directness.
- Performed without visual aids to place emphasis on speech content and delivery

Extemporaneous Speaking

Extemporaneous speaking is an exciting opportunity for the student to demonstrate a knowledge of current event topics and critical thinking skills. It is a short speech for which the student only has about a half hour to prepare (at the high school level) and the student draws the topic randomly from a hat. In addition to the NFL criteria summarized below, extemporaneous speech formats suitable for grades 3 through 5 and 6 through 8 are included in Chapters 8 and 9.

- Student draws a topic at random and adheres to it; if topic is a controversial subject, student may advocate a position or present both sides of the topic.
- Information presented should be well chosen, pertinent, and sufficient to support the central thought of the topic; content should be well organized.
- Concentrate on poise, quality, use of voice, enunciation, fluency, bodily expressiveness, gaining and holding attention of audience; notes (on index cards) are permissible.
- Preparation time is usually thirty minutes.
- Maximum speech length is usually seven minutes, but there is no minimum length.
- The overall impression should be of clear thinking, good speaking, and interesting presentation.

Humorous Interpretation

Humorous interpretation is the counterpart to dramatic interpretation.

- Five to ten minutes in length
- Selections are cut from novels, short stories, plays, or poetry; monologues are acceptable; a short introduction written by the student identifies the author and the title of the work from which the selection was cut.
- The selection and its cutting must be appropriate and suitable to the purpose and audience; adaptation of the author's words is only allowed if necessary to maintain continuity; literary merit of the selection is a factor.
- Delivery is from memory; concentrate on poise, quality and use of voice, inflections, emphasis, pronunciation, enunciation, and ability to interpret characters correctly and consistently.
- Gestures are discouraged—the emphasis is on vocal and facial expressiveness.
- Performed without costumes, props, and visual aids
- Any narrative portions in the cutting must be animated so as to be an interesting and integral part of story.
- The overall impression should be that the listener is carried away to the time and place of the story being unfolded.

Impromptu Speaking

Impromptu speaking occurs with minimal preparation. It is designed to be more of a creative speech than one supported by external information and analysis. The student draws his or her topic randomly.

- Maximum length of five minutes; no minimum length
- Original interpretation of the randomly selected topic
- Creative, imaginative
- Topics are developed in advance by the teacher from proverbs, ordinary things, abstract words, events, quotations, famous people.
- Preparation time is usually five minutes
- Student must stay on topic; cannot digress so that speech focuses on another topic
- Information presented should be well chosen, pertinent, sufficient to support the central thought of the topic; content should be well organized and logical.
- Concentrate on poise, quality and use of voice, enunciation, fluency, bodily expressiveness, gaining and holding attention of audience; speaking without notes.
- The overall impression should be a combination of clear thinking, strong speaking skills, and an interesting interpretation of topic.

Original Oratory

Original oratory is a persuasive or inspirational prepared speech.

- Five to ten minutes in length
- Original, nonfiction composition
- Persuasive or inspirational interpretation of any appropriate subject; format may be problem–solution; alerting audience to some threatening danger; reinforcing audience to an accepted cause; eulogy
- Thought and composition are considered primarily in the way they are employed to make the speech effective; vocal and physical delivery are heavily weighted. Concentrate on rhetoric and diction; poise, quality, use of voice, bodily expressiveness, directness, and sincerity; appropriate figures of speech, similes, metaphors, balanced sentences, allusions, and other rhetorical devices.
- Use of standard English should reveal a discriminating choice of words and fine literary qualities; language should be adapted to oral presentation.
- Performed without visual aids; notes (on index cards) are permitted.

Poetry Reading

The purpose of the poetry reading is to encourage students to find, understand, appreciate, and interpret selections of poetry for dramatic effect.

- Maximum of five minutes in length
- Selections may be from any printed and published poem or an arrangement of several shorter poems, but not selections from plays and dramas; a short introduction written by the student includes the title(s) and author(s).

- Interpretation is delivered from a manuscript in a neat, substantial folder (such as, a binder); reading from a book or magazine is not permitted; use of the manuscript should be an integral part of performance.
- Concentrate on technique (breathing, tone, pitch, enunciation, phrasing, pace); artistry (presentation of mood and imagery, vocal characterization); responsive use of body (spontaneous changes in posture and gesture, although all gestures should be appropriate to the selection and interpretation).
- The overall impression should be that the audience is carried into the real or imagined world of the selections.

Prose Reading

The purpose of the prose reading is to encourage the student to find, understand, experience, and share a prose work through the art of oral reading.

- Maximum length is five minutes.
- Presentation from printed or published work; introduction states title and author.
- Read/interpreted from a manuscript in a folder; not from the book or magazine itself; use of the manuscript should be an integral part of the performance.
- Concentrate on technique—breathing, tone, pitch, enunciation, phrasing, pace.
- Concentrate on artistry—presentation of mood and imagery, vocal characterization, flow of narration.
- Responsive use of body (that is, spontaneous changes in posture and gesture) permissible so long as appropriate to the selection and interpretation.
- The overall impression should be that the audience is carried into the real or imagined world of the selections.

Debate

Debate is an activity involving an assertive exchange and defense of ideas against those of other participants. Debate usually is focused around a single topic, although the individual debaters may point out numerous issues and concepts related to that topic. Unlike discussion and conflict-resolution, debaters do not attempt to persuade each other to reach a consensus or compromise. Even in parliamentary debate, which occurs in legislatures such as Congress, debate occurs and then the issue is decided by a vote, or compromises are reached in separate committee meetings. Instead, debate is aimed at persuading observers to take sides on the issue. Each debater takes a position (side) of the topic and defends it against attack from the other side. Observers later vote to express which side was most persuasive. Debate is an excellent tool for building critical thinking and persuasive speaking skills. (See the Kimberly A. Powell Interview later in this chapter—page 293.)

At the elementary and middle school level, teachers can devise a number of different debate activities. The debate formats mentioned here are also suitable for the National Junior Forensics League. Following the description of each kind of debate are sample ballot forms that suggest ways to evaluate a debate. Peer and self-assessments can also be developed and used effectively with debate. Finally, a glossary of some basic debate terms is included as Appendix 10.1 for teachers who would like to give debate a more in-depth treatment.

The Debate Topic (Proposition)

Debates tend to be more effective when the topic is carefully chosen to provide focus and distinct affirmative (in support of the topic) and negative (not in support of the topic) positions. A topic may not be suitable for debate if it is so broad that each speaker can choose a position without really having to disagree with one another. The way in which a topic is stated helps determine the scope of the debate. Generally, debate topics (also known as *propositions,* or *resolutions*) are most effective at focusing a debate when phrased in one of three forms: a proposition of fact, value, or policy.

Proposition of Fact.   A proposition of fact is a statement or question that focuses a debate on whether or not the alleged *fact* can be demonstrated with adequate evidence. For instance, the statement "Elvis Presley is alive" is a proposition of fact because even though the King's death was publicly announced and a burial was undertaken (no pun intended), it is still possible (as we have seen demonstrated on talk shows time and time again) to mount a coherent (though perhaps suspect) argument that he is alive. A proposition of fact does not seek a comparison between two or more alternatives, nor does it attempt to evaluate or persuade an audience to adopt a particular course of action. Rather, a proposition of fact merely seeks to test the likelihood that a fact-based statement is true. Some examples of propositions of fact include:

Teen curfews reduce crime.
Have aliens from outer space visited the earth?
Does pollution cause global warming?
Video games promote violent behavior.
The United States is a democracy.

Propositions of fact are well suited for debates in elementary classrooms. While challenging students to gather adequate evidence for an affirmative or negative position, a proposition of fact does not require the more complicated anticipation of alternative solutions that often occurs with a policy proposition or justification of value systems that may occur with a value proposition. As a result, debates focused on a proposition of fact tend to be straightforward and easily managed by younger students. Particularly for younger learners, propositions of fact can be drawn readily from stories where there is room for differing interpretations of the meaning of a word or picture, the cause or effect of a character's actions, or a question about whether a story accurately depicts history.

Proposition of Value. A proposition of value is a statement or question that considers the merits of an idea or compares two or more ideas. It inherently requires acknowledgment of personal and shared values in decision making. For instance, the value proposition "Dogs are better pets than cats" requires consideration of what is meant by *better*. If a debate is not to be reduced to a mere recitation of the virtues of dogs and the virtues of cats, the participants must address how their favorite measures up on at least a few common values. For instance, an argument can be made that the most important quality in a pet is loyalty, and that, using that criteria, dogs are clearly more loyal than cats, and hence, better pets. A person arguing in favor of cats, of course, could argue that cats are just as (if not more) loyal than dogs, though they express loyalty in different ways. Throughout the debate, participants can disagree over one another's choice of criteria. For example, "Certainly loyalty is important, but ease of care is also an important attribute in a pet. Cats do not need to be walked regularly every day or bathed after a jaunt in the mud. . . ." Examples of propositions of value include:

> Protecting the environment is more important than creating new jobs.
> *The Lion King* is the best animated Disney film ever made.
> Professional athletes make good role models.

In some ways, value propositions are the most difficult to debate because, at their most sophisticated level, value debates involve competition between value systems. However, for K through 8, it is possible to have successful debates on value propositions by simply foregoing the requirement that students justify their values. Instead, students may be encouraged to merely articulate their positions. If desired, sensitivity to different values or priorities can become a subject for whole-class discussion.

Proposition of Policy. A proposition of policy is a statement or question that seeks adoption (or reinforcement) of a specific course of action. In general, propositions of policy can be easily recognized because they usually contain the word *should*. Examples of propositions of policy include:

> Should our school build a new playground?
>
> Video games should be rated for violence.
>
> Loggers should not be allowed to cut down forests where endangered species live.
>
> Should highways have a 55 m.p.h. speed limit?

Depending on the proposition, at more advanced levels the affirmative speaker may offer a hypothetical plan or policy as an example of the resolution and then defend that plan. It may not be necessary to describe a plan for converting the nation's highways to a 55 m.p.h. speed limit, for example. The debate will be just as effective if it focuses merely on the advantages and disadvantages of having a uniform 55 m.p.h. speed limit. However, the proposition "Video games should be rated for violence" might not be considered so simply. The advantages and disadvantages of implementing a rating system for video games would likely depend on who required the rating (the government or private companies?), who developed the rating system (parents or politicians?), and whether or not enforcement of a particular system is feasible. In cases like this, where the proposition might require consideration of alternatives, the affirmative customarily presents a plan of action.

Argumentation

Debaters make arguments. That is, they make claims that the topic has certain favorable or unfavorable implications, and then they support those claims with evidence and reasoning. Teachers who have time and space in the curriculum may wish to require student research in the library for information that can be used as evidence. Students look for credible, recent, objective sources of information, such as, newspaper and magazine articles, and record useful information from those sources onto cards or sheets of paper for easy reference. Students record a citation for every piece of evidence they *cut*, or extract, from its original source. The quality of a debater's evidence can become an issue during the debate, so critical thinking skills are required to select only the most credible, relevant, and powerful evidence. Finally, students employ reasoning skills in using the evidence to support their claims. Students may reason deductively, inductively, by analogy, or by applying an accepted criteria to the facts of a situation. A student's use of logic may thus become an issue during the debate. For a detailed discussion of the components of an argument, see Chapter 3.

Debate Formats

There are several different kinds of debate formats. Some are one-on-one, others are appropriate for teams of two or three, and still others are appropriate for larger groups. In all debate formats, there can be two types of speeches: constructive and rebuttal. In the constructive speech, each side lays out their reasons for affirming or negating the resolution. Constructive speeches include any evidence used to support arguments, and they are usually longer in length than the rebuttal speeches, typically twice as long as a rebuttal. Not all debates have rebuttal speeches, but when they do, the rebuttal is designed to counter arguments made by the opponent and to further develop arguments made in the constructive speech. New arguments are generally excluded from rebuttals, and because the rebuttal tends to be a shorter speech than the constructive, it is more summative in nature; evidence is offered sparingly. A good way to explain rebuttals to students is to say that they are a chance to summarize the affirmative or negative position in a debate and tie it all together.

Lincoln–Douglas Debate. This debate takes place in a one-on-one format. One debater takes the affirmative side of the topic and attempts to support the topic by linking several arguments together into what is called a case. The negative speaker tries to oppose the topic by presenting his or her own case, or by simply arguing the opposite of the affirmative case. Traditionally, negative speakers do not present their own cases, but rather rely on attacking weaknesses in the affirmative cases. Because this strategy requires a great deal of mental facility and familiarity with a topic and the sources of evidence about that topic, younger children and even older middle school students might benefit more from the opportunity to prepare a negative case in advance.

After the affirmative and negative teams have had an opportunity to present their cases in Lincoln–Douglas debate, they may cross-examine each other briefly (ask questions designed to point out flaws). Lincoln–Douglas debate can occur without the cross-examination period.

Each speaker takes notes during the debate, and after the opening speeches (called constructive speeches because they construct the initial issues and arguments that the rest of the debate will follow), the affirmative presents a short rebuttal speech, followed by a negative rebuttal, and then one more affirmative rebuttal. The affirmative gets an extra rebuttal because the affirmative is assumed to have the burden of proof in the debate. A very simple method of taking notes might look something like Exhibit 10.1.

Exhibit 10.1   Taking Notes During a Debate

I raised these points:	The other side responded by saying that:	I will respond with:

Exhibit 10.2 is a sample of the National Forensics League high school Lincoln–Douglas debate ballot. It may provide some ideas for how to adapt or develop a form that meets the format you choose for your debates. You will notice that the times add up to a little over half-an-hour. That time can be shortened by the elimination of cross-examination, by paring down the length of the constructive speeches, and by eliminating the final affirmative speech so that each student has only two speeches. Most beginning debaters, however, especially younger students, rarely use the full time allotted to them.

Oregon-Style Debate.   The Oregon-style of debate is usually performed in teams of two on each side. Each person is assigned a speaker position: 1st Affirmative, 2nd Affirmative, 1st Negative, and 2nd Negative. In an Oregon-style debate, the format looks like this:

1st Affirmative Constructive	5–8 minutes
Cross Examination by 2nd Negative	3 minutes
1st Negative Constructive	5–8 minutes
Cross-examination by 1st Affirmative	3 minutes
2nd Affirmative Constructive	5–8 minutes
Cross-examination by 1st Negative	3 minutes
2nd Negative Constructive	5–8 minutes
Cross-examination by 2nd Affirmative	3 minutes
1st Negative Rebuttal	3–5 minutes
1st Affirmative Rebuttal	3–5 minutes
2nd Negative Rebuttal	3–5 minutes
2nd Affirmative Rebuttal	3–5 minutes

You will notice that the negative team has back-to-back speeches in the Oregon-style of debate. This is once again because the affirmative has the burden of proof and so is allowed to end the debate with the last speech. Exhibit 10.3 is representative of an NFL scoring ballot.

Exhibit 10.2   National Forensics League Lincoln-Douglas Ballot

Round _____   Room _____   Time _____   Date _____

Judge _____

Affirmative (name and code) _____

Negative (name and code) _____

Instructions to Judges

1. Unlike team debate, the resolution to be debated will be a proposition of value, rather than a proposition of policy. Thus debaters are encouraged to develop argumentation on conflicting underlying principles to support their positions. To that end, they are not responsible for practical applications. There is no need for a plan (or for plan attacks).

2. The burdens on the affirmative and negative positions are not prescribed as they may be in debates on propositions of policy; therefore decision rules are fair issues to be argued in the round.

3. In making your decision, you might ask yourself the following questions:
   a. Which of the debaters persuaded you that their position was more valid? (Which debater communicated more effectively?)
   b. Did the debaters support their positions appropriately, using logical argumentation throughout, and evidence where necessary?

4. Remember, there should be clash in the debate.

Circle the Appropriate Number:

	Superior	Excellent	Good	Average
Affirmative	50-49-48-47	46-45-44-43	42-41-40-39	38-37-36-35
Negative	50-49-48-47	46-45-44-43	42-41-40-39	38-37-36-35

Affirmative	Negative
Case and Analysis	Case and Analysis
Support of Issues Through Evidence and Reasoning	Support of Issues Through Evidence and Reasoning
Delivery	Delivery
Reason for Decision	Reason for Decision

In my opinion, the better debating was done by _____

   (affirmative or negative)   code

Critic's Signature _____

Format:

Affirmative	6-minute constructive
Negative	3-minute cross-examination
Negative	7-minute constructive
Affirmative	3-minute cross-examination
Affirmative	4-minute rebuttal
Negative	6-minute rebuttal
Affirmative	3-minute rebuttal

Reprinted with permission of the National Forensics League.

Exhibit 10.3   National Forensics League Debate Ballot (Oregon-Style)

Round _____   Division _____   Date _____   Room _____

Judge _____

Affirmative _____   Code _____

Negative _____   Code _____

Name	Points (0–30)	Rank (1–4)
_____	_____	_____
_____	_____	_____

Name	Points (0–30)	Rank (1–4)
_____	_____	_____
_____	_____	_____

Decision: The winning team is the _____   Side: Team Code _____

Signed: _____

School: _____

Reason for decision and comments to the debaters:

Reprinted with permission of the National Forensics League.

Other Debate Formats.   A *debate forum* consists of very brief speeches by two speakers on opposite sides of a topic. They then open up the floor for questions from the audience and answer them from their point of view. A *debate symposium* involves multiple speakers presenting speeches on many different sides of a topic.

Parliamentary debate is a simulation of a legislative session, when a speaker of the house controls the floor and parliamentary procedures are followed to determine the order, topic, and length of speeches. Topics usually revolve around a proposed policy, law, or other legislative enactment.

Teachers can use the basic concepts of debate to develop their own in-class formats. Exercise 10.5 is a debate format that was developed for in-class use at the college level, but it could be adapted for use with fifth through eighth graders. The advantages of using debate as an in-class activity are outlined in the following interview.

Using Debate to Teach Persuasion Skills

Interview with Kimberly A. Powell
Assistant Professor of Speech Communication
Luther College, Decorah, Iowa

Q: *What are the advantages of using the "Impromptu Debate" exercise in class?*

During the past six years of teaching persuasion as a part of the public speaking course, I have continually faced three challenges. First, some students are hesitant to take a position and argue it with conviction for fear of offending someone in class. Second, there are always a few students who do not understand the importance of using supporting material. Finally, in making arguments in persuasive speeches, many times the claims are made without either the evidence or the reasoning to clearly make the point. I have finally found a successful teaching tool to help students meet each of the challenges: debate.

Debate is now a permanent part of my public speaking syllabus. After we have discussed supporting material and persuasion, and before the persuasive speech assignment, students engage in debates. I provide each student with a handout that describes the six steps (see Exercise 10.5) in this debate assignment. I have found that once the clash portion of the exercise begins, students do not want it to end.

The students find this to be an enjoyable exercise and evaluations consistently express the desire to do more debates. From a teaching standpoint, this is a succesful exercise because students gain confidence and develop an understanding of how important it is to fully articulate arguments with effective supporting material. An additional benefit is that the delivery of speeches tends to improve after the debates. I believe this is because students have experienced that it is okay and even fun to get very involved in arguing an issue. As a result, they forget they are performing and instead communicate with their fellow students.

Using debates in the public speaking course has been the essential tool in helping my students experientially develop into critical thinkers and effective persuaders.

EXERCISE 10.5   IMPROMPTU DEBATES

Objectives: 1. To demonstrate the importance of using supporting materials
             2. To practice effective use of supporting materials
             3. To practice persuasion using complete arguments

Procedures: 1. Divide students, or allow them to divide themselves, into groups of four; then divide each group into two teams. Since debate is usually a new experience, and threatening to some, it helps to have a partner.

             2. Each group of four chooses a topic from a series of topics suggested by the teacher. Alternatively, students may choose their own topic but they must clear it with the teacher first to make sure it is appropriate for the classroom. Once each group has chosen a different topic, the group writes a proposition statement. This statement is the one that each team will either challenge or support. The proposition statement should be worded as a definitive sentence, such as "Chicago should impose a curfew of 10 P.M. for minors under age seventeen" (policy) or "A federal rating system for violence on television is an appropriate solution to the problem of media violence" (value).

             3. Once each group has chosen a topic and written a proposition statement, students choose sides. Two students in each group argue the affirmative, supporting the proposition, and two argue the negative, against the proposition. If everyone in the group agrees on the topic, simply explain that it is possible to make effective arguments for both sides. In fact, for purposes of debate, it can actually be an advantage to argue against your own conviction because you already know the arguments the other side will raise!

             4. The next part of this assignment is research. The teacher explains the importance of using supporting materials in debate and reviews guidelines for effective supporting materials. Each student then contributes three sources to support his or her position. Teachers can assign the research as homework or can schedule class time in the library.

             5. After students have found sources, they brainstorm with their partners and write opening and closing statements. During this time, they should decide who will deliver the opening and closing arguments of the debate.

             6. Now that the students have prepared, it is time for the actual debates. Position students with two desks on one side of the room, for the affirmative team, and two desks on the other side of the room, for the negative team.

EXERCISE 10.5 *Continued*

> Students stand to give their opening and closing arguments at a podium positioned between the desks. The opening arguments should be mini–persuasive speeches that highlight the major arguments for their proposition.
>
> The middle portion of the debate is an impromptu *clash* of arguments. In advance, the teacher explains certain ground rules: students are free to argue back and forth on the issue, but they may not raise their voices or make personal attacks rather than argue on the issue, and they must cite sources when making arguments. Arguments must include the claim, evidence, and reasoning (see the Toulmin model in Chapter 3). During the clash, all students remain seated.
>
> Closing arguments should summarize why the audience should agree with that team's side of the debate.
>
> Each debate takes twenty minutes in a class period, leaving time for discussion after each. Teachers can schedule the debates one or two per day for one to two weeks, depending on how many groups of four there are per class. Teachers can use the following format or adjust the clash portion to fit time constraints:

Affirmative Opening Argument:	2 minutes
Negative Opening Argument:	2 minutes
Clash:	12 minutes
Negative Closing Argument:	2 minutes
Affirmative Closing Argument:	2 minutes

Reprinted with permission of Kimberly A. Powell, Assistant Professor, Luther College, Decorah, IA (1995).

SUMMARY

Schools can enrich the language arts curriculum and provide authentic learning experiences through a variety of extracurricular activities and activities with parental or community involvement. At the K through 5 level, students benefit from interacting with adults as young oral communicators seeking to gather information, persuade, or entertain their audience. At the Grades 3 through 5 and 6 through 8 levels, simulations of real world communication events, such as moot courts and mock trials, can provide opportunities for integrating content from other disciplines, such as social studies and/or civics. A newly established National Junior Forensics League is an honor society for schools and students who earn points through participation in oral-intensive events, including speeches, oral interpretation, and debate. Several different forms of debate can be adapted to accommodate different numbers of speakers and purposes. Appendix 10.2 provides sources of additional information on oral-intensive activities.

REFERENCES

Graupner, J. (1993). *Minnesota Debate Teacher's Association Policy Debate Crib Sheet: Levels I and II.* St. Paul, MN: Minnesota Debate Teacher's Association.

Graupner, J., Kersten, B., and Sunne, D. (1995). *Minnesota Debate Teacher's Association guide to first steps on teaching policy debate.* St. Paul, MN: Minnesota Debate Teacher's Association.

National Forensics League. Ballots for forensic and debate activities. Ripon, WI: Author.

APPENDIX 10.1
Competitive Debate Terminology

Affirmative:	The affirmative side of the debate affirms, supports, or defends the topic.
Brief:	An outline of arguments and evidence used by debaters to keep individual arguments accessible, organized, and easy to present during a speech.
Burden of Rejoinder:	The responsibility of a speaker to directly attack or refute the other side's previous arguments.
Case:	The case is the affirmative side's logical presentation of reasons the topic should be supported. The affirmative case is always presented in the first speech of the debate.
Claim:	A claim is an assertion of truth, supported by evidence, and connected to the evidence by logic or reasoning.
Clash:	The degree of directness in countering an opponent's arguments, as in, "There was a lot of clash between the affirmative and negative arguments." Clash is essential for a good round of debate because it clarifies the differences between the affirmative and negative positions on each issue. In a round with lots of clash, there are few attempts by either side to avoid, ignore, or circumvent the arguments made by the other team; and each team presents strong arguments that tend to disprove the arguments of the other team.
Constructives:	The opening speeches of a debate round; their purpose is to establish the key points for both sides that will be defended later in rebuttals.
Cross-Examination:	In some forms of debate, a short period for cross-examination is allowed after each constructive speech (but usually not during rebuttals). A member of the opposing team cross-examines the person who most recently delivered a constructive speech. Cross-examination is designed to point out or defend flaws in a team's position, and responses made to questions during cross-examination can be used against a team by its opponent.
Evidence:	Information used to support the truthfulness of a claim. In debate, evidence usually comes from published, printed sources and is generally able to withstand scrutiny only if from relatively objective, credible sources. Debaters cite their evidence by stating author, title, publication, date, and page number, where relevant, as in "According to the *Daily Herald*, December 12, 1995, over four million people go hungry every year in our nation's big cities."

(continued)

APPENDIX 10.1   *Continued*

Extension:	A speaker extends arguments by adding new subpoints that support the thesis and/or additional evidence. Extensions usually occur in rebuttal speeches.
Flow:	The handwritten outline of arguments made throughout the round, usually on a legal pad. Judges and debaters *flow* the round as it progresses and a debater's ability to keep a good flow is especially helpful in rebuttals.
Negative:	The negative team opposes the topic and is responsible for attacking the affirmative side's case with counterarguments.
Negative Philosophy:	Negative teams do not generally present a case like the affirmative team, although in certain kinds of debate they may, but they do generally present an overview of their philosophy, which in turn undergirds all negative attacks on the affirmative case. The negative philosophy is a point of view about the resolution that acts as a cohesive force for their side throughout the debate.
Rebuttals:	The closing speeches in which each speaker attempts to hone the debate down to its essential issues. Rebuttals usually last four to five minutes.
Resolution:	The topic, proposition, or statement that serves to focus the debate, such as "Resolved: That the spotted owl should be protected at all costs against the logging industry."

Adapted with permission of Jim Graupner and the Minnesota Debate Teacher's Association (1993 and 1995).

APPENDIX 10.2
Resources

Information resources about current events suitable for middle school debate (also a limited number of materials in Spanish) are available from:

Close-Up Publishing
44 Canal Center Plaza
Alexandria, VA 22314-1592

For information about moot courts for middle school students, write these law-related education organizations:

Constitutional Rights Foundation
601 South Kingsley Drive
Los Angeles, CA 90005

Constitutional Rights Foundation Chicago
407 South Dearborn
Suite 1700
Chicago, IL 60605

National Institute for Citizen Education in the Law
711 G Street, SE
Washington, DC 20003

Special Committee on Youth Education for Citizenship
American Bar Association
541 North Fairbanks Court
Chicago, IL 60611

For information on debates for middle school students, write to:

National Junior Forensics League
Box 38
Ripon, WI 54971

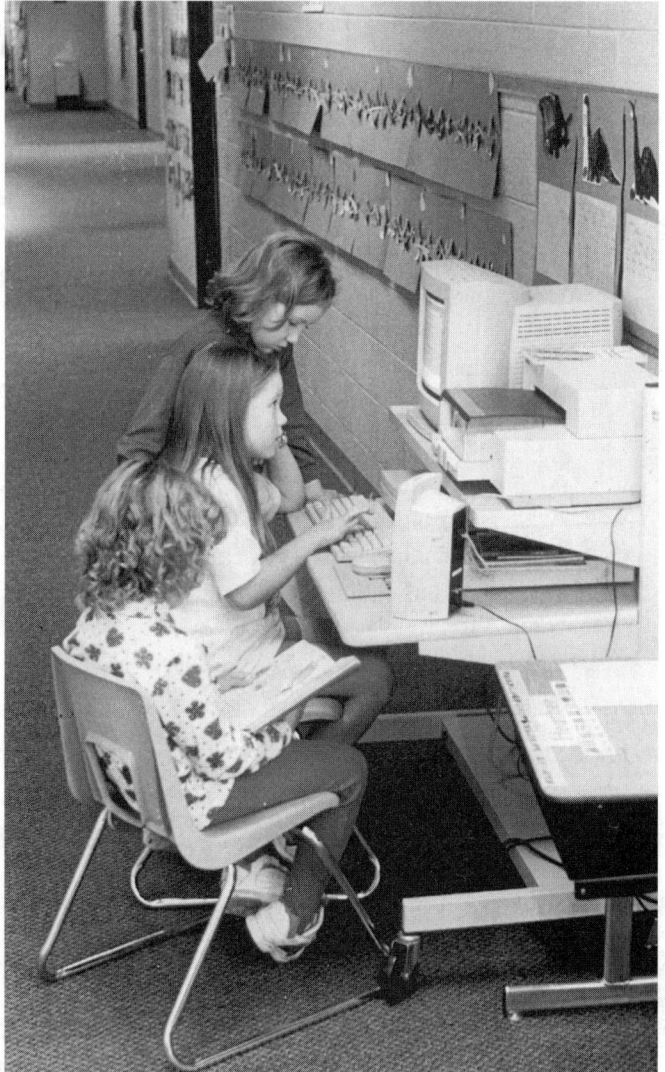

Cooperative learning around a computer

APPENDIX

Developing an Oral Communication Lab and Resource Center

As interest develops in electronic portfolios for oral communication assessment, and as multimedia technology becomes a stronger presence in our nation's elementary schools, labs and resource centers will become as important to young speakers and listeners as they have become to writers and readers. Labs can be used to assist with faculty development and support, student remedial training, assessment, self-assessment and practice, and exploratory learning. For elementary schools seeking to bolster support for oral communication across the curriculum and for a more fully integrated language arts curriculum, establishing an oral communication lab or modifying an existing reading and writing resource center might be a feasible and worthwhile objective.

WHAT SERVICES CAN AN ORAL COMMUNICATION LAB PROVIDE?

The services that an oral communication lab can provide will naturally depend on the resources a school is able to allocate in terms of equipment, space, and supervision. Optimally, an oral communication resource lab would provide the following resources and services:

1. *Audio- and videotape collection, including blank tapes for student use.* Audio- and videotapes can be used for remedial and enrichment activities. There are a number of fine videotapes, in particular, on such topics as sample speeches, listening skills, small-group discussion, and current events relevant to students. Tapes that show both sides of a controversial issue are useful for teaching persuasion, debate, and evaluative listening; and tapes that inform students about interesting and relevant topics are useful for teaching discriminative listening.

2. *Audio cassette player/recorder(s).*   Students can use audiotape capability not only to listen to tapes of interest, but also to create mass media projects, such as mock radio programs and commentaries.

3. *Chairs and tables or desks to accommodate expected use.*   Some activities will require reading and writing. For instance, self-assessment of a speech on video-tape or completion of a communication apprehension inventory will require a quiet space to write.

4. *Computer, color monitor, printer, and software capable of supporting interactive software (such as CD-ROM–based programs).*   You may want to survey the computer programs available before deciding on a new computer purchase (if your school does not already have one). Some programs are not available in both DOS and Macintosh formats.

5. *Headphones.*   To avoid disturbing others, students may need to use head-phones with audiocassette players, CD-ROMs, or video monitors.

6. *Interactive computer programs that focus on oral communication skills.*   There is a growing oral communication software market, though so far the content seems to be aimed at the secondary and university level. This may change in the near future. It is likely that we will see interactive software programs such as games and individual lessons that focus on speaking and listening. In the meantime, some multimedia encyclopedia-type programs feature audio and video about interest-ing and grade-appropriate topics. Children can be assigned to work independently or in groups using a listening and reading lesson designed by the teacher around one such software program.

7. *Microphones.*   Small microphones are needed for use with video cameras and audiocassette recorders.

8. *Musical instruments; collections of chants and songs.*   Younger children, in particular, benefit from learning and using language through music. Chants and songs are also a terrific way to build multicultural content into the curriculum.

9. *On-line software allowing access to the Internet.*   This resource can be used in cooperative learning and even discriminative listening assignments.

10. *Pictures and other visual aids.*   Using pictures and visual aids helps stimu-late discussion. Felt or flannel boards, masks, posters, and collections of maga-zines are good resources.

11. *Puppets and props.*   Students will need puppets and props for dramatization.

12. *Video camera, monitor, and VCR (portable, perhaps on a cart).*   We recommend a small (perhaps 13-inch) color monitor with a built-in headphone jack when space is at a premium and the monitor will not be used for whole-class viewing of vid-eotapes. Smaller monitors are less expensive but are still useful for one-on-one discussion with students about their communication performance; the headphones allow students to independently use the monitor at a desk or carrel without disturbing other students nearby. When resources and space are not at a premium, a cart with a larger monitor, VCR, and headphones that can be moved from the lab to the classroom is advisable. The larger monitor will allow for whole-class viewing of videotapes.

One of the primary benefits of videotaping/playback capability is the potential to create meaningful electronic portfolios for speaking and listening.

13. *Print and nonprint teaching resources.*   Teacher's manuals and assessment tools complete the oral communication lab. Teachers can use labs to administer communication and receiver apprehension tests (see Chapter 2), such as the PRCF and the RAT. The PRCA-24 (Personal Report of Communication Apprehension) and the WTC (Willingness to Communicate) tools are available as affordable, easy-to-use computer programs.

HOW CAN AN ORAL COMMUNICATION LAB BE IMPLEMENTED?

In these days of limited funding and resources, most schools will probably conclude that an independently staffed lab holding all of the above equipment and related resources is simply not feasible. In the event that some degree of staffing is feasible, however, we will present two different options for creating an oral communication lab.

Option #1: Unsupervised resource collection that can be contained within a classroom or in a separate location

Resources:

- Audio- and videotape collection
- Audiocassette player/recorder(s)
- Musical instruments
- Pictures and other visual aids to help stimulate discussion
- Print and nonprint teaching resources
- Puppets and props for dramatization
- Video camera, monitor, and VCR (portable, perhaps on a cart)
- Computer, color monitor, printer, and software capable of supporting interactive software, such as CD-ROM–based programs
- Interactive computer programs

Best suited for: K through 2 and 3 through 5 classes, when students are unlikely to be ready for unsupervised work anyway and resources are shared by a number of teachers from across the curriculum in a school.

Option #2: The lab as a separate, integrated, shared workspace for teachers and students; unsupervised or staffed part-time

Location: Location and dedicated space depends on the purposes for which the lab is used.

If the lab is to be used as a center for reading, viewing, listening, and learning, it may be located in any classroom or resource room. Plan for a space large enough to accommodate independent workstations as well as the target number of simultaneous users engaged in other activities (reading, writing, small-group discussion, peer conferencing, and so on). Headphones will be essential equipment if the dedicated space is contiguous with other workspaces, such as a reading or writing center.

If the lab is to be used for video/audiotaping simultaneously with other activities, plan for an isolated, separate room or soundproof booth. Such spaces can be as small as 500 square feet if only one to four people are using the space at a time. This can be done in two ways:

1. A soundproof booth is built against a wall of an existing reading/writing center using pressboard and sound-absorbing material or carpet; the video camera and tripod are located at one end of the booth and the student stands at the opposite end when performing. Such a space should be long enough to allow the camera to capture most of the student's body on tape. It is important to be able to see how the student uses legs, gestures, and body posture while speaking.

A space of this size is also adequate to capture students working in both dyads and small groups. For a small-group project, students should place their chairs close together in a U-shape so that no backs are to the camera.

2. A room featuring a space in the back, blocked off by carpet-covered room dividers.

If a separate area is not an option, teachers and students can take turns using the center for audio/videotaping and other activities.

Staffing: Teacher, teacher's aide, or perhaps even an older student (middle school). Staffing is necessary when the lab is to be used heavily by a number of different classes and for a number of different purposes; scheduling can be a hassle, especially if the lab cannot accommodate both audio/videotaping and other activities simultaneously. A second reason to staff a lab would be for supervision of independent remedial, enrichment, or assessment activities, especially if equipment will be used in some fashion. Some labs use student intake forms similar to the one in Exhibit A.1 for this purpose. A final reason to staff the lab with a trained representative would be to offer services of speech preparation and rehearsal—the representative could function as a tutor and coach.

Exhibit A.1   Sample Student Intake and Record Form

Date: _____

Name : _____   Teacher: _____

Grade: _____   Purpose of visit: _____

Assessment activity/tool: _____

Score: _____ Scored by: _____

Assessment activity/tool: _____

Score: _____ Scored by: _____

Assessment activity/tool: _____

Score: _____ Scored by: _____

Personal goals: _____

_____

_____

_____

_____

Resources:

- Audio- and videotape collection
- Audiocassette player/recorder(s)
- Chairs and tables or desks to accommodate expected use
- Computer, color monitor, printer, and software capable of supporting interactive software (such as CD-ROM–based programs).
- Interactive computer programs
- Musical instruments
- On-line software allowing access to the Internet
- Pictures and other visual aids to help stimulate discussion
- Print and nonprint teaching resources
- Puppets and props for dramatization
- Videocamera, monitor, and VCR (portable, perhaps on a cart)

Best suited for: Grades 3 through 5 and 6 through 8, where there is a mixture of independent learning and whole-class use.

SUMMARY

In planning your oral communication lab, you may decide on additional services and ways to share the resources with the entire school. The ones we have mentioned here are optimal for an integrated language arts curriculum with a strong emphasis on learning and assessing oral communication skills of many types. Audio, video, and multimedia capability help students develop both speaking and listening skills, and provide valuable opportunities for self-assessment and portfolio products.

Index